Praise for
The Search for the Genuine

"Exuberant, startlingly original nonfiction . . . I'm taking its essays one by one . . . just to have his inimitable voice in my head for as long as possible." **—Colette Bancroft, *Tampa Bay Times***

"Rich with Harrison's consummate humor and characteristic empathy." **—Jana Hoops, *Jackson Clarion-Ledger***

"Spanning 45 years, this new bevy of essays and musings bursts with insight, adventure, and well-lived experiences . . . his writing is always and truly 'genuine.' Forthright, perpetually curious, and compassionate, Harrison remains wholly compelling and readers will be grateful that this buoyant, observant, and caring writer took time away from his sublime poetry to create these enriching essays." **—*Booklist* (starred review)**

"Harrison was one of America's most genuine writers and his 'Search' ruminates about love, literature, hunting, fishing, border life and the magic of place." **—Bruce Dinges, *Arizona Daily Star***

"Endlessly charming . . . An essential installment in the Harrison canon." **—*Kirkus Reviews* (starred review)**

"You will see the world in a different light and soon realize you are reading the work of a genius. Many readers will also learn he was a lot like you (and me)." **—Bill Castanier, *CityPulse***

"Harrison devotees will eat this up."
—*Publishers Weekly* (starred review)

"Over the course of his long career as a writer, Jim Harrison wrote eloquently about the American outdoors in countless ways. *The Search for the Genuine* assembles 45 years' worth of his nonfiction, covering subjects ranging from Yellowstone National Park to searching for sharks. Looking for a lyrical, meditative take on the grandest subjects out there? Look no further."   —**Tobias Carroll,** *InsideHook*

"The Harrison who emerges here is recognizable, but also useful, reminding readers of the value of curiosity and range, whether in miles or mindset."   —**Glen Young,** *Petoskey News-Review*

The Search for the Genuine

Also by Jim Harrison

JIM HARRISON

The Search for the Genuine

Nonfiction, 1970–2015

Grove Press
New York

Published simultaneously in Canada
Printed in the United States of America

This book was set in 12-pt. Goudy Oldstyle
by Alpha Design & Composition of Pittsfield, NH.

First Grove Atlantic hardcover edition: September 2022
First Grove Atlantic paperback edition: March 2025

Library of Congress Cataloging-in-Publication data is available for this title.

ISBN: 978-0-8021-5722-5
eISBN: 978-0-8021-5723-2

Grove Press
an imprint of Grove Atlantic
154 West 14th Street
New York, NY 10011

Distributed by Publishers Group West

groveatlantic.com

25 26 27 28   10 9 8 7 6 5 4 3 2 1

CONTENTS

THIS IMMENSE RIVER:
NOTES ON JIM HARRISON'S NONFICTION

By Luis Alberto Urrea

> *Each morning I walk four blocks*
> *to this immense river,*
> *surprised that it's still there,*
> *that it won't simply disappear*
> *into the ground like the rest of us.*
>
> "Livingston Suite"
> Limberlost Press, 2005.

I first found Jim Harrison in a box under a stairway in the Woolworth's on Broadway in San Diego.

I was still shuffling along through bad luck and bad jobs, taking buses and trolleys for hours to hand out language tapes to Mexican students trying to learn English. Minimum wage or below. When I wasn't doing that, my Jesus complex took me into Tijuana on my free days to feed orphans. I was dreaming of literary salvation, not knowing that to get someone to read about my topics, I'd have to first have the patience to teach them the words to care about them. Basically, I was wrenched from side to side by the eruptions of my enthusiasms and obsessions. On reflection, it doesn't seem that far in its sad comedy from Harrison's belletristic expeditions.

I was low on pocket money for new books. But on the layover downtown, between the Tijuana Trolley and the northbound bus, I wandered into Woolworth's to look at the cheap parakeets and goldfish. This small pet ghetto was off to the west side of the store, and there I beheld a white bin piled with unwanted hardcovers. Very cheap. Cheaper than a paperback. A. R. Ammons—poetry; Jim Harrison—prose and poetry. Forgive me, Jim, but I might have bought Ammons's books first. I was fancying myself a Great American Chicano Polyglot Poet in those days.

I was back the next week, haunted by the memory of those classic white Harrison hardcovers adorned with Russell Chatham art. And the one-dollar-per-book price tag. For first editions. What a score: *Farmer, Wolf, Legends of the Fall, A Good Day to Die, Sundog,* and *Selected & New Poems.* I was a McGuaniac in those days, and the Harrison books kept whispering from their shadowy stall that Tom McGuane knew all about this work. Of course, they were friends. Turned out everybody was Jim Harrison's friend.

I worried that some literary pirate would beat me to the book box and I'd be left with my limp ten-dollar bill dangling from my fist. But the Typing God relented and spared my books for me. I dragged them home in a paper bag that started tearing immediately from their weight.

After being bulldozed by Harrison's writing, I found out somehow where to write to him. I probably wrote to him via his publisher. Isn't that what we did before the internet? I told him I started to cry on the second page of *Farmer* and cried for most of it. "How do you do that?" I asked. To my utter shock, some months later, he wrote back. Offered to look at my work and to introduce me to his agent. This was my first impression of the man, and it never abated.

I thanked him and did not send any work. You don't send the Buddha a basket of unripe plums. Shortly after this correspondence, I packed a duffel with clothes and books and a couple of records, grabbed my used electric typewriter, and headed out into shadowy America to find out what surprises it held in its pockets. All along the long road, Harrison books. Sometimes, a letter, or messages from mutual acquaintances at parties or readings or chilaquiles breakfasts in Tucson. I think Harrison accepted my timidity, but he didn't share it. He was the ambassador of Ikkyu, the Crazy Cloud of Zen poets—the shuffling madman and alleged drunkard, the mad lover and the raging heart, the man of wild ways—and I don't think he had the time or the constitution to be timid. A fine mentor who reached out from fifteenth-century Japan to Harrison's various hideouts and riverbanks. Ikkyu said: "Learn to read the love letters sent by the wind and the rain, the snow and the moon." And, in a thousand ways, so did Jim Harrison.

He extended welcomes and invitations until I felt ready, and that was when Charles Bowden died.

In 2015, I was invited by Chuck's family to partake in a memorial event in his honor at the Tucson Festival of Books. They told me that I'd be sitting on the stage beside Jim. If this wasn't the right moment to sit with him, there would be no right time. I recall there was a slight trepidation about what Rabelaisian outburst might escape from his mouth. As if, it was implied, I could keep the damage under control. What was more devastating than any mad quote from Jim was the way he delivered poetry and koans in his freestyle eulogy.

Chuck Bowden was a kindred soul. He was a close associate of Edward Abbey, and like Abbey, a transplanted easterner mad for deserts in all their rough and daunting beauty. Bowden found grace in harshness, and one could see Harrison in his paragraphs. But Chuck knew, just like the many writers who emulated Hemingway, for example, that those who borrowed vibes from Harrison missed something profound about his words—the tenderest heart with deep wounds and unstinting powers of regeneration.

* * *

Jim Harrison was indeed a big river in flood. Poet, novelist, gourmand, drinker, brawler, lover, genius of obscenity. Half-blind, capable of eating a fourteen-course meal without blinking his good eye, autodidact, wild creature come out of Hemingway's north Michigan woods, hunter, fisher, critic, gunman, hell-raiser, quiet in his sorrows. If a grizzly had a PhD and a bottle of the finest French wine, the moderators would be concerned when he took the podium. How fitting that nobody there knew what Jim was going to say. Bowden was the same way. Ikkyu said: "Having no destination, I am never lost."

This is a confession: I walked into the theater—they had told me Jim was already there, since he required some help getting around. They had helped him to his seat. He was wearing the years and the bad health and I could tell they were both heavy. I knew he disliked the public ritual of the famous writer. I knew he rebelled sometimes.

I took the seat next to him and before I could introduce myself, he said, "The greatest regret in my career is that I didn't blurb your novel." From then on, it was all Jim. I was just a laughing acolyte hanging on to the great tree trunk washing down the mountain on the Harrison River.

We, of course, deferred to him. I don't recall Harrison speaking about Chuck. I am sure he did, but he was off and running. He started with his famous comment about no longer counting his life in years, but in dogs. This pleased the audience. It was strangely both witty and heartbreaking at the same time.

The rest of us settled in and let the big river flow—I resolved on the spot to let Jim take up all the time he needed. Fine food and fine wine might have been in the lecture. I just sat there smiling, laughing, and occasionally feeling a tear come up as that ghastly shadow of mortality drifted over us and Jim batted it away.

Then the Ursine Jim, apparently fed up with the creeping solemnity of it all, growled: "The trouble with being a male writer," he said, "is that your dick gets in the way." Bowden would have laughed himself out of his chair. Perhaps he did.

Jim couldn't be stopped. He'd occasionally turn to me and pierce me with that good eye, and he'd make a point as he gave me a poke with one gnarled finger. I nodded: You're so right! It didn't matter what he said, it was a jazz literary essay improvised on the spot and I was trying to absorb his currents and undercurrents. There were dozens of haiku poems speeding by like cherry blossoms falling.

After about thirty minutes of his monologue, a note came down the podium from the master of ceremonies: Can you get Jim to stop? I ducked my head and simply shook it, no. Absolutely not.

I didn't care if I got to say anything or not.

Later that night, the hosts had arranged a supper in Jim's honor. It was at Janos Wilder's Tucson restaurant, where the famed chef had created a special menu for his friend. The long table was set for invited guests—members of that day's panel, donors, Festival of Books folks, and representatives of philanthropies. There might have been authors there, but I was waiting for the Big Man and don't remember if there were.

My wife and I took seats on the side squeezed against a wall, leaving the seat of honor in open space so Harrison could sit comfortably. He came in, looked around, and squeezed into the seat beside us. He was wheezing and dark in the face. I said, "Are you all right?" And he replied, "I'll never be all right again."

He leaned across me and stared at the gathered celebrants. "Who are these people?" I told him what I knew, which wasn't much. He settled back in his seat and ordered wine, poured a bit in my glass. His great pleasure seemed to be in launching a running discourse on each kind of wine, and what I needed to know as I sipped. "You want to be a sophisticated gentleman during each round of the feast," he noted. "It's all in how you do it. Don't forget." He was already composing on the fly a brilliant essay like he had done onstage a few hours before. He was in his last year of life, visibly exhausted, and out-composing everybody at the table—all their witty talk seemed to be simple babble compared to his flow. That table had become Jim's Zendo, and he was teaching me. Eating meditation for beginners.

His famous blind left eye was always turned to me in its socket, and I was unnerved, wondering if he was staring at me.

He had heard that my older brother had just died—we had buried him shortly before this event. "Tell me about your brother's death," he said. I did. He sipped his water and then his wine and stared at the ceiling. This is how I remember him best. Looking up, breathing hard, pain on his face, a finger to his lips. Utter stillness.

And when I was through, he turned in his seat and held me in place with the gaze of his good eye.

"Sometimes," he said, "God hands you a novel. You'd better write it."

I helped him outside for a cigarette.

He leaned on a low fence, gasping and smoking.

"My last smoke," he said.

The limo came for him. His friends helped him. He had drained every bit out of this day and he was tired. He was talking by sheer willpower.

He shook my hand.

"I hope I'll see you again," I said.

"Probably not."

And that was true.

But here he is, damn the torpedoes, kicking over his own headstone. Alive forever. I am still learning and celebrating at every turn of that huge churning spirit. I trust you will feel the same.

I found this magnificent collection of Jim Harrison's nonfiction impossible to read. I hope you do too. It kept striking like a rattlesnake, then making me laugh, then stopping me cold with moments of wonder and tenderness. Often in the same essay. I constantly missed Jim's wildness, his voice, his unexpected softness, his spirituality, his carnality, his critical sharpness. And then I realized he had put all these things into the book.

The preface alone is worth the price of admission. "The Man Who Ate Books." An intimate epic of bibliophilia and creativity, a philosophy that is almost a primer for readers and writers. And that voice, genuine, rueful, lyrical, sly, carries the reader (and the writing student) into the Zen of Harrison.

You will know him from the start—meet Baby Jim, chewing on the ancient family Bible. Its taste, "if not delicious, had a slightly beefy flavor, the salt coming from the hands of generations of poor farmers." Later, we accompany Young Jim on forest walks and care-less rambles, on fishing excursions on the river, rowing boats—all the while toting books. "When he ran through the fields and forest he thought about what he would read next." So engrossed in this process that he ran into the side of a barn and damaged his shoulder. Unhurried, he takes us through the years of his eternal apprentice-ship. It's a gift.

He confesses to us that when he was confronted with new books, he gave them a sniff and a slight lick.

This warm and witty meditation/confession is immediately followed by one of my personal favorite essays in the collection, "Why I Write." I search these kinds of pieces out, for I ask myself this question often, and when I first communicated with Jim, he asked me that very thing. One of his capacious and witty answers to the questions is, "Novels and poems are the creeks and rivers com-ing out of my brain." He continues, "I write as an act of worship to creatures, landscapes, ideas that I admire . . ."

This piece is followed by a meditation on Zen meditation.

Advisory: when the book seems random, Jim is interconnecting the roots of the understory—all is one epic revelation of the process of creation.

I could fill this introduction with favorite quotes and scenes and themes, but I leave this to you. Every time I pick up this book, I am surprised again. Just when I think it's going to be all about bears and fishing, Jim discusses religion, and meditation, ethics, politics, and even lit crit analyses of other writers and their work. This big river never stops flowing. Travel, writing, food, drink, sex, love, dogs, friends, confession, autobiography, sorrow. What a summation of an epic life. Honest, flaws and all.

He says, well into the book, "Deep within us, but also on the surface, is the wounded ugly boy who has never caught an acceptable angle of himself in the mirror."

As I read it, I have to put it down and write quotes from it in my own notebooks. Hardly a way to make quick progress. But one should not rush through this collection. Jim's books are always cause for meditative pauses and outright laughter. One often wrestles with his words. One begs to differ with some of his conclusions or opinions. This is a good thing. A bacchanal has broken out here: his nonfiction is as elegantly untamed as his appetite for experience, literature, good food, dogs, and unruly rivers.

—Luis Alberto Urrea
Chicago, 2022

THE MAN WHO ATE BOOKS

(2001)

It started very early, as do most bad, perhaps fatal, habits. The first incident became one of those silly family stories that bore anyone else. He was a mere baby of seven months when he crawled up on a chair and pulled the huge leather-bound family Bible off the table. The Bible fell to the floor, and he lay next to it chewing on the salty leather which, if not delicious, had a slightly beefy flavor, the salt coming from the hands of generations of poor farmers. In the back of the Bible were several pages of family genealogy, but the baby did not chew on these suspicious documents, the filigree of our existence so beloved by those of supposedly noble birth, showing the thin string of semen and egg that we have in common with dogs, apes, and suchlike.

Naturally the baby was punished, if only with screams, when he was discovered with the corner of the Holy Bible in his mouth, chewing quite happily, the pleasure equal to that of his mother's teat. The baby was not overly disturbed by the screams of the aunt who towered above him. He merely looked up her sturdy brown legs, the thighs disappearing into darkness, his twelve billion neurons recording a mystery that would later compete with chewing on books.

Unfortunately the Holy Bible was the only leather-bound book the family owned. Another story was added to the family collection when at the age of two he accompanied his mother to the public library. She was doubtless reading a lady's magazine that gave recipes on how to make tasteless food. She looked up from her reading and screamed, of course. Her two-year-old had climbed the library shelves like a primate and was up near the ceiling sniffing and licking old leather-bound volumes that were histories of Michigan describing how courageous settlers had murdered the Indians, bears, and wolves and replaced them with cows, chickens, and pigs. The library staff needed a ladder to retrieve the child. He was spanked, and shit his pants in protest.

The years passed slowly, as they always do when we are young, the torpor increased by teachers who openly wept with boredom and disgust at their miserable lot of being teachers instead of businessmen. In truth they were paid so poorly that they were at the bottom of the social ladder in any village they taught. But luckily the schools had books, and our young hero had taken to reading one every day, sometimes two, while totally neglecting his other studies. There were also many books at home, but at home he was forbidden to tear out the endpapers and chew on them, which he sneakily did at school. Endpapers were his gum and candy.

All he cared to do was read, run, hunt, and fish. He even read when he fished from their small rowboat, and he took a book along to read while resting from hunting. When he ran through the fields and forest he thought about what he would read next. He would be thinking about a book when he ran and collided with a tree or bush, and once into the side of a barn, where he hurt his shoulder.

When first picking up a fresh book he would smell it and give a random page a slight lick, then check out the page for the secrets of life. He had looked up "life" and "sex" in the encyclopedia but the encyclopedia was old and musty and words were inadequate. The words were not causally related to the life he knew. The information on sex bore no relation to looking up his aunt's skirt or fondling the girl next door, or to the beauty of dogs, cats, and farm animals coupling.

He was about eleven when he snuck away with his father's copies of Erskine Caldwell's *Tobacco Road* and *God's Little Acre*, which finally revealed sex in its rather fundamental glory which struck him as similar to eating roast chicken or frying fish or deer meat, a pleasure equal to reading a good book!

From that day onward he would read only fiction and poetry, which meant he would do poorly in chemistry, mathematics, biology, and history, all of which dealt with abstractions that were meaningless to him.

The die was now cast. He flunked high school and college, repeated and barely made it through because he imitated in writing the grace of what he read, which pleased the teachers because other students wrote so poorly. The teachers passed him even though they knew this young man was ignorant of anything other than the contents of his own galantine brain.

He bummed around the country checking if writers from dozens of states knew what they were talking about. He chewed endpapers from books borrowed, bought, and stolen, in every region of the United States. He was fired from every job for trying to read while working. Once in San Francisco he was reading a Saroyan book in the public library and one of the pages smelled like lavender. He was not satisfied until he found a girl who smelled like lavender. He had a brief affair with a very tall, thin girl because she was reading Stendhal on the library steps in New York City, another because she was reading Faulkner while eating chocolate ice cream, a red-haired girl (he didn't like red hair) because she was reading Valéry and soaking her pink feet in the fountain in Washington Square. In those days not many girls read books, so you had to make do. His

sexual possibilities were also limited because the girls had to be reading good books, not trash. He had figured out that good literature
had serious side effects.

In his early twenties his life became hopeless. He had to do
manual labor—carpentry, cement, and farm work—which required
his hands, so he couldn't read. He met a lovely girl who also read a lot
and was pleased to see her smell a new book when she opened it. She
didn't chew the endpapers, but then you can't have everything. The
day he impregnated her they had been talking about Dostoyevsky's
Notes from the Underground, not a sexy book but one that made you
turn to your body for solace. They had a baby, who began reading
books in the cradle, which demonstrates that the disease may be
genetic, then another baby, who was equally obsessed with literature.

He was fired from two good office jobs because he neglected his
work in order to read fiction and poetry. He couldn't help himself and
did this openly. The young couple were in despair from eating only
macaroni while reading. (Even forty years later he can remember
what he was eating back then from food stains in old books. Grouse
and wine stains on Mishima and Cioran.) Finally the young couple
accepted their grim fate on this bloody voyage of life. They took
vows of voluntary poverty for a decade so he could continue to eat
books and, finally, write them. There was nothing else for him to
do. The moral of this story is to keep leather-bound Bibles well out
of reach of your babies, but if it's too late and they've already begun
to chew, try to teach them that sex, food, and books aren't in the
same category (though they probably are).

(Télérama)

DOGS IN THE MANGER:
ON LOVE, SPIRIT,
AND LITERATURE

WHY I WRITE
(1970)

To answer this question has put me into a sump, a well-pit, a quan-
dary I haven't visited in years. Here are a number of answers. My
love of life is tentative so I write to ensure my survival. I try to write
well so I won't be caught shitting out of my mouth like a politician.
To the old banality "Eat or die," I add "Eat and write or die." After
writing I often read Brillat-Savarin, also cookbooks, on the toilet.
Then I try to cook as well as I hope I write. After a nap, I write again,
in the manner of an earthdiver swimming in the soil to understand
the roots and tendrils of trees. I anchor myself to these circular life
processes so as not to piss away my life on nonsense. I hunt and fish
because it helps my writing. Novels and poems are the creeks and
rivers coming out of my brain. I continue writing in bleak times to
support my wife and daughters, my dogs and cats, to buy wine, whiskey, food. I write as an act of worship to creatures, landscapes, ideas
that I admire, to commemorate the dead, to create new women to

love. Just now while listening to the blizzard outside I poured a huge glass of Bordeaux. This is what I call fun! Rimbaud said, "Everything we are taught is false." I believed him when I was eighteen and still do. Writers are mere goats who must see the world we live in but have never discovered. I write to continue becoming an unmapped river. It suits me like my skin.

SITTING AROUND
(1993)

I've had truly mixed feelings about writing this little meditation, but then it is not costumed as a dispensation. We apparently drown in discursive texts and lists of principles and, on occasion, turn in despair from recondite Buddhist studies to the poetry of Han Shan and Gary Snyder and many in between. As the Acoma Pueblo poet Simon Ortiz has said, "There are no truths, only stories." Perhaps that is why we are drawn back to *The Blue Cliff Record* and the *Book of Serenity*. After all, we live within a story and our own story is true. This is only to say what I have to offer is a tad simpleminded compared to what has been offered to me.

Why sit? I tend to sit every morning in the Sōtō tradition because I was taught to do so back in the seventies by Kōbun Chino Sensei and he appeared on an immediate basis to be the master of a superior secret. I have a *zafu* in the granary study of my farm in northern Michigan, also one in the loft of my log cabin in a rather

remote area of the Upper Peninsula. There is a river right outside
the door of the cabin, and other than being a truly fine river it is also
a reminder of a Tung-shan quote Jack Turner, a student of Robert
Aitken, sent to me:

> Earnestly avoid seeking without,
>   lest it recede far from you.
> Today I am walking alone,
>   yet everywhere I meet him.
> He is now no other than myself,
>   but I am not now him.
> It must be understood in this way
>   in order to merge with suchness.

I also sit on logs out in the forest, big rocks in gullies, stumps,
three pillows in hotels, car seats, hard plastic seats in air terminals,
soft cushioned seats in offices, while staying still for a long time—
I would sit on my head if it were possible. I once saw a Chinese
acrobat do this and was quite envious. I've always lived far away
from a teacher so it is possible you will not think this is formal Zen
practice. But then I am willing to call my practice "bobo" after a
comic religion I've been inventing lately, or if you wish, just plain
dogshit, an indication that a dog has passed this way. As a matter of
fact, when outside I often sit with my dog. When you have reached
the ripeness, or deliquescence, of fifty-five years, you are less concerned about what things are called. It is the liberation to be found
in mouthy old geezers everywhere, and is uncomfortably close to the
liberation in the energy of youth.

I have sat in all these places for twenty years because I didn't
want the act to become another version of the Lord's Prayer or a
private church service—in other words, to keep the ritual fresh.
As a young man I was a Christian zealot and managed to suffocate
my faith in theology and textual squabbles. Too bad the great Buddhist poet and scholar Stephen Mitchell hadn't published his *Gospel*

According to Jesus before he was born so I could have eaten the wheat rather than just breathing the chaff.

Frankly, when I first started sitting so many years ago it was for the selfish reason of stopping my head from flying off. It did so nearly every day, and I was becoming more than a little frightened. To crib from Aristophanes, whirl was king, a not unusual state for a young poet to find himself in. (I say "himself" because it's me. I cannot humanly countenance forms of Zen that involve gender considerations.) A poet's livelihood is in his moods and if there is not a larger, selfless backwall to these moods he tends to end up in madness and death. A number of family deaths had told me that life was a great big house fire of impermanence. What's more, all my habituation and conditioning, my gluttony, alcoholism, drug ingestion, and neuroses weren't helping one bit. And it is easy for a young poet to be obsessed with Yeats's notion that life is a long preparation for something that never occurs. Sitting told me immediately that life was a preparation for itself, something I had already suspected from my lifelong immersion in the natural world. Perhaps poetry helped create the freedom that must be there before there is freedom.

So much for piths and gists, the junkyard of apothegms, the plodding oinks of wisdom. Sitting on a stump I feel a little closer to the idea that I'm a member of just one of possibly thirty million species. Some people don't like to count bugs because they are frequently obnoxious. A stump or log seems to help me assume. Zen as a glyph for the vehicle of reality, the water that just happens to be contained by a glass and a myriad of other containers. Mistakes are made when students are led to believe that the water pipes, the steel culverts, the plumbing are the river.

Stumps and logs help me forget the world of achievement, disappointment, rewards—the illusion of being right, struggling to hold the world together—and help me shed many of the illusions that the very notion of "personality" is heir to; there is a frequent mistake here in equating personality with "ego," which is a Freudian term and unfortunately rather Prussian. The point seems to be to rid yourself of vanities in order to understand your true character. In sitting, the host returns to the original mind while the guest dithers. Then the dithering stops.

For years I've had a quote by Deshimaru pinned above my desk: "You must concentrate upon and consecrate yourself wholly to each day, as though a fire were raging in your hair." What a ruthless statement. But maybe not. Both you and a piece of wood burn up, and at the end of the day you have ashes which don't return to wood. This is wonderfully obvious but can be forgotten for years at a time. Sometimes the statement wears out and I put it away for a while to rest, though it doesn't take long for it to refresh itself. I use similar statements by Foyan, Dahui, and many others to zap myself. They are excellent cattle prods to the wayward ox who might be spending too much time in front of the butcher shop window wondering at the way it all ends.

There is a particular problem for the artist, writer, poet who begins early to separate himself for vision and lucidity, also to get the work done, and then this separation can easily become distorted, a "fiction" in itself, a personality egg he drowns in juices of his own making. Thus, the artist's Zen can become the arhat's Zen—harsh, dry, attenuated, remote, somewhat selfish. Frequently he would be better off at an American Legion barn dance or sitting in a country bar talking to farmers.

I have to travel a great deal to earn my livelihood, and there is nothing quite like travel to make you a victim of moods. It would be nice to carry a shoebox to store these moods in—then you could abandon them in a locker at LaGuardia. The reason why moods are so hard to locate and identify is they don't exist, though popular culture teaches us to indulge them. National culture seems mostly interested in teaching values that get us to work on time. When you sit, all of this cultural habituation and conditioning drifts away.

I'm reminded daily that I'm no great shakes as a thinker and doer in the philosophical arena. I was taught in college that ontogeny recapitulates phylogeny but I still have to keep looking up the meaning. I know four or five teachers, and where would they be without plain old sitters? Often my life seems too monstrously active and I'm learning that there is no need to be in a hurry if you can only do one thing at a time. Professionally, I've shown no expertise outside the arena of imagination. One of my "amusements" is to try to find and follow black bears, which have always been a dharma gate for me, aside from being bears. Black bears aren't remotely as dangerous as grizzlies, but it is best to be in a state of total attention, because, frankly, the bear is. We want to fully inhabit the earth while we are here and not lose our lives to endless rehearsals and illusions. Perhaps my sitting is more like that of an addled bird, but the bear is always out there, not calling to me, just a bear.

(*Tricycle*)

DOGS IN THE MANGER
(2000)

It is rare when experience so freely offers an apt metaphor but years ago while driving through western Nebraska on a state highway in late April I had slowed down one early evening the better to hear the profusion of meadowlarks through the sunroof and windows. At the outskirts of a small village with an abandoned bank and grain elevator, really the shell of a village holding less than half the population of its former self, there was a brindle mutt barking from the open mow door of a disused barn. I stopped for a moment thinking that he or she must be stuck up there at which point the dog began to strut in barking fury. I stopped at the local bar to tell anyone who might care that there was a dog stranded in the second story of the barn. There were only three people in the bar, including the proprietor, a very old man, his wife in a wheelchair eating from a large plate of fried food, and a burly young cowboy who was a dozen beers ahead of most of the rest of the world. The old man thanked me for my concern. The dog was the only one in town that could climb the ladder to the mow which he did daily in the late afternoon then spent an hour or two barking at the world. The beery lout kept repeating, "It's just what he does," until hitting him over the head with a bar stool would have been a gift to silence. To be civil I had the two-and-a-half-dollar "snack plate" of deep-fried chicken gizzards and calf nuts, a local specialty, much tastier when pinkened by organic hot sauce. When I was finished the drunk told me that if I was looking for women, Alliance, a hundred miles to the west, was "chock-full of them." A geographical invariable is that women are always freer in distant valleys, counties, cities.

Robert Filliou, a Frenchman, said that "art is what makes life more interesting than art." I take this to mean art in the larger sense, including music and literature and so on, and the statement becomes unquestionably true on long road trips. The pleasure of these jour-neys is added to immeasurably by a good sense of both natural and human history in areas through which you pass, and I think equally so by a knowledge of the literature of each locale.

My barking dog was in the land of Willa Cather, Wright Mor-ris, John Neihardt, Mari Sandoz, and the living poet Ted Kooser, who adds his own peculiar lucidity to the Nebraska landscape. If I drive from Montana to Oregon and Washington I see in part the countryside through the eyes of A. B. Guthrie, Wallace Stegner, and, more recently, Raymond Carver, Tom McGuane, and Bill Kittredge, among others. Certain areas of the Deep South nearly suffocate with the weight of William Faulkner, Flannery O'Connor, and Eudora Welty, and driving through Greenville, Mississippi, you can clearly imagine Walker Percy and Shelby Foote in third grade together. Of course Richard Ford presents the uncomfortable example of a writer who is both southern and western.

This is all pleasant enough in terms of the garden-variety tour-ism that lifts you out of your homebound ruts. Writers tend to emerge from their landscapes and often never really leave them except physically. Van Wyck Brooks's *The Flowering of New England* was properly renowned but as the years passed, along came dozens of scholars who said that life for these New England folks (Emerson, Hawthorne, Melville, Thoreau et al.) was less than picturesque. Preposterous creatures lived under New England's covered bridges and, as Robert Richardson pointed out, Emerson did not hesitate to lift the lid weeks later on his lovely wife's coffin, you know, just to make sure that death is death. In other words, geographical origins tumble way down the list in levels of our interest.

Barking dogs are most often comic, and thinking of writers as barking dogs is a leavening influence on our sodden incomprehension about what really makes writers function. Most of them seem not to want to know they are mammals, and in America in particular they are born Balkanized, often quite remote, and as memories of college fade, they hear the echoes of their barking in empty barns.

Is a dog really barking if no one hears him? Scholars and irritated writers look wistfully at the coherence of Europe. In England, France, and Italy, all roads lead to London, Paris, and Rome. New York appears to be the singular locale of publishing and criticism and I certainly thought it to be the center of everything in my youthful period in the Village, or later, in my brief two years on the faculty at Stony Brook, from which, for reasons of temperament, I fled back to the lakes and forests of northern Michigan.

The view from everywhere is different and coherence is but a by-product of history most often forced by the critical and academic communities. For a brief year in college I was an art history major mostly because you spent weeks in a dark auditorium looking at slides and were momentarily safe from your hormones. It was quite an eye-opener to learn that the grand cluster of French Impressionists didn't spend all that much time together. And recently in the exhumation of Beat studies it is amusing that a central figure, Gary Snyder, was mostly solitary in Japan preoccupied with the study of Zen Buddhism. Despite vaunted associations, friendships, correspondences, and an often begrudging sociability, writing is a solo flight that lasts a lifetime.

It is fun when visiting my fellow dogs throughout the country to see how quickly they embrace the notion that in a literary sense we are at least six countries: East, Midwest, South, Southwest, West, and Northwest. The East is stickball, black clothes, Yuppie Boston, air pollution, and they eat millions of hot dogs. The Midwest, alas, is cornfields, forests, mosquitoes, ugly cities, and dumb people à la the movie *Fargo.* The South runs to parody—heat, magnolias, racial cruelty, crude businessmen, a sexual stewpot, and, as a Chicago writer said, "Southern writers have traditionally aimed their crotchless panties at New York." The West is mostly vacationland, faux cowboys, banal mountains, they hate outsiders, and cows are the most important citizens. The Southwest is dry heat, cactus, rattlesnakes, right-wing hideouts, border drugs, the twin Babylons of Los Angeles and Las Vegas. The Northwest is the relatively simple concoction of big forests being cut for the Japanese, an oil soaked ocean, it rains every day, the culinary torpor of pen-raised salmon, Microsoft dweebs.

Without question writers are most resentful about being considered "regional" by those in Gotham. My own irritation about this began to pass years ago when I noted that writers in Brooklyn and the Bronx, not to speak of New Jersey and eastern Pennsylvania, are also occasionally thought to be regional oddities.

I have noted, though, along the way that literary life tends toward the catty and trashy if very much alcohol is involved. Tom McGuane once said that drinking is the writer's black lung disease. Barking and booze are aggressive bedfellows. This is why I've been to only one writers' conference in my entire career. A few collective drinks and the specter of xenophobia arises. Not only does New York *suck a dirty sock* but so does everyplace else other than where the writer at hand resides. On your walk the next morning there is the sense that you might have spent the evening in Yugoslavia.

You see a stray mongrel trotting down the street, quite happy to be ignored, going about his doggy business. In all the arts it has to be the song, not the singer.

In recent years I've become a little fatigued with my long road trips and have turned to other countries where there is a blessed relief from our own Empire and the writers don't remind you so much of those right-wing businessmen who feel held back by unknown forces. It is a delight in Canada, Mexico, and France to immediately lose our evidently spontaneous feeling that our literature is currently the most interesting in the world. It is, however, difficult to explain to foreign writers why we are no longer as interested in publishing them as we used to be. I suggest that we have truly become an Empire like the Roman and our interest has waned, if not disappeared, in the literature of other countries. In Canada, Mexico, and France the barking tends to be more muted. The biggest blinders are always worn by the horses of nationalism.

There is a comic and unnerving notion that in everything we write we are making a case for ourselves, and this most often includes the locales where our perceptions are centered. In the ages of a writer (ambitious then morose then puzzled) how quickly the short run becomes the long run. You realize with some amusement that there has never been any even ground or parity in the Alpine regions of poetry and the literary novel except that, inevitably, the landscape is eroded by time. My memory stuns me when I think of all the "prominent" writers of the sixties, seventies, and eighties who have simply disappeared from notice, quite irrespective of where they lived or wrote, or who published them.

I am writing this in the Morvan region of Burgundy. Lizards are crawling up the walls of the ancient manoir, eating flies among the rose vines. On the lawn the guard dog, Eliot, is barking at a herd of Charolais cattle. In the distance I see the mountains of Morvan, where two Caesars slept while conquering what is now called France, the country where Balzac said that "fame is the sunshine of the dead." Time makes a joke of all of us, albeit a serene joke, or so we envision the void that might await us all—dogs, flies, lizards, butcher, baker, candlestick maker, and writer. It is certain that you'd better have a life to accompany your art. Meanwhile, if you wish to bark into the distance during cocktail hour, try to remind yourself that it's just barking.

MY LEADER

(2008)

Now in the dog days of summer Sirius is making a dawn peek over the mountains, or so I think being fairly ignorant of stars. It's been over 90 degrees for thirty days and here in Montana the earth has begun to burn. I recall a hot late morning down in Veracruz in a poor-folks cemetery waiting for a restaurant to open so I could eat my lunch, a roasted robalo with lime and garlic, a beer, a nap, and then to start life over again watching ships in the harbor that needed to be watched. The old cemetery keeper points out a goat in the far corner and shrugs, making hand and finger gestures to explain how the goat crawls over the stone fence or wriggles through the loose gates. I follow the goat here and there and he maintains what he thinks is a safe distance. He eats fresh flowers and chews plastic flowers letting them dribble in bits from his lips. A stray dog trots down a path and the goat charges, his big balls swinging freely. The dog runs howling, squeezing through a gate. The goat looks at

me as if to say, "See what I have done." Now he saunters and finds
fresh browse in the shade of the catafalque of the Dominguez family.
I sit down in the shade and he sits down facing me about ten feet
away, his coat mangy and his eyes quite red. I say, "I'm waiting for
my roasted fish." He stares, only understanding Spanish. I say, "In this
graveyard together we share the fatal illness, time." He stretches for
amouthful of yellow flowers quickly spitting them out. Baptists say
the world is only six thousand years old, but goats are fast learners.
They know what's poisonous as they eat the world.

(*In Search of Small Gods*)

NESTING IN AIR
(1994)

I think it was Santayana who noted that all people seem to have a secret religion hidden beneath, perhaps surrounding, their more public worship. Our consciousness paints our world. The obvious fact that there is no actual connection between our senses and the world around us is troubling indeed. The fact that the discomfort is there whether or not you wish to take responsibility for your perceptions is also troubling. With ten thousand rituals I paint time and mortality, not only to make them endurable but to give them the dimension, splendor, resonance, perhaps beauty, that I sense they deserve.

That said, we may return to earth and discover we like one rock better than another, and sometimes imbue rocks of certain shapes with religious significance. We are not far here from the cross and swastika. Land configurations have always drawn religious interpretations. We frequently choose to live in a place by inkling, intuition, and our dogs will follow the same process in choosing their best spots on our places.

I awake as a mammal, and it usually takes some time before I remember that I am a college graduate or a writer. "With all its eyes the creature world beholds the open," said Rilke. As my consciousness begins its paint job I frequently, but not always, go outside and bow to the six directions, mindful of the ironies involved. I don't mind if the gesture appears absurd to someone else as I eventually have to die all by myself. After coffee I often do zazen for a while because most of what we think about never has happened, and probably won't. This culture-oriented brain foment is a part of consciousness I like to skip. I also say my own version of the Lord's Prayer just to cover the bases, as it were.

Of course bowing and prayer, even the verbless prayer of zazen, are a specific form of consciousness running counter to the time. Our time is a vast and anguished picture show, as have been all other times. Individually, we have always been like that very rare Brazilian bird that nests in air.

In the area of the food I eat, the consciousness and rituals become a tad esoteric, particularly when the food is wild in origin. Some of this I can trace to my youth up in the country. I am dark complected and tended to become chocolate brown in the warmer months. This and my one blind eye gave me a somewhat "exotic" look. When we chose up sides to play cowboys and Indians I always had to be the Indian and get killed because of my appearance. I suppose to compensate for this I spent a great deal of time sneaking around in the woods, and still do, for that matter. It's just fate, that's all. But what I remember is one afternoon when I was seven and cleaning a pail of bluegills I had caught, I felt bad because there were too many. My Dad misinterpreted my sadness and said, "If you feel so bad just tell them you're sorry." Surely this was an accident more than anything else, though my dad had given me the works of Ernest Thompson Seton. Fifty years later I am still talking to any fish or game I have killed, or any fish or game I've received as a gift (even if only because someone else doesn't want the bother). The main part of these conversations (which can become real two-sided depending on my mood) involves my imagining the lives, the *otherness*, of the creature at hand. Maybe like so many rituals it is simply a gesture to allay fear, dread, guilt, whatever, though just the other day in Arizona I spoke at length to a roadkilled roadrunner. I am also at the age where I no longer care if I'm nuts.

There are occasionally spooky aspects to this process. I have noted eating bear meat tends to produce bear dreams. Last fall at a tavern in the Upper Peninsula of Michigan I was given a big chunk off the hindquarters of a black bear. I asked how the bear had died, and the hunter said it had stood up with its paws on a deadfall and howled at him. This fact was quite troubling when I was talking to the meat that I certainly couldn't throw away.

(*Northern Lights*)

FIRST PERSON FEMALE
(1999)

Why did I think I might be able to write in the voice of a woman? Anyone who knows a novelist or poet very well has probably figured out that they are not dealing with a true intellectual. Intellectuals have a compulsion to be right and this urge is inimical to what John Keats called "negative capability," the capacity a poem or novel must have to keep afloat a thousand contradictory people and questions in order to create the parallel universe of art. Rationality, to borrow from Foucault, may be an inferior level of discourse. This is a very high-minded thing for me to say, keeping in view the recent moment when my wonderful mother, who is eighty-four and of 100 percent Swedish derivation, said, "You've made quite a living out of your fibs."

She and her four sisters grew up on a small, poor farm in northern Michigan with a rather strong and domineering father. However, all the daughters became rather strong and domineering themselves, with not a weak sister in the lot. God pity the man, and hopefully He did, who ever tried to pull a fast one on these women. At this point I somehow remember that there is a reason I'm not supposed to call them ladies. They were not averse to having a good time and neither were their husbands who, though they all fished and hunted strenuously, would never describe these particular activities as "manly." That idea seemed to derive from writers of city origin like the tortured Hemingway, who, though a very great writer, seemed to suffer from a prolonged struggle with his manhood. Faulkner was a bit more nonchalant and colorful on the subject, what with his lifelong fascination with the "pelvic mysteries of swamps."

So I have often wondered about the peculiar female umbrella I grew up under and what particular effect it had on my work, what drove me to write in a female voice in most of *Dalva*, all of the novella "The Woman Lit by Fireflies," and a large portion of my most recent novel, *The Road Home*. I could always ask the analyst I've been visiting in New York City for more than twenty years, but I never have. That would be poking needlessly around the sacred veil of art herself. The answer is always in the entire story, not a piece of it. And on a wretchedly therapeutic level there's the idea that my capability to write as a woman saved me from death by drugs and booze, in that manliness in our culture can paint you into a corner where the only thing left to do is eat roadkill and bite the moon.

Back in the late seventies the character of Dalva came to me in a dream. This is not the sort of thing that is fashionable with literary critics, but then they have their lives and I have mine. In fact she appeared several times in dreams. At first her voice was beyond my ability to hear, as if I were indeed deaf or could hear only the rhythm of modulations, but by strong inference her dream language seemed to say, "Listen to me now, I've been waiting for you a long time." Perhaps it takes a culture as slippery and venal as our own to discount the dream life that was so vital to people for thirty thousand years. Dalva appeared at a time of great emotional stress, after I had taken a very long nondirectional car trip. I fixed on the particularly unknown state of Nebraska, a place that had always fascinated me as a stage for the collision of European and Native cultures that culminated at Wounded Knee in 1890 but still survives in vital remnants today. If you're blind to this in our past, you're liable to be blind to it in the present and future.

I wrote my grand historical scheme into the life of this woman, who herself was part Lakota, and whose father, grandfather, and great-grandfather had truly lived our history. She, finally, lives it too, no less than they—not as a pawn but as a particularly vivid human being.

Of course, the raw meat on the floor, the mystery, is how to convincingly enter another's voice. At nineteen I was a poor scholar indeed, but I owned most of the Bollingen volumes of the collected works of Carl Jung. Rather than study the text I mined it for my own purposes, though it would be a couple of decades before I had the wit to use the material. One very troubling idea was Jung's question of what we have done with our twin sisters that the culture forces us to abandon at birth. This is a reduction, but then I'm a novelist and poet, and I'm talking about fiction, not accuracy. But perhaps in my work in the voice of a woman, I was trying to revive this ghost that the culture steals from us.

An additional source was my sometimes casual but lifelong study of the roots of American Indian culture. This is scarcely an abstraction in northern Michigan, where the closest reservation is only a half dozen miles from our farm and mixed bloods was common. Again, this was not a scholarly impulse but a search for fuel, for answers to our behavior that seemed not to exist in white culture. A pervasive theme in many Native cultures is the freedom of shape changing, where the man or woman becomes a coyote, a bear, a wolf, a bird, a flower, tree, creek, rock, the wind. This is somewhat more attractive to a loony young writer than to an MBA, much less an MFA, and I unwittingly traveled these dangerous waters most of my life. The merest suggestion of emotional limits drives me into a sodden funk. In *The Road Home*, Dalva can say things, simply enough, that a male character can't, and in areas in which I can't bear to be voiceless. Talking about loutish cowboys, one of whom she errantly loved, she says: "By the first midnight in a Hardin bar it occurred to me that these people made Brooklyn Sicilians look like English gentlemen. There's a terrible illusion that the grandeur of landscape contributes to grandeur of personality." I have too many cowboy friends to say such a thing, but Dalva was up to it.

I tend to think that art is essentially androgynous and that gender is a biological rather than a philosophical system. I doubt that there is an intelligent straight man who hasn't at times envied the seeming emotional latitude of either women or gay friends. On a perhaps comic level for a novelist, once you have decided to make this emotional latitude your own, you have already committed your act of hubris. You are way up there on the high board, and now you will discover if the pool is empty or full. On an almost absurd level I thought once that because of my blind left eye, I was missing half of life—and if I'm writing only as a man, I'm cut in half again. Being down to a scant quarter isn't enough to sustain my life.

The pool appears to have been full, but in literary matters the jury is out for a great deal longer than writers might wish. Dalva began her public life rather slowly but is still thriving ten years later. Clare, in the novella "The Woman Lit by Fireflies," has even been included in a feminist anthology. Clare's situation was scarcely unique though not often noted. A young woman marries a liberal, high-minded young man. She retains her ideals but watches his degenerate, deliquesce, until she can no longer bear it and abruptly leaves.

Dalva's reappearance in my recent The Road Home did quite well, especially in France, where the novel first was published and marked my first appearance on a national bestseller list. I have no specific ideas on why my work has done this well in France. Of the hundreds of letters and reviews, there have been only two real objections to my writing in the voice of a woman. This surprises me, though I thought that many of the political-minded might think of me as beneath contempt or essentially harmless, or that possibly women might prefer stories to politics, or that a literary novel rarely raises anyone to anger unless there is unpardonable sexual mayhem.

And maybe I could describe the cages in which my heroines lived because as a male I unconsciously helped to build these cages. Dalva was free to be an inordinately strong woman partly because I have known a number of them, easily as many as the inordinately strong men I have known. You have to look more closely, because men have generally defined the terms of strength.

If you can agree with the notion of the twin sister you abandoned at birth, the almost intolerable problem is access to her mind. It is here that we deal with aspects of the creative process that appear decidedly nonrational. If many of the culture's presumptions about women are wrong, and they are, you must certainly abandon any habituation and conditioning if you want the slightest access. Oddly enough, the first presumption your mind must demolish is that women lack the latitude of individuality of men. This is not the less difficult for being so obvious. I suspect that the source of so much feminine anguish in political and social terms is the same for anyone who is purposefully misunderstood. From birth to death someone is always yelling a name in your face that is not your own.

After *Dalva*, "The Woman Lit by Fireflies," and *The Road Home*, I'm willing to give up the quest, but then in an interview I once said that I didn't want to write about "nifty guys at loose ends," the fodder for so much of our postmodernist fiction. Men and women alike as writers may wander lonely as a cloud, or simply scratch their tired ironical behinds, quite unmindful that the neofascists hope to make us only workers in a theme park for the convenience of the global economy.

To show how confused the unconscious well out of which a writer draws material can be, it occurred to me while writing this that whether it is Clare in "The Woman Lit by Fireflies" or Dalva herself, perhaps I am trying to revive the presence of my beloved sister, Judith, who died with my father in an auto accident when she was nineteen. We used to talk about Dostoyevsky and Rilke, Modigliani and Gauguin, while burning red candles and listening to Berlioz. Who knows? In fiction I try to make life live itself. Judith was an indomitable young woman, and it is very likely indeed that this still-living spirit contributes to my efforts, however short they fall. Ultimately, the perception of reality in a culture is consensual, and so it must be if its peculiar civilization is to function. You have to excuse all the question marks thrown in by the artists, whether they are poets, painters, composers, novelists, or sculptors. Their calling from the beginning has been to maintain the vitality of the human spirit whether by saying no in thunder or assuming a voice not of their own sex.

(*New York Times Magazine*)

WILLIAM WORDSWORTH.
1850.
MARY WORDSWORTH
1859.

GREAT POEMS
MAKE GOOD PRAYERS
(1993)

A frequent and flawless 3:00 a.m. thought is, *How and to what extent have we betrayed our lives?* I do not use the popular phrase "the gift of life," as that notion would be viewed as suspect by three quarters of the globe's population, those drowning in the hunger and blood we only watch and read about. As William Butler Yeats said:

> Now days are dragon-ridden, the nightmare
> Rides upon sleep; a drunken soldiery
> Can leave the mother, murdered at her door,
> To crawl in her own blood, and go scot free;
> The night can sweat with terror as before
> We pieced our thoughts into philosophy,
> And planned to bring the world under a rule,
> Who are but weasels fighting in a hole.

Yeats is not specifically talking about the US Congress here or in the following:

> The blood-dimmed tide is loosed, and everywhere
> The ceremony of innocence is drowned;
> The best lack all conviction, while the worst
> Are full of passionate intensity.

This is all certainly more poignant information than we receive from the media, and it arrives in a form that is actually memorable. The media are excellently equipped to pose enormous questions followed by puny answers. For enormous answers we have always turned to poetry, whether it is by Isaiah, Sophocles, Tu Fu, Shakespeare, Whitman, Neruda, or Ginsberg, though even in poetry the answers are grassy hills compared to the vast and gloomy Everest of the question.

But let's retreat to a place that is more comfortable, albeit dimly lit—ourselves, and our probable regret that we may have betrayed our lives. Despite its intensity, our regret is apparently unable to change the past or to change the essential texture of Yeats's "foul rag-and-bone shop of the heart." Gary Snyder and others have pointed out that Native Americans tend to see all biography as similar and that it is the healing dreams and insights in one's life that are to be cherished. This is fascinating in that most of our own societal correctives are directed to the cash register and our death-bed scenes have everyone mentally flipping through the portfolio or the lack of one.

So what? When I was young and left-leaning (still am) and believed desperately in John Keats's notions of the truth of the heart's affections and the imagination, I disliked very much these lines of Yeats: "Those men that in their writings are most wise / Own nothing but their blind, stupefied hearts." I could not stomach this, as I knew that in the distant, golden future, probably by the time I hit thirty, everything would be made clear to me. The doom I read about

in the ancient *Elder Edda* was more acceptable, as it was penned by
my own Nordic ancestors:

> Hard it is on earth,
> With mighty whoredom;
> Ax-time, sword-time, shields are sundered,
> Wind-time, wolf-time, ere the world falls;
> Nor ever shall men each other spare.

This little strophe is not only true but admirably written, and it
reminds me of Heidegger's idea: "Poetry proper is never merely a
higher mode of everyday language. It is rather the reverse: Everyday
language is a forgotten and therefore used-up poem, from which
there hardly resounds a call any longer."

Poetry tells us that the uninformed experience is not worth
enduring. It is the polar opposite of political language, in which
nothing we hear is causally related to anything we know. It is the
most difficult, the highest art and singularly undemocratic—for every
hundred thousand who try, we get one really good poet. Jimmy San-
tiago Baca, a notable Latino poet, identifies a member of the calling
as one who gives birth to himself over and over, certainly a perilous
obsession and oddly gender-free—Emily Dickinson and Rilke had
more in common with each other than they had with anyone else,
before or after.

Just yesterday I was way out in the boondocks, taking a snooze
in a depression in a dune after a long hike. I wasn't cross-training or
improving myself as far as I know, just dozing, catching my breath
after a couple of hours of walking, letting the sweat dry on a brilliantly clear but overcrisp June day.

I had been tracking ravens in the sand, also a small yearling
bear, thinking of a statement by the poet and philosopher Neil Clare-
mon to the effect that reality is an aggregate of the perceptions of
all creatures. Only a poet could say such a thing. As I began to fall
asleep, I questioned why I love to fall asleep out in the wilderness.

Maybe because I'm a mammal and belong there? Perhaps it is equally likely that a bear will bite off my sleeping face as that I'll die in a plane crash on the way to LA, but I prefer the former. What do I look like to the ravens wheeling overhead? What did I look like to them forty years ago when I hoed those endless rows of corn and other vegetables? There is apparently a fragile bridge between expecting nothing and wanting everything. I was reminded again, as I often am during such harsh but lunar moments, of a poem by Yeats, the most distinctly true poem I have taken to memory, both a corrective and a grace note:

The Witch

Toil and grow rich,
What's that but to lie
With a foul witch
And after, drained dry,
To be brought
To the chamber where
Lies one long sought
With despair?

(*Esquire*)

PETER MATTHIESSEN AND A WRITER'S SPORT
(1974)

It probably begins with a child who has more than a passing fascina-tion with maps, studying them by the hour in a geography text or frayed world atlas in his grammar school. At first the usual places are interesting enough—France, Spain, Germany, Russia—places intricately connected with his lessons. Perhaps some war draws his attention to parts of Asia, say Mongolia and its great Gobi Desert, the Tibetan Plateau in Nepal, or the bare spots which cartographers call "sleeping beauties" within the island boundaries of New Guinea. And then Africa with its redolent place names: Mombasa, Dar es Salaam, the Serengeti, Addis Ababa, and the Congo. But the most fabulous names of all are in South America—the Mato Grosso, Patagonia, Tierra del Fuego—and they send tremors of curiosity through him. Maybe the child begins reading tales of adventure in

Richard Halliburton or the books of that most refined exoticist W. H. Hudson. If he is less literate he might only read the safari tales in sporting magazines, such as "Bushwhacking the Swamp Jaguars of Quintana Roo" or any of those characteristic fabrications that have giant pythons sliding forth from the dark recesses of a "kopje." The photos in the books and magazines show boas that are easily confused with lianas and vice versa: every tree is weighted with snakes, if not gorillas. In the comics he sees Tarzan riding his five-thousand-pound elephant Tantor past the vine-covered monuments of the inevitable lost kingdom.

So the child might come to love the extremes of sport, from Jonathan Slocum's antique, globe-encircling sloop to the ascent of Annapurna, from Frank Buck facing elephants forever poised on the verge of charging to those first encounters with marlin and swordfish on rod and reel in Van Campen Heilner and Zane Grey. Impassable rivers, endless jungles, brushes with death on the high seas.

But most of us who love what we clumsily call the "outdoors" are content eventually with a forty-acre woodlot, a civil backpacking trip into a national or state park, a canoe ride down a lazy river. If we deer hunt in Michigan we are among six hundred thousand others and we have justifiable fears that our brilliant orange parka will be mistaken for a whitetail. There might be a few days each fall or a fully ritualized duck or grouse hunt. Even among bird-watchers there are many lazy fibbers.

Peter Matthiessen is a singular man. There is the air of the nineteenth century about him, something uncompromising, unbending. He is a combination of the thoroughly self-made man and the adventurer, the artist, the explorer, the naturalist, and, probably most accurately, the pilgrim. At forty-five, he is tall and slender, graceful; a bit weather-beaten and wary but well on top of it all.

Matthiessen lives out on the eastern tip of Long Island, in Sagaponack, a small rural enclave not far from Bridgehampton. One can see what a solitary and beautiful place it was until recently,

when a number of rather garish vacation homes were built imped-
ing the view of the salt marsh. But just beyond the marsh is the
Atlantic and on a recent evening a thousand or so geese descended
outside Matthiessen's house from a red and wintry evening sky.
There aren't many people around except at the height of summer,
and behind its tall privet hedge the house seems a splendid spot to
rest after returning from places as varied as Tanzania, New Guinea,
the Amazon basin, the coast of Nicaragua, and the Great Barrier
Reef. Rest. Write. Get ready for a long trip with George Schaller
into the Tibetan Plateau country of Nepal in search of the snow
leopard. Dr. Schaller, well known for his work with the mountain
gorilla and Serengeti lion, has advised Matthiessen to prepare himself
for extensive walking and climbing at sixteen thousand feet. This is
a trifle hard to comprehend, as altitudes from five to ten thousand
can be lung-wringers for most any effort.

We aren't used to our writers being able to do anything particularly well other than write, and Matthiessen is first and primarily
a literary novelist. Ordinarily if a novelist is a fine wing shot, he is
probably only a fine shot "for a novelist." Of Norman Mailer it could
be said, "He's one of the best fifty-year-old arm wrestlers in the arts."
You know very well that every grain elevator and feed store in Kansas
boasts a lout that could put him down in minutes.

Ernest Hemingway was a rare exception, and this tends to irri-
tate every critic who has written about him. Critics are notoriously
sedentary. They have been known to divorce wives who are unable
to carry them from the desk to the dinner table, whereas sport was a
large part of Hemingway's life. Few novelists can write for more than
four hours a day, and if you don't teach and aren't interested in literary parlor tricks or drinking yourself to death you become an amateur
sportsman of sorts. And Hemingway, whose basic athletic skills were
not large, became a first-class wing shot, a big game hunter, a skier,
a boxer of some skill, and a master angler. He could be an arrogant
and unruly brute on occasion but this does not diminish the number
of things he did well.

But you quickly run low on names and the claims become strained: Vance Bourjaily is a good shot. Harry Crews is reputedly competent at karate and falconry. Larry McMurtry rode a horse. Galway Kinnell plays a fair game of tennis—for a poet. James Dickey hits a target with his bow with some regularity (a sport that can give you some profitable material). George Plimpton has been known to hit a duck and plays an underwhelming game of golf, though very good tennis. Tom McGuane is an expert flycaster. J. D. Reed is one of the best trenchermen on the Eastern Seaboard. William Styron watches his wife play tennis. After a fifth Richard Brautigan can do three push-ups without stopping. Thomas Berger used to drive fast. The author is the third-best pool player in a village of two hundred. William Hjortsberg does bird calls of the four birds he recognizes (crow, starling, ostrich, pheasant). Robert Ruark was no doubt a better shot than writer.

The art of the novel is usually so all-consuming that there is very little energy left for mastery of anything else. Matthiessen plays fair tennis and inferior squash, swims very well and skis; but it is his driving curiosity and what it drives him to that set the man apart. Some might be led to idly question his sanity at times.

You are pretty sure in the metal cage under the ocean's surface off Australia that the huge white shark is able to burst the bars, but in the impact of its rushes the shark is losing teeth and the cage is rocking like a puppet. Or on the Harvard-Peabody New Guinea expedition it becomes conceivable that you are not going to get out either dead or alive and you move up a hillside and sit behind a rock until the fear passes. The turtle schooner shipping out of Grand Cayman for the Miskito Cays isn't seaworthy and the food is vile so you get off and make your way home from Nicaragua. You notice the Indigenous Peruvians who accompany you down the river on a balsa raft are chewing coca leaves, from which cocaine is derived, and it occurs to you that they are doing so to gain both relief from the cold and courage for the horrendous rapids just ahead. In the Sudan you are stuck at a small outpost the day after the assassination of Patrice Lumumba. Near Lake Manyara in Tanzania the open Land Rover stalls a few feet beneath a lioness crouched and spitting along a tree limb.

Within this framework the old phrases about taking a chance become euphemisms. But the alternatives, in fact, don't seem to exist for Matthiessen. Descriptions of states of fear in sporting literature bear similarities: there is an immediate icy clench of the bowels, a brief daze descends, then adrenaline moves through the system like a shock from an electric fence. Some of us know this set of emotions only unavoidably, through war or a near auto wreck, or from hearing a rattler while hiking. But for Matthiessen, who insists that he hates fear and is often afraid, there's sometimes no choice. He acts as if one life isn't sufficient and nine might not be. If you truly want to know about rhinos, Cape buffalo, or elephants, it is altogether reasonable that they are going to force you up a tree.

Despite the appealing surface drama of these trips, most of the knowledge of the flora and fauna and the human history of an area has to be there before Matthiessen leaves the States. Since Matthiessen was an English major at Yale he has picked up his information through subsequent study and experience. The fact that he is first of all an artist lends an unusual charm and sensuousness to his prose in matters of natural history. However, no details are sacrificed in either *Wildlife in America* or *The Wind Birds*. You have no sense of the whole without knowing with some precision the separate parts.

Many of us don't see much on our travels because we don't know what we are looking at. (Recently in Tanzania a Cleveland gentleman complained that it was sad that all these animals couldn't be in Mexico and thus closer to home.) Often we enter a piece of wilderness somewhat like a scuba diver entirely ignorant of marine biology. As an instance, hunters tend to concentrate on the quality and variety of their weapons rather than on a close knowledge of the habits and habitat of their prey. A field naturalist such as Matthiessen, and even more so George Schaller, would make an alarmingly successful big game hunter. But something in the process of truly knowing about mammals makes one less likely to shoot except for food, and lessens the degree of difficulty so essential to the objectives of sport. Those expressions like shooting a "sitting duck," a "treed grouse," or "fish in a barrel" unfortunately reflect a lot of the activity in outdoor sport. But if you know that a Maasai kills a lion with a spear or that Leakey, to prove an archaeological point, killed a number of the antelope species by stalking and striking them with a sharp stone, your three-hundred-yard shot with a .270 doesn't seem so impressive.

Matthiessen has an unfair reputation in the literary world as a stern and haughty Brahmin (he, in fact, took himself off the New York Social Register at age eighteen, after which he joined the Coast Guard). There's certainly that side that gets all of the work done, and the wary reticence and caution that keeps him from getting his neck broken in some far-off place. But he is also very whimsical, essentially a romantic, with far fewer conservative tastes than the most ardent freaks half his age. He owns a large rock and folk record collection and was not above trying the South American psychedelic ayahuasca fourteen years ago, a trip that led to experiments with LSD, mescaline, and psilocybin, all undertaken with a sense of curiosity and privacy. It has always seemed silly to me that so many anthropologists would try to penetrate the mysteries of Native American peyote rites without simply trying it out themselves.

When he was twenty-two Matthiessen tried to bring a small fishing sloop all the way from the Gaspé Peninsula down to Manchester, Massachusetts. The seas became so violent he tied a line from his ankle to the wiring on the decrepit motor so that it would stop in case he was swept overboard. When he finally gave up after three days and made it to shore, the tip of the mast caught a bridge over the tidal river and snapped the mask at the deck. Matthiessen waded across a mud flat and got very drunk in a small village with a logger who in the fire of the moment offered to haul the boat the

hundreds of miles on his logging truck. The logger gritted his teeth
when sobriety came, but by that time they were well on their way.

There is a charming crankiness to the man verging on the
eccentric. Matthiessen avoids newspapers and TV, short of an occasional pro football game. A few years back he and his wife Deborah
marched around their predominantly Republican neighborhood
advising people to support Eugene McCarthy and dump President
Johnson. After a few days of this a kindly soul informed them Johnson had dropped out of the race the week before. And during a
recent visit of mine, a Hollywood producer arrived in Sagaponack
to talk about a movie deal. The producer was energetic, slick, and
florid, looking a little like the grandest golf pro on earth. To relax
the atmosphere, he began with some involved stories about what
had happened to him on the morning of the Los Angeles earthquake
but was brought up short when Matthiessen admitted that he hadn't
heard anything about a Los Angeles earthquake.

Writers have elaborate notions about paying their dues, an obsession
with struggle that comes from the knowledge that good work never
comes by accident. Long ago Daniel Defoe said, "Easy writing makes
damned hard reading," and a literary writer like Matthiessen, as
opposed to a more conventional novelist, earns an audience slowly.
His first three novels—*Race Rock*, *Partisans*, and *Raditzer*—earned
critical success but not much else. To supplement his negligible
income as a writer he turned to commercial fishing and operating a
charter boat for blues and tuna out of Montauk. This is a distinctly
unglamorous business though it later helped him write about sea
changes and marine biology with great skill. The books that followed
the apprenticeship of the first three novels enable one to gracefully
make elaborate claims for the work. It is not awkward or inaccurate
to speak of Matthiessen in the same breath or in the same terms in
which one discusses the other justifiably vaunted writers of his gen-
eration, from Barth, Barthelme, and Berger down through Updike
and Vonnegut. And a certain amount of the slowness of recognition

and critical confusion is caused by Matthiessen's versatility. As with Edward Hoagland and Edward Abbey, the power and popularity of his natural history work has tended to overshadow the less accessible novels.

It was not until 1965 and the movie sale of *At Play in the Fields of the Lord* that Matthiessen had any success that could be stored in a bank. On the surface the novel is a violent adventure tale set in the jungles of Peru. But beneath its skin we have a hero, Merriwether Lewis Moon, who deeply troubles us. Moon is a half-Indian adventurer from the United States and when he decides not to go back but to stay with a local tribe it is a disavowal of everything we Americans hold on to. We want Moon to return because he is necessary to our ideas about what America *should* be like but we are utterly sympathetic to his refusal. Much of the texture and the background of this novel were absorbed on extensive travels through the wilderness areas of South America when Matthiessen was thirty-two. The original journal of this trip was published as *The Cloud Forest*. The voyage through the steep canyon of the Pongo de Mainique rapids of the Urubamba River forms the most exciting pages of the book. By the time Matthiessen reaches this location, there aren't enough supplies for the return trip, leading to another of those "How in God's name did I get here?" situations on a balsa raft held together with vines and with no idea what lies ahead.

Two years later Matthiessen joined the New Guinea expedition out of which came *Under the Mountain Wall*, an involved account of a Stone Age tribe persisting in the twentieth century. On the way to New Guinea he traveled around Nepal and the Sudan, Kenya and Tanzania, where the idea for his latest book, *The Tree Where Man Was Born*, was formed. This book required additional trips to Africa. It is an informal travel chronicle and perhaps the finest book on the East African experience extant. In recent years Matthiessen has also written the text for *The Shorebirds of North America*, revised and reissued as *The Wind Birds*, and *Sal Si Puedes*, a book on César Chávez, whom he much admires and still works with. Another recent book,

Blue Meridian, concerns itself with the *Blue Water, White Death* film expedition in search of the great white shark off the coasts of Africa and Australia. This last book makes Peter Benchley's *Jaws* seem like a silly fairy tale.

It seems in character that though he has many friends in the literary world (including William Styron, Terry Southern, and George Plimpton, all of whom were involved in the early days of the *Paris Review*), Matthiessen tends to shun literary society except for a very occasional cocktail party, believing that there is simply not enough time.

We are used to profound and often justified pessimism. Time is running out. The Atlantic shows signs of rot from Maine down to the Virgin Islands and beyond. Concentrations of plankton, necessary for the ocean's food chain, decrease in water that is well oiled. The most far-flung islets have their nests of refuse and beer cans. Matthiessen has an almost Zen attitude of calm about this; but it is the attitude of a man who is doing what he can to remedy the situation. He seriously thinks it might take a state of total plague to wake people up. Back in 1959 he published *Wildlife in America*, a detailed study of our people's impact on the wildlife population in America from the time we got off the boat. This was well before the ecological movement gained momentum, only to lose much of its energy in the mire of Congress.

Finally, what the man has is style in the old sense, an unmistakable grace of bearing that comes from surviving odds, both real and invented, that would appear hopeless to nearly all of us. If you travel nine days on foot into the Tibetan Plateau of Nepal because you are interested in snow leopards and Tibetan Buddhism the dangers are obvious, but the power of your curiosity makes you what might be called an "accidental adventurer." You take responsibility for where and what you are and dismiss the severe discomfort and occasional fear as the price to be paid for the trip. Perhaps feeling cold and sick and utterly frightened on Everest or a balsa raft is not nearly so

injurious to the spirit as feeling cold and sick and utterly frightened
sitting at a desk in an office building.

Most recently Matthiessen is at home and tired of travel. His
wife Deborah died two years ago and he takes care of his small son
Alex. His three other children are off at school and college. He
has just finished the galleys of his new novel, *Far Tortuga*, his first
in a decade. The book is based in the turtling fishery out of Grand
Cayman and seems to me even more black and overwhelming than
At Play in the Fields of the Lord. Matthiessen wants to sit still for a
while but talks with interest of the Kerguelen Islands in the Indian
Ocean, and then there are those inhabited islands just south of the
Philippines . . .

THE PLEASURES OF
THE DAMNED
(2007)

Poetry shouldn't tell us what we already know, though of course it can revive what we think we know. A durable poet, the rarest of all birds, has a unique point of view and the gift of language to express it. The unique point of view can often come from a mental or physical deformity. Deep within us, but also on the surface, is the wounded ugly boy who has never caught an acceptable angle of himself in the mirror. A poet can have a deep sense of himself as a Quasimodo in a world without bells, or as the fine poet Czesław Miłosz wrote:

> A feast of brief hopes, a rally of the proud,
> A tournament of hunchbacks, literature.

Charles Bukowski was a monstrously homely man because of a severe case of acne vulgaris when he was young. Along the way he also had bleeding ulcers, tuberculosis, and cataracts; he attempted suicide; and only while suffering from leukemia in the last year of his life did he manage to quit drinking. Bukowski was a major-league tosspot, occasionally brutish but far less so than the mean-minded Hemingway, who drank himself into suicide. Both men created public masks for themselves, not a rare thing in a writer's paper sack of baubles, but the masks were held in place for so long that they could not be taken off except in the work.

Throughout his life, Bukowski held a series of low-paying jobs so dismal that they are unbearable to list, though he did keep a position as a mail carrier for many years. Early on he was a library hound, and there are a surprising number of literary references in his work. (Quite by accident while I was writing this, the French critic Alexandre Thiltges paid a visit. He confirmed my suspicion that Bukowski had closely read Céline.) Even more surprising in this large collection are the number of poems characterized by fragility and delicacy; I've been reading Bukowski occasionally for fifty years and had not noted this before, which means I was most likely listening too closely to his critics. Our perceptions of Bukowski, like our perceptions of Kerouac, are muddied by the fact that many of his most ardent fans are nitwits who love him to the exclusion of any of his contemporaries. I would suggest you can appreciate Bukowski with the same brain that loves Wallace Stegner and Gary Snyder.

It is uncomfortable to realize that I have been monitoring American poetry for fifty years and am now even a member of the American Academy of Arts and Letters, which a friend refers to as "the Dead Man's Club." All the scaffolding around the five-story building of this poetry is actually a confusing blemish and should be ignored in favor of the building itself, but this is probably impossible until a date in the future far beyond our concern. Time constructs the true canon, not critics contemporaneous to the work, whether they are the Vendlerites of the Boston area, the Bloombadgers of New Haven, or the Goodyear Tires of New York City.

Bukowski was a solo act, though his lineage is fairly obvious. You detect Whitman, Bierce, Mencken, Sherwood Anderson, Kenneth Patchen, William Carlos Williams, perhaps Villon and Genet, and strongly Céline. He loved classical music, and there is an amusing poem in which he feels for Bruckner because he wasn't a better composer. He despised Fitzgerald because to a man from the lower depths, Fitzgerald seemed sensitive only to the sufferings within the upper class. Bukowski seemed far more worried about his cats' health than his own. One had been shot and run over but survived, though its front legs didn't coordinate with the back, a metaphor for something, probably Bukowski's life. He had several failed marriages—but then historically, poets are better off with imaginary lovers. He observed birds, but one cannot imagine anyone less a nature poet, if you discount the infield of a racetrack, where you could see him in the long line at the two-dollar window. He was deeply enthused about bars and keeping company with whores, and seemed to like the spavined landscapes of the nether regions of Los Angeles, which I myself used to visit. They are so resolutely charmless compared with the slums of New York I knew in the late fifties, which I visited because I was advised not to.

I have wondered, when asked about Bukowski in Brazil and France, if that's not why so many foreigners admire him: he's simply the American of their imagination, a low-level gangster as poet. Some are Abel poets and some are Cain poets, and Bukowski is clearly the latter (there are those who think of themselves as Cain poets but shift to Abel when they get a job in academia). It is clear from reading him that Bukowski didn't live in a gated community, whether academic or economic. His was the hard-found music of the streets.

But then, *fuimus fumus*—it all drifts away in smoke. It is not poetry that lasts but good poems, a critical difference. An attractive idea is that the test of poetry should be the same as Henry James's dictum for the novel, that it be interesting. Pasternak said that despite all appearances, it takes a lot of volume to fill a life. Bukowski's strength is in the sheer bulk of his contents, the virulent anecdotal sprawl, the melodic spleen without the fetor of the parlor or the classroom, as if he were writing while straddling a cement wall or sitting on a bar stool, the seat of which was made of thorns. He never made that disastrous poet's act of asking permission for his irascible voice.

The Pleasures of the Damned is an appropriately long collection because it is likely to stand as the definitive volume of Bukowski's poems. It is well edited by John Martin, the publisher of the estimable Black Sparrow Press, who was Bukowski's editor for most of his working life.

It is hard to quote Bukowski because there are virtually none of those short lyrics with bow ties of closure that are so pleasant for a reviewer to quote. I will excerpt a poem evidently written quite near the end of his life:

> it bothers the young most, I think:
> an unviolent slow death.
> still it makes any man dream;
> you wish for an old sailing ship,
> the white salt-crusted sail
> and the sea shaking out hints of immortality
>
> sea in the nose sea in the hair
> sea in the marrow, in the eyes
> and yes, there in the chest.
> will we miss
> the love of a woman or music or food
> or the gambol of the great mad muscled
> horse, kicking clods and destinies
> high and away
> in just one moment of the sun coming down?

I am not inclined to make elaborate claims for Bukowski, because there is no one to compare him to, plus or minus. He wrote in the language of his class as surely as Wallace Stevens wrote in the language of his own. This book offers you a fair chance to make up your own mind on this quarrelsome monster. It is ironical that those who man the gates of the canon will rarely if ever make it inside themselves. Bukowski came in a secret back door.

(New York Times Book Review)

STEINBECK
(2002)

I think I was twelve or thirteen when my father, Winfield, gave me *The Grapes of Wrath*, describing it as his favorite novel. Winfield was an agronomist specializing in land and water conservation but he read widely. I suspect that part of his sympathy for Steinbeck came from his own hard life including living in a tent for two years digging on a pipeline to save money for college. After *The Grapes of Wrath* in the ensuing high school years I read the total Steinbeck oeuvre in the company of my younger sister, Judith, who was a total Steinbeck adept. When I was twenty-four Winfield and Judith died together in an automobile wreck and I've often wondered if some of the poignant feelings I have for Steinbeck aren't tied up in our broken circle of admirers.

Steinbeck is a writer who has truly stayed with me, along with Melville, Whitman, and Faulkner. Just recently I reread *Sea of Cortez* and was again amazed at his knowledge of the natural world, to which I must add his broad knowledge of the world in general that far surpassed that of his fellow writers at the time. Steinbeck never seemed to use characters as tools to prove a point as did Dos Passos or Hemingway, both considerable writers.

Contrary to the modernist tradition which often seems on the verge of finally suffocating writers Steinbeck dared not to disappear into himself. I suspect that here lies the core of critical attacks on the man, in the simple fact that he clearly stood outside the pervasive literary narcissism of both his time and our own. He also strikes me as being outside the permanent love affair with self-importance that afflicts so many major writers. Both Steinbeck and Faulkner had a dimension of personal humility that beneficially pervades their work.

When I was nineteen I hitchhiked from Michigan to California hoping to become a beatnik, whatever I thought that was, but also to see Steinbeck country. I picked beans around Salinas, ate oranges on hot afternoons, and clearly recall describing the glories of the countryside that bore and nurtured John Steinbeck to Winfield and Judith on my return.

(John Steinbeck: Centennial Reflections by American Writers)

LAUREN HUTTON'S ABCS
(2007)

When you hear that banal old line "Take my hand, I'm a stranger in paradise," it occurs to you that such emotions are rarely accessible. Romantic gullibility is, however, characteristic of songwriters and poets, and I happen to be, among other things, one of the latter. The onset of a crush or infatuation is a nonmilitary surge, a rather blowsy tsunami in the brainpan so that the soul develops twinkle toes, the heart enlarges to the size of the Pacific Rim. If you're married, it is far safer if the object of desire is a photo in a magazine, or on the silver screen, rather than within the somewhat rigid confines of your actual life.

You wonder how pheromones can emerge from the pages of a magazine and infect the mind of the viewer. It's not just me who has experienced this affliction. Early in my mediocre screenwriting career I dined several times with Orson Welles in Patrick Terrail's Ma Maison in Hollywood. Over the usual caviar, a whole Norwegian poached salmon, a leg of lamb, and several French Premiers Grands Crus, I asked him if the Rita Hayworth stories were true. Of course. He told me he was in Brazil and had seen the fabulous photo of Rita on the cover of *Life* magazine, jumped the next plane to Los Angeles, and soon married her. How heroic, though I was cynical enough to question whether it was really "the next plane." Didn't he have business in Rio to tidy up? In any event, the marriage was a "disaster." Orson also warned me never to fall in love with a hatcheck girl—valuable advice, though I never met one.

I've had a number of such experiences of varying intensity. Lucky for me I'm half Swede and Swedes are slow studies, brooders. They're more likely to walk in a rainy forest for a month and then miss the next plane because they tried to expunge their perilous emotions with herring and aquavit.

After boyish infatuations with Deanna Durbin and Jeanne Crain (*State Fair*), Deborah Kerr (tied to the stake in a negligee in *Quo Vadis*), Ava Gardner (*The Barefoot Contessa*), Cyd Charisse (kicking sky-high in *Deep in My Heart*), I hit a vacuum for a while before Lee Remick twirling her baton in *A Face in the Crowd* hit me hard below the belt.

There was a hiatus for a time in my wanton but abstract affections because of a very happy marriage sexually and the general busyness of my life. I had spent two mostly miserable years as a poet, a writer of reviews for the *New York Times Book Review*, an administrator of an English department at Stony Brook University on Long Island. I simply didn't have time to let the devil into my life until we moved to northern Michigan on the grace of two grants and I had my first extended leisure since I began working at the age of twelve. We lived in an idyllic stone farmhouse for seventy-five bucks a month on a hill overlooking Lake Michigan. I was finding it hard to write in a state of total freedom, and one idle summer morning, probably with a hangover, I picked up my wife's *Vogue* and stared long and hard at a Richard Avedon display of a young model named Lauren Hutton. It was shot in the Bahamas, and in one photo I seem to remember Lauren was on her tummy reading Ezra Pound's *ABC of Reading*, one of my favorite books at the time. For some strange reason asses can be more memorable than books and to be frank her butt was extremely bare. There was the "involuntary shudder" in my body that we read about in novels but rarely ever get to feel. It was akin to getting suckered into peeing on an electric fence in my farm-boy childhood. Since I was a literary type, I doubtless thought of Lucrezia Borgia or the nudes of Botticelli or Modigliani to try to raise lust, the brain's hangnail, to higher ground. Far later in life I learned that male chimps will give up lunch to look at photos of female chimp butts, but at the time I tended to want desire to be somehow connected to the English Romantic movement. I'm sure my unruly but silky hair was sweating as I turned and re-turned the page. This was clearly the finest flower of womankind, as they say.

In my heroic posturing as a young American poet of note, I naturally wrote her a letter, and she wrote back saying, "You sure can turn a girl's head with that typewriter." I wrote again but received no answer. A certain slippage entered my fantasy, which, after all, was mostly literary. Would I have been so awestruck had she been reading *Peyton Place* rather than Ezra Pound? Also, having lost my left eye at the age of seven to an angry girl wielding a broken bottle, I had lost any impulse to push myself on a woman. Pheromones again. They either like you or they don't. Stalkers have always been a mystery to me. Why pursue a woman unless she gives you some sort of welcome sign? And my somewhat unstable mind was distressed one morning remembering the last night's dream wherein Lauren lived in a house on a small causeway out in a harbor somewhere. I was anyway recovering from a severe back injury and writing a novel, having determined that the few hundred bucks in royalties delivered by my books of poems wouldn't support my family.

Our fantasy neurons can burn out, but they can also revive themselves, sort of like the attempt to bring back the two-dollar bill, or the idea that chapters of life don't close but smear and blur themselves into the next. About half a dozen years after the "Pure

Poet in Northern Michigan" chapter, I was in Key West tarpon fishing and made friends with Phil Clark, about whom Jimmy Buffett wrote his song "A Pirate Looks at Forty." These tarpon trips lacked wisdom, as drugs, booze, and other nonsense were integrally woven into our sporting life. Clark was a wonderfully raffiné character involved in commercial fishing and smuggling, not a unique combination of vocations in the Keys in those days. Clark told me that when he lived in New York City he had roomed with Lauren Hutton, though they weren't romantically connected. That didn't quell my hot jealousy as I imagined them passing each other in and out of the shower. I think at the time Lauren worked briefly at the Playboy Club.

Half a dozen years later I was in Hollywood as an accidentally successful screenwriter, though it was some years before my mediocrity at this difficult form would be revealed. While in Hollywood, when not taking meetings I'd stay with Jack Nicholson. When I brought up Lauren Hutton he said that she was utterly lovely but tough and that he had once sent her roses but she had sent them back. He also warned me that while actors are usually three people, actresses are always at least five.

My memories of my Hollywood years are, not surprisingly, blurred, as the 1980s were not a time of rehab. I somehow managed to get an informal date with Lauren at an intensely private club, On the Rox, up above the Roxy Theatre, where one would run into a sparse crowd of people like Jagger and Belushi or find James Taylor jamming. I sat there at the bar with my fat heart going pitty-pat. In came Lauren, splendid in cowboy boots, Levi's, an open white satin blouse, a tweed coat, and uncapped teeth. I'm normally voluble, but I recall stuttering a bit. We had a drink and talked about Ezra Pound, William Carlos Williams, and Faulkner for an hour, and then she left.

That was that for another half dozen years until in New York City a magazine was giving a party at '21' for George Plimpton and me, who were columnists for it. I recall that no one recognized me when I entered, because I was wearing a camel hair coat and a

three-piece suit. Lauren had been an old friend of George Plimpton's ever since *Paper Lion*, and when she arrived we talked about
my cooking dinner at her place, but nothing came of it. I excel at
taking naps, pouring drinks, lighting my cigarettes, writing too many
novels, and, some say, cooking.

The last I heard of Lauren was at the Tosca Cafe, a bar I like
in San Francisco. The owner, Jeannette Etheredge, is an old friend
of Lauren's and said there had been a severe motorcycle accident
and Lauren was badly injured. I sent along my sympathies and in my
melancholy I wondered why people ride around on these skinless
rockets, but then I also question the efficacy of internal combustion,
photography, movies, mirrors. Our affections are up for grabs in our
nontraditional society, but then this isn't new. A couple of years
ago I visited Dante's house in Florence and questioned again how
he could spend his entire life on a work dedicated to Beatrice, an
eight-year-old girl he met when he was nine and was never to sleep
with. I can sit in my studio and look at a blank wall and see all the
heroines of my novels march past, carefully ignoring their origins,
mindful that James M. Cain said, "I write of the wish that comes
true—for some reason, a terrifying concept."

It is a comfort to know that women also suffer this fantasy
affliction. Nearly fifty years ago during a bridge game with another
couple in our squalid married-housing apartment our friend stood
up and shrieked at her diminutive husband, "You shrimp, you miserable little turd, you're nothing compared to my true love, Marlon
Brando."

(Playboy)

INTRODUCTION TO
RESIDENCE ON EARTH
BY PABLO NERUDA
(2004)

Genius always leaves us wishing the meal could continue. Why didn't that layabout Shakespeare produce twice as much? How grand it could have been if Dostoyevsky had written a novel about what happened after he died. We were severely cheated when Caravaggio and Mozart fled earth so early in their lives.

Neruda achieved his full dimensions if any poet did. He led a whole life both publicly and privately. It is boggling to read his *Memoirs* and try to map his exterior and interior voyages, from the rawest perils to the Stockholm ceremony that reminded him oddly of a school graduation, to his transcendent Buenos Aires "poetry slam" with Federico García Lorca which will raise the hairs on your

body as if they are throwing off infinitesimal lightning bolts. That
evening both poets stood athwart poetry's third rail.

I lost my first copy of Neruda's *Residence on Earth* in Key West
in the midseventies. I left it in one of a dozen possible bars on a
verminish hot night during May tarpon season with the air dense
with flowers, overflowing garbage cans, the low tide deliquescing
crustaceans, and where, while swimming before dawn off a pier, the
moonlight illumined a deadly shark whose face looked like a battered
Volkswagen. I retraced my steps the next day but found nothing. I
had underlined too much of the book anyway.

At that time back in the twentieth century I was addicted
to Spanish-speaking poets such as Neruda, Vallejo, Hernández,
Lorca, Parra, and Paz, whenever I could find translations, but also
Yesenin, Rilke, and Yeats. What a sacred mishmash. In northern
Michigan I was far from a good library but my brother John was a
librarian first at Harvard and then at Yale at the time and could
send me anything. Naturally I read our own poetry on both sides
of the farcical Beat-academic sawhorse, and all of those poets in
the Midwestern middle like myself, but then nationalism in literature is stifling indeed as are our varying fads of poetry. Earlier in
my life it was fashionable to spend your life and career not being
particularly enthused about anything, and now there is an affecta-
tion of artless sincerity where after the high adventure of graduate
school poets settle down in a domestic trance. On my rare visits
to colleges and universities I keep expecting to see men carrying
caskets out of the welter of brown brick buildings. Of course any
poet is semi-blind to the ocean of trivialities he swims through and
basks in like a nurse shark, the important magazine publications,
the books and chapbooks, the readings, the awards, the miniature
parades he organizes for himself in the backyard among the flower
beds and house pets, and then finally on nearing the empty pantry of death he sees clearly the formidable odds against any of his
poems surviving. This is all to create the atmosphere in which I
continue to read Neruda.

It's important to offer here what constitutes Neruda's credo:

Some Thoughts on Impure Poetry

It is worth one's while, at certain hours of the day or night, to scrutinize useful objects in repose: wheels that have rolled across long, dusty distances with their enormous loads of crops or ore, charcoal sacks, barrels, baskets, the hafts and handles of carpenter's tools. The contact these objects have had with man and earth may serve as a valuable lesson to a tortured lyric poet. Worn surfaces, the wear inflicted by human hands, the sometimes tragic, always pathetic, emanations from these objects give reality a magnetism that should not be scorned.

Man's nebulous impurity can be perceived in them: the affinity for groups, the use and obsolescence of materials, the mark of a hand or a foot, the constancy of the human presence that permeates every surface.

This is the poetry we are seeking, corroded, as if by acid, by the labors of man's hand, pervaded by sweat and smoke, reeking of urine and of lilies soiled by diverse professions in and outside the law.

A poetry as impure as a suit or a body, a poetry stained by food and shame, a poetry with wrinkles, observations, dreams, waking, prophecies, declarations of love and hatred, beasts, blows, idylls, manifestos, denials, doubts, affirmations, taxes.

The sacred law of the madrigal and the decrees of touch, smell, taste, sight, and hearing, the desire for justice and sexual desire, the sound of the ocean, nothing deliberately excluded, a plunge into unplumbed depths in an excess of ungovernable love. And the poetic product will be stamped with digital doves, with the scars of teeth and ice, a poetry slightly consumed by sweat and war. Until one achieves a surface worn as smooth as a constantly played instrument, the hard softness of rubbed wood, or arrogant iron. Flowers, wheat, and water also have that special consistency, the same tactile majesty.

But we must not overlook melancholy, the sentimentalism of another age, the perfect impure fruit whose marvels have been cast aside by the mania for pedantry: moonlight, the swan at dusk, "my beloved," are, beyond question, the elemental and essential matter of poetry. He who would flee from bad taste is riding for a fall.

(translated by Margaret Sayers Peden)

How is an ordinary mortal to look at this statement? I am reminded that at the Hard Luck Ranch on the Mexican border where I have a little studio, a number of cows died of thirst several years ago in clear sight of Lake Patagonia across the fence. Neruda ran through every fence he encountered except Stalinism over which he tripped grotesquely. But earlier in his life, in his twenties, when he began *Residence on Earth*, he was trapped in a variety of minor consular posts in the misery of Rangoon and Burma and other remote outposts. It is lucky for us that he hadn't been dispatched to a place he would have loved like Paris. He was lonely well beyond desperation but with an energetic anguish that sent him on the inner voyage of *Residence on Earth*. There was no ballast for him except the next part of this long poem. In every line you trace with great difficulty the bruised consciousness that produced it because unlike most poetry it proceeds from the inner to the world outside the poet.

Of course I'm not an astute critic. Perhaps *Residence on Earth* is one of those very rare poems you must drown in. You don't understand it in discursive terms, you experience it. To read *Residence on Earth* is to take a long exhausting swim across the Mindanao Trench, which is said to be the deepest part of the world's oceans. In other words, the territory could not be less reassuring or secure. For me the poem is the most palatable and grand of all work immersed in surrealism, lacking as it does the French hauteur of intellect. It always returns to earth.

Once, in my thirties, I thought I had invented a brilliant definition of metaphor but then I misplaced it and decided recently that nothing is worth searching the contents of seventy cartons of papers. Boris Pasternak inferred that metaphor is the shorthand of the gods, those who with overfull mental plates must move in leaps rather than walk like other mortals. When midway through *Residence on Earth* you read "Ode to Federico García Lorca," you are startled to discover that it was written a year before Lorca's execution because the metaphors so perfectly illumine and presage Lorca's death. In the past century there is no poet so profligate and exquisite in the realm of metaphor as Neruda. Neruda haunts our bodies on an actual earth with the same power that Rilke haunts the more solitary aspects of our minds. Rilke holds no one's hand while Neruda, like his idol Walt Whitman, attempts to hold everyone's.

There is a troubling matter when we reread Neruda's apologia in "Some Thoughts on Impure Poetry." In my own lifetime our country had reversed the quotient of 70 percent of people being rural and 30 percent urban. In an interview with Robert Bly in the 1960s, Neruda joked, "Perhaps I am a foolish writer of nature like your Henry David Thoreau." In recent years I have noticed that two Buddhist magazines I read have largely abandoned their traditional dependence on the language of nature in favor of nounless abstractions. It is less pronounced but I have also noticed this in the language of poetry in my own lifetime. I recall as a teenager in reading Robert Graves's *White Goddess* how young poets under the tutelage of a female ollave, a witch of poetry, would learn all the names of trees, plants, flowers, birds, and animals. Once in reaction to the anemic MFA programs I've come in contact with, and while being banally prescriptive in the manner of northern Midwesterners, I conceived of a program

in which poets would work for a year in the country, then a year
in the city, all the while keeping journals and studying the perhaps
three hundred central texts of world poetry, and after that a third
year at the university. Our bifurcated and predatory culture crushes
and strains the economically nonviable language of earth from our
lives. In contrast, Neruda, in his monumental *Residence on Earth*,
superbly and sincerely translated by Donald Walsh, tells us to break
down all barriers of language, that there are no poetic subjects per
se, and that we aren't romantic soloists on this sky island of earth.

For more years than I clearly remember I have had photos of
Faulkner, Dostoyevsky, Whitman's tomb, Rimbaud, and the stun-
ning Jill Krementz photo of Neruda holding an immense chambered
nautilus on the wall of my home studio. They belong together.

(New Directions edition of *Residence on Earth*)

WHY I WRITE, OR NOT
(1998)

Standing outside the Metropolitan Museum of Art in New York several years ago, feeling sodden and perplexed over the Goya show, I ran into an old friend, the poet Charles Simic, whom I hadn't seen in twenty years. Among other things that we talked about, he said, "I thought I'd understand everything by now, but I don't," and I think I replied, "We know a great deal but not very much."

I'm not saying that we throw in the towel on our rational mind, one that we only had two fingers on in the first place, but with age, the processes of my own art seem a great deal more immutable and inexplicable to me. For instance, even without my eyes closed, specific ideas usually carry an equally specific visual image for me. The act of writing is a boy hoeing a field of corn on a hot day, able to see either a woodlot or, more often, an immense forest where he'd rather be. This is uncomplicated, almost banal. He has to hoe the corn in order to be allowed to reach his beloved forest. This can be easily extrapolated into the writer as a small god whose birthright is forty acres in which to reinvent the world. He cultivates this world, but then there is always something vast and unreachable beyond his grasp, whether it's the forest, the ocean, or the implausible ten million citizens of New York or Paris. While he hoes or writes, he whirls toward the future at a rate that with age becomes quite incomprehensible. He leaves a trail of books, but he really marks the passage of time by the series of hunting dogs he's left behind. His negative capability has made the world grow larger rather than shrink, and not a single easy answer has survived the passing of years.

It is more comic than melancholy because the presumptions are so immense. No matter how much you've read, something has been left out that you aim to fill in yourself. This takes a great deal of hubris and frequently a measure of stupidity. Our large family read widely if indiscriminately, the movie theater in our small town in northern Michigan changing features only once a week. I began with the usual Horatio Alger, Zane Grey, Hardy Boys flotsam, graduated to my father's passion for literate historical novels, especially those of Kenneth Roberts, Hervey Allen, and Walter Edmonds, and then also to his taste (he was an agriculturist) for Hamlin Garland and Sherwood Anderson and Erskine Caldwell, before continuing on my own so that by nineteen my obsessive favorites included Dostoyevsky, Whitman, Yeats, Kierkegaard, Joyce, Rimbaud, Apollinaire, Henry Miller, and Faulkner. Such a list might very well lead an intelligent soul to keep his mouth shut, but then a curious arrogance has always been the breastplate of a young writer's armor. At this stage humility is a hobble you can scarcely afford. The only fuel the ego receives is interior. You might wander around in a thunderstorm, hiding out and repeating *Non serviam*, but then no one has asked you to do anything, and no one is looking for you, least of all those whom you have tormented with your postures.

Despite early forays to New York, Boston, and San Francisco, I have been preoccupied in my writing with rural life and the natural world. I must say that I don't see any special virtue in this. You are pretty much stuck with what you know, and Peter Matthiessen with his obsessive preoccupation with the natural world balances nicely with a taste for the more urbane James Salter or Don DeLillo. It is the artfulness of the prose and construct I'm looking for, not someone's fungoid wisdom. Good writers seem to know that we are permanently inconsolable.

It is the mystery of personality that seizes me, the infinite variety of human behavior that thumbs its nose at popular psychologisms. Even our dreams seem to wish to create new characters as surely as we do in our fictions, and our creation of our own personalities is most often a fictive event. In creating an environment for certain of my characters, I often find myself trying to create an environment for my own soul. It is a daily struggle against the habituation and conditioning that bind us and suffocate us, destroying the fascinating perceptions that characterize the best writing. You continue under the willful illusion that the world is undescribed, or else you need not exist, and you never quite tire of the bittersweet mayhem of human behavior.

Except, of course, for the fatigue brought on by our collective behavior, both political and economic, the moral hysteria we are currently sunk in. Last May without an inkling I found myself saying in a French interview that we are becoming a fascist Disneyland. This is seeping into our fiction and poetry in the form of a new Victorianism in which a mawkish sincerity is the highest value. At one point I thought it was simply the way academia had subsumed serious fiction and poetry, but now it seems that academia and the small presses are the only barriers against totally market-driven work, despite the other obvious shortcomings of the MFA pyramid scheme, a sad breeder of middling expectations and large disappointments.

Poetry comes when it will, and I've never had any idea of how to cause it. Way back during the Tang dynasty, Wang Wei, a phenomenal poet, said, "Who knows what causes the opening or closing of the door?" There has always been a tendency among poets in slack periods to imitate their own best efforts, but this is embarrassingly obvious to their readers. It's a bit like raping your own brain, or trying to invent a convincing sexual fantasy only to have the phone ring and it's your mother wondering why you're still a "bohemian" at age fifty-nine. The actual muse is the least civil woman in the history of earth. She prefers to sleep with you when you're a river rather than a mud puddle.

I wrote my first sequence of novellas in the late seventies and had some difficulty getting them published, as "no one" was writing them in those days. My own models in my search for an intermediate form were Isak Dinesen and Katherine Anne Porter. I've never been able to write a short story, which used to make me a bit nervous, as magazines kept prattling that this was the "age of the short story." I became less nervous when it occurred to me that these selfsame magazines couldn't very well publish novels or novellas, though the *New Yorker* did publish my story "The Woman Lit by Fireflies" and *Esquire* printed the novella "Legends of the Fall" in its entirety. A publisher who turned the latter down suggested I increase its mere hundred pages to five hundred and then we'd have a best seller—no matter that, unchanged, it has eventually sold quite well for twenty years. Novels seem to take care of themselves if you offer them up an appropriate amount of time. I've never written one without first thinking about it for years. This is probably a peculiar method, but I can't function otherwise. I just did a year's research for the second section of a novel and ended up using very little. This is what the film business aptly calls "backstory," without the knowledge of which it is difficult to proceed. If a character is thirty-seven, you still have to figure out the nature of her personality when she was a child, even if you have no intention of using that.

I've also written more screenplays than I should have, but then I've been fascinated by movies since I was a child. Admittedly, this fascination has never been very mainstream, which has caused me problems when looking for work. I doubt if there are proportionately any more first-rate novels than good movies in a particular year, but given the intelligentsia's scorn of Hollywood, this is not an acceptable idea. I admit there is a cynicism and perfidy in Hollywood that almost approach those of Washington and are probably equal to those in book publishing, but I have also noted evidence that some of the loathing for Hollywood is a veiled form of anti-Semitism, and being a mixture of Swedish, Irish, and English, I can say this without paranoia.

I suppose the main problem in screenwriting is that you're separated from the possible director until later in the series of drafts. This is a waste of time and money, especially since you have a good idea of a suitable director from the inception of the story. Another pronounced difficulty is that film-school graduates are definitely short on the varieties of human experience in favor of cinematic technology. Despite the fact that very bright movies tend to do well, there is a relentless and collective effort to "dumb down" the story. There is always the fear-maddened search on the part of film executives for a reliable formula story line, with inevitably sad results. On the plus side, no matter the whining, there always has been more oxygen in the West. Even Bill Gates wouldn't have done very well in Connecticut or Gotham. To be even as peripherally involved in the film business as I am, you have to have a taste for insanity and vulgarity, insecurity, hideous disappointments, spates of beauty, being fired over and over, and very good pay. It is usually a shuddering elevator far above ground, but I prefer it to intense domesticity. Yeats used to say that the hearth killed more poets than alcohol did.

I've recently had the uncomfortable feeling that despite my rather harsh Calvinist will, I've had less control over the trajectory of my life than I had presumed. I suppose it's because of the semireligious nature of the original period of the calling. Without going into the anthropological aspects, the beginning of the calling, when I was in my early teens, was similar to a seizure. I had abruptly given up on organized religion, and I suspect that all of that somewhat hormonal fervor merely transferred itself to what I still think of as Art, whether painting, music, poetry, sculpture, or fiction. Keats and Modigliani seemed excellent models for a life! The fact that neither

of them lasted very long is a nominal consideration for a teenager.
If you spend hours and hours listening to Stravinsky while reading
Rimbaud and Joyce, you are fueling a trajectory that is inevitably
out of immediate control. If you reread all of Dostoyevsky on Grove
Street in New York City in a seven-dollar-a-week room with only an
air vent for a window, you are permanently at age nineteen changing the nature of your mind. In your self-drama you are building an
intractable wildness that you'll have to live with.

Of course, in geological terms we all have the same measure
of immortality. The heartbeat that is your own, that you occasionally hear while turning over in bed in a cramped position, doesn't
last very long. The immediate noise your book might make is woe-
fully impermanent, and self-importance is invariably an anchor. In
immediate literary history, say the last fifty years, by reading lists of
prizes and remembering vaunted reputations, you see how even the
grandest fame is usually written on water. News magazines for years
liked to refer to Faulkner as Old Mister Cornpone; when I was a
teenager, he was far less favored than James Gould Cozzens. Finally,
what happens to your work is not your concern. Thinking about it
gives your soul cramps that resemble amoebic dysentery.

The mail over the years has brought me thousands of manu-
scripts and galleys and letters from young writers. It is possible to
drown in paper, but even more dangerous is the nasty mood of feeling put-upon. Other than recommending quantities of red wine and
garlic, I am without advice for these young writers. The closest I
can come is, Don't do it unless you're willing to give up your entire
life. Despite the Human Potential Movement, there is no room for
much else. And Einstein was on the money when he said that he
had no admiration for scientists who selected thin pieces of board
and drove countless holes in them. You should always want your
work to be better than your capabilities, as settling for less is a form
of artistic death.

I'd also rather err on the side of creating humans as more than
they are than as less. There is a whining penchant for lifting the

bandage, for forgetting that a body is much more than its collective wounds. In any culture, art and literature seem terribly fragile, but we should remember that they always outlive the culture. In an age of extraordinary venality such as our own, when the government is only a facilitator of commerce, they come in for a great deal of general contempt, as if every single soul must become bung fodder for greed. But then we are nature, too, and historically art and literature are as natural as the migration of birds or the inevitable collision of love and death.

(*Why I Write: Thoughts on the Craft of Fiction*)

THOREAU
(2010)

I have a deeply idiosyncratic relation to Thoreau mostly because he is enmeshed so thoroughly with my childhood memories. My father was a governmental agriculturalist in northern Michigan driving around a fairly remote area giving advice to farmers. Luckily for me Osceola County was a very poor farming area so that there were many forests to wander and hunt in and rivers, lakes, and creeks in which to catch trout and other fish. My father, Winfield Sprague Harrison, was a Thoreau obsessive. The only other writer who seemed to equally move him was John Steinbeck and there is a specific rural connection between these authors.

There has always been a great deal of urban, critical ridiculing of country idylls such as Thoreau's as if he were to be confused with Rousseau's ideal of the noble savage. The fact of the matter is that during my childhood millions of people lived very simply. This was a time of family farms rather than immense agribusiness, the virtual factory farms that have overwhelmed American agriculture.

The ideal behind family farms was as much as possible to be self-sufficient. In short, you grew and preserved your own food from tomatoes to pork. Far earlier in our history this was Thoreau's motive in *Walden*. The hundred-year road between Thoreau and our family was short indeed.

Concord in Thoreau's time, 1817–1862, though within twenty miles of Boston was overwhelmingly rural and forested with small farms surrounded by large blocks of woods. It was here that Thoreau had his small but epical experiment in self-sufficiency on the shores of Walden Pond. And it was in this area that he developed his explosive ideas of civil disobedience so predominant in the lives of Gandhi, Martin Luther King, and others. In America now we seem to have a moneyed oligarchy more than a democracy. It is ironic indeed that Walden Pond was preserved in recent years through the efforts and money of Don Henley, a member of the former rock and roll group the Eagles. The landscape of America so revered by Thoreau is always imperiled if a dollar can be made off it.

So I grew up deeply fascinated with Thoreau, learning, up to a point, from his example. For more than twenty years I had a remote cabin and during our entire fifty years of marriage my wife and I have never been without an ample vegetable garden except for the two years we lived in Boston. I am addicted to walking every morning, a fundamental teaching of Thoreau. Somewhat comically I am without my hero's abstemiousness. I never have a day without French wine or an attempt to make a good meal. Early in life when I attempted to be more ascetic I noted that life lost its Technicolor.

I am talking about the general question of influence to focus on the improbable vitality of Thoreau's work nearly two hundred years later. This is a lucid case of magnum élan vital. D. H. Lawrence said, "The only aristocracy is that of consciousness," and Thoreau had an uncanny level of perception botanically, of flora and fauna, but also historically. He knew minutely what he called the "tawny grammar" of the natural world. Most literary writers, frankly, are Romantic generalists, possessing a great deal of anecdotal knowledge, while Thoreau was a profound student of both literature and nature. Unfortunately at present my friends in pure mathematics and physics are more likely to be familiar with literature than my writer friends are to be knowledgeable about the sciences.

Thoreau's experiment in remote, survivalist living lasted two years during which he remained in contact with his great mentor, Ralph Waldo Emerson. This is important because it is fashionable now for those who retreat into the natural world to wear an anti-intellectual costume which was never Thoreau's intent. To him the life of the mind was as natural as a tree. Sad to say, Thoreau died in his forties or one might have expected his already unique insights to become more penetrating and idiosyncratic with age in the manner of the great French mind Bachelard.

It's extraordinary to watch the waxing and waning of reputations during one's lifetime. It's certainly not worth much of your time but then a great deal of curiosity is idle. A friend who spends a vulgar amount of time on the Internet says that you start out checking on the health benefits of flax and end up reading about the number of Russian prostitutes in Madrid. When you sharpen the blade of your curiosity you come to the conclusion that the nineteenth century gave us three figures—Thoreau, Whitman, and Melville—that the twentieth century never equaled. Comically enough Thoreau was only average as an agricultural survivalist but his writing is still implacably vivid and his natural contemporary heirs Peter Matthiessen and Gary Snyder are predominant in our literary landscape.

It was Wittgenstein who said that the miracle is that the world exists. Thoreau goes to great lengths to remind us of the nature of nature, the grace of the landscape's donnée. He resisted our government's stupidities. He was put in jail for refusing to pay taxes for our war against Mexico. Emerson visited him and said, "Henry, what are you doing in there?" and Thoreau answered, "What are you doing out there?" His gift is still with us as proved by the volume you have in hand. His words are beautiful but dangerous to your mind.

DREAM AS A METAPHOR
OF SURVIVAL
(1994)

"Whirl is king."
—*Aristophanes*

Come to think of it, the world has taken me out of context—physically, mentally, and spiritually. There is a not quite comic schism inherent in the idea that on a daily basis the *New York Times* and *All Things Considered* tell us everything that is happening in the world, but neglect to include how we are to endure this information. If I had not learned to find solace in the most ordinary preoccupations—cooking, the forest, and the desert—my perceptions and vices by now would have driven me to madness or death. In fact, they very nearly did.

It should be understood at the outset that a poet's work (like that of an analyst) frequently parodies his or her best intentions. The following is decidedly "creationist" rather than informed, bearing up as it does under the burden of a mind that creates its living out of a perceptual overload rather than out of a gift for drawing conclusions. As an instance, the memory of a mother's angry slap quite naturally suggests the flour on her hand: *She was making bread and I was eight. I said I didn't eat the seven Heath bars in the pantry though the wrappers were under my bed, and I didn't break the hen's eggs against the silo. Sent to my room I crawled out the window never to return and found Lila. We lay down on the wood bridge and tried to count fish but they kept moving in the green water. I felt my face where mother slapped me. I sat up and looked at the back of Lila's knee. She said "thirty-three" when I looked up the back of her blue skirt to where her underpants drew up into the crack of her butt. Lila didn't mind my injured eye because her dad had been shot in the war and maybe he had been shot right through the eye, she said. The girl who cut my eye moved away. I got back through the window just before I was called to dinner, a pocket full of violets for my mother, who asked me how I picked them in my room.*

In other words, what a mess, but then a dozen years ago I couldn't remember "everything," and all the memory knots were tiny claymores that blew up on contact or, more accurately, on encounter, as the miniature explosions were frequently accidental, causing all sorts of personal havoc.

It only gradually occurred to me that our wounds are far less unique than our cures. There is a specific commonality in the nature of the specter of anguish that arises and expands within us that makes us seek help, whether from an analyst, guru, roshi, shaman, preacher, even a bartender, those experts at symptomatic relief. In the north country of my youth, mental pain was implicitly tautological—omnipresent and unaccounted for—something to be endured with quiet manliness, another hazard to test the mythical fortitude of country folk (Michael Lesy's *Wisconsin Death Trip*).

The bottom line, as they like to say nowadays, is that we no longer feel at home either within, or without, our skins. There are thousands of ways to adorn this fact. It is largely the content of modernist and postmodernist literature and art, not to speak of the relentless fodder of self-help books and columns in newspapers. Rilke, that grand master of dislocation (he moved virtually hundreds of times), said, "Each torpid turn of this world bears such disinherited children / to whom neither what's been, nor what is coming, belongs." Alienation, so ubiquitous as to be banal, fuels our nights and days, our hyperactive adrenals gasping from fatigue. Where, and how, do I belong?

But then there have been quite enough general assessments of this theory and practice of dread. One nearly envies the bliss-ninnies, the New Agers, proclaiming from mountaintops that help is on the way. How can so many ladies have been Pocahontas or Mary, Queen of Scots in a previous life? It seems no one was the serf's child who was fed to the lord's hounds on a whim. On a recent pass through Santa Fe for a bite to eat (broiled chicken with red chile sauce), I saw a huge crystal for sale for $10,000. In a time and country when absolutely everything is possible for those with sufficient greed and power, this crystal in the shop window was so wildly awful as to be somehow comic and comforting.

What do I mean by dream as a metaphor of survival, even, in fact, as the path toward home? I am certainly not qualified to describe the way the unconscious struggles to heal wounds, and such published descriptions strike one as finite indeed, in that they try to render a magnificent fiction (the dream itself) into an immediate, therapeutic solution. (So what, of course, if it helps?) Part of the struggle of the novelist is to convince the reader that the nature of character is deeply idiosyncratic to a point just short of chaos, that the final mystery is the nature of personality.

In my own not very extraordinary case the biographical details are explicit: There was a severe eye injury causing blindness at age seven (I had been playing "doctor" with an unkind little girl). My instability was further compounded by the deaths of my father and nineteen-year-old sister in an accident when I was twenty-one. These were the two people closest to me, and in the legal entanglements of the aftermath, I was witless enough to look at the accident photos left on an absent lawyer's desk. Both of the death certificates read "macerated skull."

These were the main events along with a number of other violent deaths of friends and relatives, including seven suicides. The capstone seems to have been the accidental death of my brother's fourteen-year-old daughter about a dozen years ago. There had been a hundred-day vigil while she was in a coma, and a wintry funeral near Long Island Sound. Much later I dedicated a long poem to her called "The Theory & Practice of Rivers," of which this is a small part:

> Near the estuary north of Guilford
> my brother recites the Episcopalian
> burial service over his dead daughter.
> Gloria, as in "Gloria in excelsis."
> I cannot bear this passion and courage;
> my eyes turn toward the swamp
> and sea, so blurred they'll never quite
> clear themselves again. The inside of the eye,
> "vitreous humor," is the same pulp found
> inside the squid. I can see Gloria
> in the snow and in the water. She lives
> in the snow and water and in my eyes.

(Only now do I connect the eye material to my wound at seven.)

There was, quite naturally, a cycle of predictably severe depressions, beginning at age fourteen, then nineteen, twenty-three, twenty-seven, thirty-three, thirty-seven, and forty-three. Curiously, this cycle of lows, along with what dogs, cats, horses I owned at the time, is the way I ascribe "chapters" and carve up my life. It is evident to me now that the first of the depressions was caused when my father had to move our family of seven from a rural, heavily wooded area in northern Michigan south to near East Lansing so we could ultimately attend college. I remember that my first reaction to our new quarters was that there were no trout, the rivers were muddy and the lakes were warm, and the pheasants in the field behind the house were no substitute for the herons, turtles, bobcats, deer, coyotes, loons of my early years. And even more poignant for an utterly self-conscious twelve-year-old, a new community would have to adjust itself to my wounded left eye.

This is only the skeleton of a life, albeit a tad melancholy. I should add, before I reach the heart of the matter, that I attacked this life with a great deal of neurotic arrogance and energy (fifteen books, fifty or so articles, twenty screenplays), though I certainly would not have survived without the help of my beloved wife, my daughters, my remaining family, and a group of faithful friends. And (of course) a psychoanalyst in New York, whom I began to visit the year before Gloria's death. Coincidental with her passing was the death of my father-in-law, the diagnosis of my mother's colonic cancer, and the quite pathetic fracture of my foot while I was chasing my bird dog. In addition, after ten years of averaging twelve grand a year, I noted amid these disasters that I was making exactly as much that year as the president of General Motors. However, my first success had become quite meaningless within the framework of my life, and I added cocaine to an increasing alcohol problem. My sole survival gesture at the time, other than infrequent visits to my analyst, was to drive north into the Upper Peninsula of Michigan and buy a remote log cabin on a river. Typical of my behavior, I didn't bother going into the cabin before I wrote the check.

It has dawned on me that we appear to make certain specific decisions on a subconscious level far before we realize them, then simultaneously war against these decisions on a conscious level. This is only to say that pigs love their mud, and unless one is sufficiently desperate one continues to fritter away at the perimeters, re-creating the problems of the neglected core on a daily cycle that is shot full of self-drama. As an instance, after five years of treatment in New York, I took back to the hotel the extensive correspondence that had developed and was appalled to discover that I had created a serial of repetition of complaint, a "Volga Boatmen" dirge of whining about the same things: drinking, drugs, the loss of my loved ones, life as a continuum of defeat despite my apparent worldly success. Compulsive, ritualistic behavior, no matter how self-destructive, tends to hold back chaos. As Yeats asked, "What portion of the world can the artist have, who has awakened from the common dream, but dissipation and despair?"

Slowly, and mostly in my imagination, I had begun to swim in waters that sensible folks would readily drown in, mostly in the area of consensual reality. The therapy began to take effect, and my outward life gradually became more and more absorbed in hunting and fishing and walks in the undifferentiated wilderness of the Upper Peninsula that began as short, lazy jaunts and lengthened with the years to ten miles or so. There were quite wonderful comic aspects of a brown, burly man fighting crotch chafe plunging through swamps, thickets, over steep hills, down a gully that held a startled bear. I rewarded these exertions by preparing enormous, complicated dinners. Concurrently my work began to revolve around more "feminine" subjects, the acquiring of new voices, and away from the concern with "men at loose ends" that tends to characterize the fiction of most male writers.

It was in the dream arena of mortal play that these changes had their source and increased in volume. Dream life has always struck me as curiously Buddhist, as the dream points toward the feeling that "the path is the way," rather than toward Western geometric constructs such as ladders, steps, guideposts, the "ten" commandments. I became absolutely convinced that barring unfortunate circumstances we all are, in totality, what we wish to be, and if something was quite wrong, the "wrongness" came from a radically skewed and wounded core that had to be approached.

I'm a little hesitant to admit that the majority of the striking dreams occurred in the last few days of the waxing moon and at the cabin rather than my home, hesitant because the notion of any relation between dreaming and the moon is too daffy and hopefully accidental. Perhaps I am closer to a dream life in the wilderness. The time span involved is about twelve years in this sampling.

1. There were slides of glass in my spine preventing the free flow of whatever flows up and down the spine. This is too obvious to comment on, other than the way an "Ur-dream" may release the possibility of others. I knew nothing of Kundalini yoga at the time.

2. For the first time I saw the faces of my father and sister, not as torn or macerated, but normal, except they had the bodies of mourning doves. They were serene.

3. A comic one but not at the time. An enormous, glistening-faced wild boar appeared at the foot of my bed in the cabin loft and told me in a radio baritone, "Change your life." I began doing so by starting the generator and turning on the lights.

4. I went into a room that was full of a dozen rather soiled and sweating women, some lean but mostly really chunky. My dick was sticking out of my trousers, and I was embarrassed. They put me at ease and mentioned with laughter that it was a hard life being immigrants. We wallowed, sucked, and screwed for hours, and I awoke exhausted and happy. Since I have a fantasy penchant for austere "ice queens," this was a little puzzling. Versions of this dream reappeared and years later it occurred to me that our culture tends to treat older women as immigrants.

5. I was out in a wilderness of extreme cliffs and sharp-edged boulders. I leapt off a cliff with the manuscript of my new novel (*Sundog*) in my arms. I was injured horribly but survived, crawling around to pick up the pages. I looked up at

the cliff edge far above me and was rather pleased with myself. I wondered why my dread of publication took itself into the wilderness.

6. At dusk one rainy autumn evening I saw a timber wolf near my cabin after hearing her howl several evenings. A few days later I dreamt I found her out near the road, her back broken by a passing car. I knelt beside her, and she flowed into my mouth until I held within myself her entire body. I remember idly thinking in the dream that I had tried so hard to lose weight and now I was pregnant with a female wolf.

7. My father and sister are being driven down the middle of a river in a soundless car by two Native Americans. The four of them are quite happy. The driver pulls up to the shore and tells me flat out that I was never supposed to be a chief in the first place, but a medicine man. I interpreted this to mean that though I was a miserable failure at life I was doing quite well in my art, and if I pursued my art strongly enough I could heal myself and might help heal others. Soon after I began to write a long poem called "The Theory & Practice of Rivers."

8. A very disturbing dream. I was with two medicine men who were dressed in leather and furs. One was mortally wounded and embraced me, asking me to take his place. Again, I interpreted this as a message to bear down on my art. I've been a student of Native Americans since my childhood but would not dream of trying to "become" one. As Charles Olson implied, a poet must not "traffick" in any but his own sign.

9. I was surrounded by a crowd of people who were trying to kill me. My skin began to ache, and I crouched there with feathers shooting painfully out of me. I became a bird and flew away. This reminded me of the "ego" as an accretion of defenses that no longer function. When we are alive, we are always ahead of it.

10. This dream occurred while I was staying in New York City with my agent. Both of us were having a difficult time. One afternoon we decided to play gin rummy though we were unsure of the rules. While playing cards we watched the progression of a massive excavation next door. My agent asked what was even further below the five-story excavation. I told him there were watery grottos full of blind albino dolphins. He is accustomed to such explanations from me. That night I dreamt that we were playing cards and a monster came out of the excavation and broke through the window of the ground-floor apartment. It was towering above us but we continued playing cards because the monster was only me. My eyes were lakes, my hair trees, my cheek was a meadow with a river (I first thought it was a scar) flowing across it. In any event, I had become the landscape I most loved.

11. A more didactic dream, like the wild boar, beginning with a voiceless lecture to the effect that there were three worlds and I only knew two of them. I remain unsure of this. Then the dream downshifted into a hyperreality where alternately a cobra and a coyote entered into my chest cavity, taking the place of my spine and skull. In my youth I enjoyed snakes, but then was frightened of them for a long time. After this dream they didn't bother me. I remembered that in my childhood I was somewhat confused over the difference between people and farm and wild animals. Once while we were fishing I asked my father and he said, "people live inside and animals live outside." I accepted this explanation as adequate.

12. A wonderfully obvious dream. I am in New York City in the form of an ordinary red-tailed hawk, the most common hawk in the northern Midwest. I am trapped in a narrow opening between buildings where I have been investigating the evident fact that there are secret, unrecorded floors in New York City

apartment buildings. I thrash my wings, tearing feathers and spraining a pinion. My analyst discovers me and draws me out of the wedge. He holds me as a falconer would, smoothing my feathers, and allows me to fly off.

13. I am in a clear glass coffin, dead amid soil, moss, vines, and flowers, being looked at by a crowd. A slender, brown youth breaks through the crowd and breaks the coffin open with a club, and I jump out. At first I thought the brown youth was me, but on a closer look I saw it was my fifteen-year-old daughter, whose recent problems had brought me quite painfully back to life.

14. I was in Los Angeles working on a movie project and felt quite literally peeled in body and mind. I dreamt of a crow I had stared at a long time at my grandfather's farm as a child. The crow grew larger, and I noticed that there was a belled harness around its breast. I got on, and we flew to a sandbar in the Manistee River where we fished and bathed. The crow did not fly me back to LA, so I had to get on a plane.

15. One night I thought I was awake but wasn't. I heard someone crying and discovered it was a weeping boy lodged behind my organs and against my spine. When I awoke I immediately realized that this weeping boy, retained from post-trauma times, had caused me a lot of problems, and I set about getting rid of him.

16. This is a recurrent dream, though only once was Judith there, and only once was the dream resplendent. The hillside continues to reappear. My dead sister, Judith, was in a gown on a hillside, which was bare except for a dense thicket that was virtually throbbing with life. She beckoned me to this thicket so I might be restored.

17. A comic, literary incident. I was in an estuarine area near the seashore. A combination crypt-vault-septic tank floated up. I was urged to put all literary jealousies, ambitions, anger in

it. I did so and nudged it seaward. Far from shore it got stuck on a sandbar along with others and I wondered who else had done the same thing.

18. Last winter I suffered a period of extreme exhaustion from writing two novellas plus six versions of two screenplays within a year. On April Fool's Day I began a month's car trip with no specific destinations, highlighted by wandering through the canyon country of southern Utah. But when I opened the cabin in early May I was still exhausted in spirit and body. I dreamt several nights in a row that I should walk the "edges," the fertile area in terms of flora and fauna, between the darker forest and the open country. There was also the suggestion in the dream that the birds of North America are largely mis-named. I took off on foot, discovering again that the surest cure for mental exhaustion is physical exhaustion, though only if you keep it "light." Dream advice must not be taken as another sodden nostrum.

19. I am way back in terra incognita with a friend. At the edge of a black spruce bog in a thicket we find a moss-covered cement slab with iron rings. We are fearful. We wonder what's under it—hell, a snake pit, the repository of nightmares? My friend indicates that it's up to me—I mean the contents. We lift the slab aside. The pit is full of brilliant blue sky.

20. A huge Italian miner from the western Upper Peninsula is sit-ting at a laden table with his family. He points to a large glass of red wine and pronounces, "Anything more than this is an emotional hoax." I found this recent dream quite disturbing as I like a before-dinner whiskey or two, though on occasion it makes me unhappy with its "stun gun" effect. Wine, by comparison, is gentle.

21. At home I have insomnia, falling asleep finally an hour before dawn. I am jolted back awake by a dream in which I am whirl-ing on the bed, shedding and sloughing layers of skin in a blur. Now I am much smaller and painted half bright yellow, half

pitch black. Out the window above me I can see far into space to thousands of multicolored galaxies far beyond the Milky Way. I feel totally at home in this universe.

The above represents about one-third of what I think of as the key dreams since I first visited my analyst. They seem curiously simpleminded, like surreal children's stories. But within a sociohistorical framework, it is the primitive aspects of psychoanalysis that appeal to me. There never was a culture (except our own) in fifty thousand years that ignored dreams or wherein, as Foucault puts it, a healthy mind did not offer wisdom and succor to a weak and sick one.

Of course it is difficult to avoid trying to screw the lid on too tight, to find closure where there are maybe only loose ends. I see the evident attempt of my dream life to relocate me, to protect me from an apparent fragility I tried to overcome with drugs and alcohol, the overdominance in my life of "manly" pursuits. I no longer try to "guts out" anything.

Ultimately, in Zen terms, "to study the self is to forget the self." We wish, ultimately, to understand everything and belong everywhere. I have learned, at least to a modest degree, that I must spend several months a year, mostly alone, in the woods and the desert in order to cope with contemporary life, to function in the place in culture I have chosen. In the woods it is still 1945, and there is the same rain on the roof that soothed my burning eye, the same wind blowing across fresh water. The coyotes, loons, bears, deer, bobcats, crows, ravens, heron, and other birds that helped heal me then are still with me now.

I locate myself freely when I have the courage to ask myself a koan I devised: "Who dies?" What does this man look like to himself when he is away from the mirror? When I walk several hours the Earth becomes sufficient to my imagination, and the lesser self is lost or dissipates in the intricacies, both the beauty and the horror, of the natural world. I continue to dream myself back to what I lost, and continue to lose and regain, to an Earth where I am a fellow creature and to a landscape I can call home. When I return I can offer my family, my writing, my friends a portion of the gift I've been given by seeking it out, consciously or unconsciously. The mystery is still there.

> Who is the other,
> this secret sharer
> who directs the hand
> that twists the heart,
> the voice calling out to me
> between feather and stone
> the hour before dawn?

(Psychoanalytic Review)

BLUE PANTIES
(1999)

Early one recent morning far up a canyon near our "casita" on the Mexican border of Arizona, I found two things of singular beauty: a rattlesnake and a pair of sky-blue panties. After making a large circle with my English setter, Rose, I was in a hurry to get out of the canyon because of the growing heat which in turn brings out our seven local varieties of crotalids, the rattlesnakes, of which one must be wary. I have almost enough intelligence to avoid them but Rose runs so fast that I fear she might stumble on one and there is a particular subspecies, the dread Mojave, that is certain death for a dog, and its venom is even capable of killing horses and cattle.

The snake was half-emerged from a rock formation near my path. My heart leapt at the buzz of its rattle, the way its head jerked testing the air after sensing my inimical footsteps. I was relieved that Rose was a hundred yards distant. Then, on the two-track, the narrow dirt road that led to my vehicle, I saw a pair of blue panties lying in the grass near three yellow California poppies. It is due to the occasional wretchedness of the English language that panties are called a "pair," certainly a partial cause of our sexual schizophrenia.

You should know that back in the seventies I was a private detective for nearly a week before I sensed specific dangers in the profession and went back to writing. I picked up the panties and examined them. They were very clean and made of cheapish cotton and had a very slight scent of lilac. I looked up at the heavens which were equally blue but doubted the panties could have been dropped by God, or from an airplane, as it is a bit perilous to open an airplane's windows. I dismissed the idea that they had been tossed from a motorcycle because it's hard for a woman to take off her undies on a motorcycle, is it not? I examined a set of tire tracks determining that they were not Michelins, but Firestone steel belted radials, definitely an American product.

Rose came running up but then slowed to approach the panties cautiously where I had tossed them back in the grass. She looked at me for an answer, which I could not offer. There was obviously no connection between the panties and the rattlesnake, but how could I help drawing conclusions as a poet? Our great literary critic Kenneth Burke had identified part of the soul of beauty as threat: high cliffs, elephants, great thunderstorms, huge waves, exploding red galaxies, Gauguin's vahines, grizzly bears, the fer-de-lance, a million femmes fatales in blue panties are all overwhelmingly beautiful though they can and will destroy us.

The etiology of the power of panties is quite clear. I've been a lifelong poet but the very first poem I remember is the schoolyard chant:

> I see London,
> I see France,
> I see somebody's
> Underpants.

I'm sure that William Faulkner, remembering the delta wilderness, was thinking of underpants when he referred to the "pelvic mysteries of swamps."

Of course I prefer cotton because I emerged from the proletariat, the farm or peasant class. White cotton. But then I don't quarrel with any material a woman wishes to wear though I understandably hedge at the nun's burlap or sackcloth. Naturally I sympathize with Republican wives whose craven husbands force them to wear panties made of aluminum foil. Recent history tells us that these men are inconsolable over the fact that they possess genitals.

We brainy primates, in natural but rare moments of stillness, ponder the origins of our clothing and accoutrements, but then perhaps it would be as difficult to write the history of panties as it would be to write the history of rain. What is the soul of this garment? Was it devised early in history to protect women from insects and snakes, or the undesired probing of males? Perhaps near Sarlat, the birthplace of the Occident, a young woman wore panties woven of leaves, tender filaments of bark, spiderwebs, to repel Orf, the ogre, but then she would willingly take them off for Arf, the gallant one.

We are 99 percent genetically identical to chimpanzees who quite notably don't wear panties except in movies and circuses. In the final 1 percent rests our implacable inventiveness. Everything emerges here, from Mozart to the hydrogen bomb, from quantum theory to panties which may cost anywhere from one dollar to a thousand. They might be embroidered with the names of the days of the week. When I snuck into the bedroom where my lovely aunt was taking a nap I saw her panties embroidered with the word "Tuesday." My little brain roared like a locomotive engine, or perhaps simply surged with the emotion a nun might feel on first seeing the holy Shroud of Turin.

Meanwhile, back in the canyon the blue underpants sleep in the grass. Perhaps they are a discarded trophy. Did some American version of Emma Bovary throw them away before making love to her Latino yardboy in the back of a pickup truck? Possibly. I somehow know that the presence of these blue panties on this remote trail is not a solo act. Fingers were hooked around the elastic waistband to remove life's central barrier. Perhaps tonight in the light of the warmish full moon the dread Mojave will emerge from its hiding place and coil around these blue panties, breathing in the ineffable night air.

WISDOM
(2004)

At this moment in geological history the idea of wisdom seems archaic, something we vaguely remember that was taught in college by demonstrably unwise people.

Just the other day I was staying in a motel in a cow town near the interstate to write in peace in the delicious anonymity of a shabby room with a painting of a donkey wearing a garland of roses that looked curiously like our president. This town became famous in the press because the deputy police were caught shooting stray dogs for pistol practice. Anyway, while I was there I turned on the television because I am without it for nine months, thus without exposure to the real America. I was told in a fungoid baritone that my country is in "high alert" for a terrorist attack. We were warned that the attack could come anywhere in America or, of all places, Yemen. This is geographically a wide latitude but I was a good citizen and kept my single eye open for the evildoers.

Late in the afternoon I sat in a thicket for an hour and watched sandhill cranes flapping in for a landing with their lovely prehistoric honks and screeches. This is wisdom to me, sitting in a thicket where you can see out but no one can see in, not the media or the government or the terrorists. After the thicket you will have a bottle of wine in your room, a Domaine Tempier Bandol, and then eat a dinner so mediocre that it reminds you of nothing.

The only wisdom I have come in contact with lately is in a book called *The Birds of Heaven* by Peter Matthiessen in which he brilliantly extrapolates all dominant world problems by studying the fifteen crane species on earth. Curiously, three of these species have found safe haven only by living in the DMZ between North and South Korea. They are huge birds but still too light-footed to set off the fatal land mines that litter the earth like hidden cow plots, real explosive shit.

I love these birds; a few of the species I've known since childhood. Frankly, what we are doing to them is what we are doing to ourselves fueled by greed and stupidity. There is still an imponderable wisdom in sitting in a thicket for an hour, banishing both the world's noise and your own. Then you drink your French wine, smile, and say to the impenetrable ceiling that hovers over all of us, "When was it otherwise?" The government offers you nothing but apprehension. Only you can offer yourself peace.

DOG YEARS:
ON HUNTING

DOG YEARS
(2004)

*"All knowledge, the totality of all questions and answers,
is contained in the dog."*

—*Franz Kafka*

Our greatest politician, Thomas Jefferson, said that "good wine is a necessity of life for me." I agree but he should have said, "Good wine and good dogs are necessities of life for me."

Maybe it's as wrong to call a great man like Thomas Jefferson a politician as it is to call a grand sporting dog a dog. It's too categorical. For instance the best dog of my life was an English setter named Tess over whom I shot at least twelve hundred birds, including grouse, woodcock, four kinds of quail—bobwhite, Mearns, Gambel's, and scaled—and also sharp-tailed and Hungarian grouse. Bird hunters are invariably sentimental about their dogs unless the animals are outright incompetent. With Tess the actual proof was simply in the numbers though with a dog, that's never more than part of the story.

To start at the beginning, I've always trained my own dogs but I wouldn't offer this as a necessarily wise move. My first bird dog in 1966 was an extremely full-chested and muscular English pointer bitch named Missy. From the moment we picked her up in northern Michigan she essentially became our trainer. As a pup she could scale tall bookcases to play with the cat. We were quite poor at the time, living in a drafty rental for forty bucks a month in Kingsley, Michigan, with a furnace that couldn't raise the heat past fifty-five on the coldest winter days. I'd been trying to grouse hunt with Verl McManus's old beagle who had a singular talent of pattering around the woods treeing grouse—at which point he'd yip. I'd pretend the grouse had just barely landed or were on the verge of taking off when I popped them out of trees, and then one day I shot one on the fly flushing down between aisles of pines. The beagle naturally looked at me with admiration.

By the time Missy was six months I knew I was outfaced and took her to a trainer, who said euphemistically, "That's a lotta dog," as she climbed—with some success—a fir tree in his yard to get at a squirrel. That fall we moved to New York's densely crowded Long Island just after Missy had learned a new trick. After I ran her she'd reenter the yard at top speed and leap over the entire hood of our car, then brake with her front paws while her momentum would pivot her ass around so fast it would drag her backward a few feet. Quite a dog.

A university community is no place for a sporting dog or a sporting gentleman. Missy had taken to excavating our suburban yard; after I came home from a wretched day at the university she'd hear my car and explode from under the ground like a creature in a horror movie. We had two years of solvency but at the price of boredom for someone who had grown up around woods and water. I was in my midtwenties and never took a real job again. The rest of my life has taken place in the immediate area of trout fishing and bird hunting, where I could train a dog on wild birds right out the back door.

Sad to say but soon after coming back to northern Michigan Missy developed fibroid cancer and died. When I dedicated a novel to her many people assumed that one of our children had died and were further confused when they discovered it was "only a dog." How can I forget the way she entered a pasture woodlot as if it were full of grouse and then the ground shook as she drove a big herd of Holsteins toward me like a gift, wondering why I didn't lift my shotgun?

There was an interim then when I only hunted with friends and their bird dogs as if I couldn't quite bear the memory of Missy. Starting around 1970 my friend Guy came up every fall for grouse and woodcock shooting. He had a lazy, incredibly neurotic Lab bitch named Rain who despite her "put-upon" attitude was a superb upland game dog with an uncanny nose. She was equally good at ducks down on Lake Okeechobee in Florida though she had to be lifted gently into the boat.

To fill our dogless space at the time we bought two Airedales, the male, whom I called Hud, coming from a bear-dog strain in Arkansas. Hud was well named because his favorite activity was screwing the garbage cans at midmorning every day. It didn't look like all that much fun to the owner but Hud obviously enjoyed it. He was a big boy and soon got into trouble for ripping off a barn door to get at a female in heat and tunneling under a kennel to mate a neighbor's pretty boxer. He also knocked men off snowmobiles when they crossed our yard. The other Airedale—Jessie, a female—hoarded the bowels of entire cows the neighbors butchered. She would hunt but getting a bird back from her was a wrestling match.

My hunting life changed for the better when Guy sent us a young yellow Lab from England's Sandringham breeding facility. I properly called her Sand and she was hunting well by the age of seven months, learning more from Guy's dog Rain than I could teach her. This is a rarely mentioned item in a trainer's vocabulary, but a young dog learns very well from watching and hunting with an experienced dog. You are "guiding" rather than training the animal and your most important function is to discourage bad habits. Once the dog comprehends that you are partners, the process is three-quarters of the way home. An occasional light spanking can be in order on young dogs, but it too severely wounds the dignity of an older animal. The best tactic I've developed is a stern word and a light ear pinch. If you love to punish, pick on someone your own size. Many hunters carry over illusions of control from their day jobs. They want what some call "lawyer dogs," kenneled animals that get to hunt only a couple days each fall and are still expected to cover the ground in a ticktock, metronomic fashion. They are expected to be as efficient and obedient as a legal secretary. The half dozen top bird dogs I've known in my forty-year hunting life have all been dear companions of their owners' daily lives.

I got so used to following Sand's superb nose that I'd occasionally get lost—which is no fun at all in Michigan's Upper Peninsula where my favorite area is a dozen miles from anything. I soon could tell from the way Sand's butt wiggled if it was a grouse or a woodcock. She often retrieved birds that I was unsure I had hit. She went through a short period where I caught her trying to bury grouse and then she would sit on the dirt pretending she couldn't find the bird. I thought this peculiarity might have come from her convalescence after being hit by a snowplow, with her medical bills coming to $10,000 in today's money. We called a trainer in Pennsylvania, a friend of Guy's, who said, "Kick her in the ass. She's trying to hide the bird to eat later."

She did have "eating problems" as many Labs do. Once on the way north I stopped at a tavern for a much-needed drink and on returning to the car I noticed Sand had eaten a pound of butter, a dozen eggs, and some bananas. The next trip I put all the sacks of groceries on the car roof when I went into the tavern, then forgot them. I recall clearly the sound of three magnums of good wine crashing to the street when I drove off.

A singular charm in Sand was never losing a downed bird even in the thickest Michigan cover, a common event with big-running pointing dogs that only wish to find more birds. The biggest problem with Sand other than that she was part pig was her fear of bears. Dozens of times I would drive to an area I wanted to hunt and she would jump back in the car if she scented bear. If I forced the issue she would walk behind me tight to my legs. Once in Sand's late years when I was hunting with both her and Tess we came upon a bear in an alder thicket who growled before running away. Tess growled back and Sand disappeared. I said to Tess, "Where's Sand?" then followed her more than a mile to find Sand hiding behind a stump and still shaking. I was always mindful that an English setter had been killed on my Upper Peninsula property before I bought it. Small bears tend to be underestimated. A bear hunter I met had a hound that needed 280 stitches after a run-in with a bear that was not that far beyond cub stage. When you skin an adult bear you see a musculature that makes Arnold Schwarzenegger look like Mary Poppins.

The arrival of Tess brought on the true glory days of my hunting life. At the outset I was lucky to have Nick Reens as a friend, neighbor, and hunting partner. Nick has managed, along with a few others, to breed a select number of litters out of an Old Hemlock strain. These are big-lunged dogs ranging from 70 pounds for a bitch to 110 pounds for a male. Utterly docile and sweet in the cabin or house these are big-running setters suitable for the Southwest and Montana though they shorten up in the denser cover of northern Michigan. When cynics say that our dogs are "too far out" we've learned to give a pat answer: "That must be where the birds are." Nick hunts as many as five at once and they act as a massive vacuum cleaner for the game birds in the area. One day on Drum Hadley's 500,000-acre Gray Ranch in New Mexico three of us bagged thirty quail on a cold, windy day while another group hunting short-running eastern setters only shot four. The possible downside to this strain of setters is that the owner must be in fairly good walking

shape. Though of serene disposition, these dogs don't care if you
have a sore foot or a hangover.

Curiously, it took some time before I did as well with Tess as I
did with Sand. A fine pointing dog can promote a certain laziness in
your attention span. With Sand I had to watch her every moment.
I knew Tess would hold the point but I was a little slow in learning
how to approach her while hunting solo. With a hunting partner
the avenues of escape are more limited. I gradually figured out it
was better to come up on her from the side rather than directly
from the back. This afforded me a clue as her eyes often followed
the scent line. Sometimes in sparse cover she would lie out flat on
her point which setters did earlier in their tradition and when she
had to reposition she would often crawl very quickly on her belly.
Like any good grouse-and-woodcock dog Tess kept a sharp eye on
the direction missed birds were flying in order to repoint them. I've
long given up this practice under the idea that if a bird escapes once
it's sporting to let it be home free. There are specific exceptions to
this rule. One day in Montana it was blustery and the Hungarian
grouse wouldn't hold to the point but would flush wild well out of
range. Because Tess had such a sharp eye we were able to pick up
fifteen singles.

Once on the ridge summit of Hog Canyon near the Mexican
border we were sprawled on the grass resting from the steep climb
when Tess, also prone on her side, went into a full point in that
position. My hunting partner noticed it first and nodded and at
this same moment a Mearns quail cock marched past her nose and
then between us.

It was an extraordinary afternoon as a little earlier Tess had
pointed a few feet below the crown of a hill too steep for us to
scramble up, then held the point as she slowly slid backward some
hundred feet or so to the bottom where we stood. We call this being
staunch to point. Another desirable characteristic is intensity.

Her main drawbacks were a weakness for rabbits and ground
squirrels though this penchant was usually under control. Chasing

a jackrabbit can blow out a dog on a warm day. I have never understood the attraction of ground squirrels for dogs unless it's the peculiar sharp squeak these rodents make. My cabin can have a half dozen red squirrels in the yard and the dogs yawn but they can't resist ground squirrels. And dogs can have additional oddities. Tess never once acknowledged the presence of a horse or cow. I could also tell when she was a bit bored and then I would take her to new cover, which delighted her. Many dogs don't figure out how to control running Gambel's quail but Tess did, circling way out like a good pheasant dog and turning them back in my direction. This is pure hunting instinct rather than simple intelligence. Despite my affection for English setters there are a dozen breeds with more apparent intelligence. My wife's English cocker, Mary, would have made Tess look like Big Dumb. (Mary has even figured out the proper time for me to get up in the morning and when it's time for my afternoon snooze.) But Tess's sole interest in life was finding game birds, with chasing ground squirrels and eating dinner a distant second and third. The only food she ever begged for was the skin of a fried whitefish. If I gave her my leftover breakfast oatmeal with raisins she would finish the oatmeal but leave the raisins in a neat pyramid. She turned away in disgust and embarrassment when I offered her yogurt as a joke.

Our last hunt together was a tearjerker. We were over a mile from the car in a rough canyon near the Mexican border. She gave me two points and then quite suddenly collapsed. I carried her out over my shoulder with some difficulty and a week later had to have her put down. I thought I was mentally prepared for this moment but then I simply broke down. This has been true with the death of all our dogs, I suppose because I have never had any impulse to rate animals by level of importance. We are fellow creatures.

In the late years of Tess's career I got another puppy from Nick and we named her Rose. The mother was Sam who had a problematical early career after the trauma of being confined in a dog trailer while some kids were setting off firecrackers. Sam mostly tagged along with

us for two years until we were hunting one morning in South Georgia
and Sam decided she was over her trauma and began hunting beauti-
fully. Back home she would regularly run the half mile from Nick's
house, scratch at our door, say hello, turn around, and run home.

Frankly, I'd had some doubts about getting another setter
because I was by then in my midfifties and the early training period
can be a real workout—which translates as "you are going to bust
your ass." I've thought that Rose had no more than 80 percent of
the intensity of Tess but this is partly because my own intensity had
begun to wane. Tess regularly hunted perhaps seventy days a year
or more in Michigan, Florida, Montana, and Arizona. With Rose I
started hunting half days and reduced my kill. One August morning
in the Upper Peninsula Rose had twenty-nine woodcock points in
less than two hours. I was slow to admit that I enjoyed this training
run as much as hunting. As I became a little more squeamish I'd
simply yell "bang" at the flush and that was fine by Rose whereas my
Lab Sand would look at me with disappointment whenever I missed.
She liked the flavor of everything.

Rose's biggest drawback is that she's what's called a competitive bitch and doesn't like to hunt with other dogs, and if she does,
she tries to beat them to the cover. We lost her for three days in the
vast area south of Safford, Arizona, when she successfully outran all
Nick's males. I'd like to say she learned something from this harrow-
ing experience but I don't think she did. After that I only hunted
her alone or with dogs who didn't mind her being out in front.

I gratefully accept that Rose learned a lot more hunting with
Tess than she ever did from me. She learned to honor Tess's points
because when she broke a covey Tess growled and snapped at her.
This one-day lesson wouldn't have worked without her stern aunt.
Rose has also been spectacular at singles. One day in New Mexico
after a friend's dog had bumped a quail covey I shot six singles while
my friend took a hungover nap.

Rose's downfall came last summer in Montana in her ninth year
when she was struck twice by a rattlesnake in our yard and one fang

broke off in her right eyeball, blinding her. She was already half deaf but her recovery from the snake took several months. The venom affected her brain or sense of smell, or both. In the Upper Peninsula she bumped woodcock though she held steady to a number of grouse. On a few occasions she seemed not to recognize me. I didn't push but let her try to recover at her own speed. She'll point doves in high grass though she flags a bit and turns around to look at me explaining, "dove." She's had some nice quail points this winter but not many, mostly because of the precipitous decline of birds in our prolonged drought. Many times when her beeped collar signals a point I've found her lying down looking at the mountains.

Rose is now ten and I'm vaguely shopping for another pup. I'm thinking of ending my hunting life with an English cocker like my wife's Mary whom I could easily teach to be president, or at least a senator, or to run a corporation, or write my novels. One day on a walk Mary scented quail and crawled like a Marine toward a covey. This breed of dog could definitely become a multispecies expert.

The other day near the end of the season Rose flounced around and trotted back to the car like a gaited horse after pointing a large covey of Mearns quail. I suddenly remembered reading that in the seventh century the Church decided dogs couldn't go to heaven because they didn't contribute to the Church. If that's true then I don't want to go either. I'm very poor at dates and numbers and what happened at what time in our life. But if my wife mentions the name of a dog we've owned and loved, I can re-create the dog's life with us, and consequently my own.

(*Field & Stream*)

A NEW MAP OF
THE SACRED TERRITORY
(1992)

In the past few years I've been preoccupied with a study, a meditation as it were, on the sickness I call the "time disease," of which I'm a terminal victim. There haven't been any profound insights, only a few flare-ups from the kind of smudge fire built to keep bugs away from a campsite. It's touchy how we slice up our lives, and you needn't be very bright to note that duties and obligations are added, never subtracted, unless you die or get fired. Ultimately, under too much mental pressure, the time disease wafts away into a theological cranny where it nests on a bed of tears and regrets, but also some joys so shot full of primary colors that, years later, they are literally breathtaking, so vivid with pleasure that a superb word like "joy" is only the humblest of glyphs beside the experience itself.

Some time ago, during a period of ill health, I wrote seven drafts of two screenplays that didn't get produced, a dozen columns, and two novellas, all within fourteen months. The meat was coming out of the slicer pretty thin and pale, and what brain was left was bruised on its wobbly stem, or full of sour air like a rubber ball—an experience shared with millions of other alpha nitwits one sees ricocheting through life. Just plain burning up all the wood the first two months of winter. That's what it is.

But looking through my journal, or when I'm in the middle of the usual night thoughts, I see that there were some grand and curious moments that year. After spending more than a year of days in the tidal flats off Key West, I caught a twenty-five-pound permit on fly. I know how to make the throw, but the luck involved has a tinge of the lottery. Later that spring, after years of trying, I finally snuck up within twenty yards of a pair of sandhill cranes in the outback of the Upper Peninsula, a feat that involved two hours at a heart-thumping crawl and a hundred blackfly bites. Perhaps a month after that I glassed a black-bear cub on repeated rolls down a sandbank to swim in the river while its mother watched and grazed on blueberries. That fall, my setter bitch Tess approached a small poplar-and-elder covert and pointed, then backed away with her belly scraping the ground in a wide half circle, repositioning at the end of the covert with an eyeball directed like a strobe at me. There were two woodcock, one at each end, and in my surprise I not only missed the double, I missed both, then gave Tess a kiss, which she prefers over biscuits.

It would be pretentious to say that these experiences saved my life that year, but they probably did. Note that none of them took place indoors. The phone wasn't ringing, there was no refrigerator, a contract wasn't involved, and I was not strapped to the dentist's chair before CNN's top one hundred world ream jobs of the year. I was outside, far outside, and I was paying attention. The experiences didn't prepare me for anything except more of the same, which is quite enough. If I came away feeling much better, which I did, it was because I had been back in a landscape where I felt I belonged. If I felt somewhat freshened for what Republicans describe as the "real world," that was because I unwittingly, perhaps subconsciously, took that vow of obedience to awareness that Jung said primitive man took for survival.

We come to the natural world from an unwieldy number of directions, a comic stew of expectations. It always seems remarkable that most of the best anglers I know come from distinctly urban areas. This has to be ascribed to a hunger for the experience, a lack of presumption, and a nonabsorption of regional dogma. Tom McGuane observes that everyone in Montana assumes a knowledge of horses as a birthright, whether or not he has ever owned a horse or ridden one. The same is true with hunting and fishing. If you can't locate a Natural Resources employee, you are usually far better off with a set of topographical maps than with any local advice, unless it comes from a guide you have paid. A map is without sentimentality, also without the misdirection of locals who have hot spots they naturally wish to conceal.

Back to time-slicing. For reasons of distance and time, most of us are pliant victims of spectator sports. Why is it I'd rather read a book about worm farming than one about baseball, about warbler aggression than about basketball, about stream morphology than about football? And this despite the fact that, due to the curse of memory, I can recall dozens of ancient names from the rosters of the Detroit Lions, Tigers, Pistons, and Red Wings (curiously "Pistons" is the only appropriate name here). The only clue is that, anthropologically speaking, all major spectator sports are considered "war surrogates": replicas, renditions, minimalizations, even parodies of actual battle, whereas spectator anxieties are resolved in play. And this is not to detract from their occasional splendor—from the intricacies of the game—only to say that a life spent watching lacks content.

I suspect that the most profound nightmares about hunting and fishing come from calling them sports, which, properly understood, they are not. Fishing tournaments own a particular obscenity, as do the rich Americans who head south to permissive countries to shoot thousands of ducks and white-winged doves. Both these groups should play in the NFL without helmets or pads. But these death spectacles come from trying to make a ritual into a contest, from a competitive obsession that ought not be resolved by killing. Mortality is almost no one's favorite subject, save for funeral directors, casket makers, pathologists, homicide detectives, and a few especially lachrymose ministers and priests. Hunting and fishing involve trip-hammering our fellow creatures into eternity. This mute fact is not meant to exclude the supermarket as a mausoleum, which the anti-hunting and -fishing factions do. If there is virtue in distancing yourself from what you eat, I do not perceive it.

Quite literally you belong in the outdoors because your people spent five million years there, only recently emerging into nation- and city-states. The rituals of hunting and fishing, like those of gathering, are archetypally in your blood. Mushrooming and berry picking are closer to hunting than skeet shooting is. So is gardening, for that matter. And with all rituals there are right and wrong ways to go about them, and the wrong ways invariably involve bad attitude, bad "spirit." In the nineteenth century it was a matter of singular horror to Native Americans to see white people having photos taken with a foot stepping on a fallen elk, moose, or deer. There is no such thing as genetic virtue vis-à-vis natives, only a specific set of attitudes that ensures that hunting and fishing are carried on in the right spirit. In *Make Prayers to the Raven*, Richard Nelson made an appropriate point: "The Koyukon won't say, 'I'm a good hunter.' First, that would be bragging. Second, it would be taking credit for something given to you. If your friends give you a lot of gifts at Christmas, you don't say, 'I'm really good at Christmas.'"

Of course, this assumes you're going to take the trouble to learn what you're doing when you enter the woods and water. A cautionary note is offered only so you won't lose consciousness in your enthusiasms. In no arena other than hunting and fishing can knowledge be so directly equated with power. The old saw that 10 percent of hunters and fishermen have 90 percent of the success is never questioned, but it is probably true. What the 10 percent shares with itself above all else is a familiarity with the habitat and the behavior of the prey unshared by the other 90. The skills of shooting and casting can be very easily learned, though there is a region of excellence in both that very few reach, and those who do tend to become gentle souls—"The predator husbands its prey." But it is a knowledge of habitat and behavior that makes the difference, and this comes only from reading and experience.

Snobbism isn't appropriate; neither is trying to buy your way in with heaps of expensive equipment. You will end up with good equipment because it is comfortable and works better. After a few decades, you may also wish to give up hunting and fishing for bird-watching and nature study, which for some appears to be a genuine step in the life process. Whatever, it is sacred ground we enter, and we are cursed if we don't mind our manners. The urge is to go home, to give a larger slice of time to living where we feel we belong. Gary Snyder, a true incarnation of the natural world, said in *The Practice of the Wild*, "For those who would seek directly, by entering the primary temple, the wilderness can be a ferocious teacher, rapidly stripping down the inexperienced or careless. It is easy to make the mistakes that will bring one to extremity. Practically speaking, a life that is vowed with simplicity, appropriate boldness, good humor, gratitude, unstinting work and play, and lots of walking brings us close to the actual existing world and its wholeness."

(*Esquire Sportsman*)

DELTA HUNT
(1970s)

We picked up Robin Swift and Jack Lufkin in Atmore, Alabama, before dawn. Now there were four of us, including Geoffrey Norman, Robin's nephew, who lives in New York but is from Atmore. I was notably the only "Yankee," and on my first trip to the Deep South, the deepest South in fact, just northeast of Mobile where the Alabama and Tombigbee Rivers join to empty their rich mud into the Gulf. It is a part of the rural South altogether unknown to us northerners who, hellbent for Florida, only get fleeting glimpses of Georgia.

It was barely light down at Robin Swift's sawmill where we stopped to pick up the bird dogs, transferring them from their large kennel into the portable kennel on the back of Jack's pickup. When Robin and I got back in the car to follow the truck I looked at the sawmill with the special vividness that typifies déjà vu, that unsettling resonance of emotion that tries to convince you that you've been somewhere before. And as we began to cross the farmland of the coastal plains north toward the hills of the Piedmont it occurred to me my sense of déjà vu had come from my early obsession with the literature of the South. Lena in William Faulkner's *A Light in August* had a boyfriend who worked at a sawmill. There were sawmills in Erskine Caldwell. Now with the landscape passing in the ground fog other names slid through my mind, fulsome, redolent with the books they wrote, books inextricable from this sort of countryside and the names of the small towns that dotted it: Eudora Welty, James Agee, Ralph Ellison, Truman Capote, Carson McCullers, Flannery O'Connor, Peter Taylor, Reynolds Price, Barry Hannah. And the ineffable music in the names of the towns themselves: Bay Minette, Rabun, Perdido, Coy, Crumptonia, Nellie, Nettleboro, Lower Peach Tree, Fatama, Mexia, Burnt Corn, Bashi, Megargel, Perdue Hill.

This sense of place made the hunting as uniquely beautiful as my first trips to Paris, the Lake Country in England, or Saint Petersburg, where the genius of the native writers, whether Baudelaire, Wordsworth, or Dostoyevsky, added immeasurably to the experience. We passed deer hunters unloading their hounds in the dim light, abandoned sharecropper's shacks, small settlements that obviously hadn't changed since the Depression. A few faded antebellum homes stood out barely against the bruised greens of early winter.

We finally reached Jimmy Henderson's farm up in Wilcox County in the Black Belt, a reference to the richness of the soil in the area. We were going to start the day with quail, a bird I had never hunted. My main intention was wild turkey, also a bird I had never hunted, but I was roundly teased about trying to shoot a turkey in the fall. The classic way to hunt wild turkey, therefore the only acceptable way to an experienced turkey hunter like Jack Lufkin, is to hunt them in the spring when the gobbler can be called toward the hunter with an imitation of the hen's voice. They were all mindful though tolerant that I as a Yankee would be ignorant of this sense of turkey etiquette. They would, nevertheless, try to find me some

turkeys in the afternoon, after the serious business of quail hunting
had been taken care of. In fact, a forester cousin named Claude Swift
was already scouting turkey for us. There seemed some general doubt
that I could hit a quail let alone hunt the wary turkey.

Jimmy Henderson met us near his corrals and toolshed. He
asked us if we preferred to hunt from horseback or truck. I had a quick
shot of panic about my horsemanship but everyone opted for the
pickup with a raised seat in the back built over the box which held
cages for the dogs. Henderson's farm proved spectacularly idyllic—
some eight thousand acres of mixed cover, with woods and swamp
broken by hedgerows and fields of mowed soybeans, winter wheat,
pasture holding twelve hundred cattle. My shooting was somewhat
less than spectacular. Every grouse and woodcock hunter deserves
the brute shock of flushing a covey of quail in front of a pointing dog
with three other setters honoring the point. At first you are lulled as
you walk in on the dogs. The cover is so open you think you are on
the verge of a real piece of cake. But then ten to thirty quail flushed
and my first impulse was to cover my eyes and my shots were only
reflexive. Luckily a single bird dropped.

Throughout the morning I found it impossible to adjust to the
uniqueness of the flush. It seemed like I should be able to see the
birds in the thickets immediately in front of the dogs. No chance.
Each covey flush was like a cattle prod in the butt. I always missed
the first shot, then would pick up a single going away. In full flight
quail seem no faster than woodcock, and much slower than grouse.
But the quail easily beats grouse and woodcock in the opportunity
to watch the beauty of bird dogs working, making long energetic
casts, sometimes hundreds of yards away, then coming stylishly to a
crouched halt on point.

I felt chastened and exhausted by lunchtime when we quit
due to the extreme mid-December heat. At a fine roast beef meal
at Henderson's I witnessed an apparently not very arcane ritual in
Alabama—a continual bragging and arguing about the comparative
merits of Auburn and University of Alabama at football. My sole

offering, a comment about Bear Bryant avoiding a real bowl contest, was not given the dignity of a reply.

By the middle of the afternoon Jack and Robin dropped Geoffrey and me off at Claude Swift's home. Claude had located some turkeys and we quickly put on camouflage clothing and drove over to Claude's hunting lease near Rabun. The three of us entered the forest only after Claude had given specific instructions to keep our mouths shut and walk quietly. As a babbling writer and Sagittarian I wanted to offer an oblique question about the presence of rattlesnakes and fictive thousand-pound charging wild boars but thought better of it, not wanting to be a two-hundred-pound bore in strange territory.

We walked a mile or so then sat quietly near the appointed area. The turkeys weren't there. We cut through a swale along a creek bed, the cover and thorns so thick that you feared turning suddenly and getting a mortal puncture for your efforts. Then with appalling suddenness it seemed like we had flushed a flock of eagles which quickly became the turkeys I had never seen in my life. Claude yelled, "HENS!" and we all spotted the lone gobbler at the far edge of the flock sailing along perhaps a hundred yards from us. Claude told us that all we had to do was to simply be back here at dawn when the flock would regroup. Claude shared Jack Lufkin's prejudices against the bad etiquette of fall turkey hunting. The next day was Sunday and he intended to go to church.

On the way home we stopped and had a drink with Jack and Robin. Jack said he would meet us at dawn for fear we would totally screw up as foreigners and not even *see* the turkeys let alone get a shot. Geoffrey and I were staying in Pensacola and had to set the alarm for 2:30 a.m., an hour when I'm not usually in bed. And after a sociable evening I got a full fifteen minutes of sleep before we headed back toward Atmore.

We picked up Jack and reached Claude's spot with no real difficulty—we had marked all the turns with fluorescent red tape. But Geoffrey who had been in the Green Berets for four years in

Vietnam couldn't quite remember the exact spot to enter the woods and I was as useful as a Venusian. Jack hissed politely at us. We made a guess and quickly flushed the gobbler though Jack didn't tell us in the dark whether the bird was a gobbler or hen. An experienced turkey hunter can tell by the sound. We sat quietly in the woods at dawn and heard the heavy fluffing sound of the hens leaving the roost in an attempt to rejoin the flock. One flew straight overhead and I idly led it with my shotgun. Jack rose to his feet and said if we hadn't been two hundred yards out of whack the gobbler would have been easy pickings.

On the way back to Atmore for more quail hunting we detoured to look at some of Jack's favorite turkey spots. On a gravel-and-sand log road we followed the tracks of what Jack said was a group of four hens and a gobbler. It was obvious that in the degree of stealth and woodsmanship required, turkey hunting was more akin to hunting some incredibly delicate and sensitive mammal. The tracks looked like the blue heron tracks I had seen on the marl bottom of a lake in Michigan.

The wild turkey had been largely extirpated from its habitat by the turn of the twentieth century. The efforts of game biologists in many states have resulted in a dramatic comeback for this game bird. Anyone caring about the bird should join the Wild Turkey Federation which, in a manner similar to Ducks Unlimited, Trout Unlimited, and the Ruffed Grouse Society, is the only recourse the serious turkey hunter has to ensure the future of his hunting.

Meanwhile, in a small fish shack back at Perdido Bay near Pensacola I am eating fried mullet and hush puppies, playing pinball, drinking beer, feeling the easy moist warmth of the Gulf, and thinking about turkey and quail. They weren't what I expected them to be—they were far nobler than any notion my imagination could muster. But all those writers had made me ready for the Deep South, and come April on my way to fish in Key West I will stop in Alabama to hunt turkey with Jack Lufkin the proper way.

THE MISADVENTURE
JOURNALS
(2008)

When we were still twerps, we could manage rather heroic views
of ourselves. I grew up in northern Michigan in the 1940s and the
landscape held everything a nascent sportsman could wish for except
the talent to take advantage of it. The simple fact that you had
to develop fishing and hunting abilities can be discouraging to a
youngster who has a vaunted idea of his potentialities, especially
when he's catching smallish bluegills and perch and the single arrow
shot from his twenty-pound-pull bow on an early August morning
fell about fifty yards short of the buck across the gully. My father
taught me well but in rare moments of absolute honesty, I am still
struck by the wide variance between my imagination's vision of a
sporting venture and what actually happens. I suspect this is partly
because I'm a novelist and my livelihood is my imagination, which

is as uncontrollable as a four-month-old English pointer. The key idea is always "not what I expected."

January 7, 1991
A Snake in the Grass

A fair cool morning on the Empire Ranch, Sonoita. I'm hunting the Cienéga hoping my pup, Rose, honors her aunt Tess. She's only failed once, but that was on a big covey of Gambel's. I am distracted because the dogs are "running off their bloom," meaning they are a quarter of a mile away hauling ass. I crawl under a barbed wire fence and there, a foot from my nose, is a foot-long baby rattler. Before I have time to react, I note that in the cold grass the only thing about the snake that moves is its eyes. I rise up violently and a barb from the wire penetrates the collar of my hunting vest and neck, so when I back up the vest pulls over my head and bloody neck. Only shot two of ten quail this day. Nervous.

January 13, 1997
Lost in the Dark

Up in the foothills of the Patagonia Mountains (southern Arizona) with Phil Caputo, his setter, Sage, and my Rose. We're finding a fair number of Gambel's and Mearns, but the going is rough as we cross many arroyos laterally, following covey flushes. For some reason I think of what's going to happen before it happens. My friend Nick Reens, the best bird hunter I know, says that if you're going to get lost it will likely happen when the hunting is good and you're not paying attention to the landscape and it's time to turn around. I have a fairly good visual on where our vehicle is to the northeast, and I try to guide us on a possible shortcut, but within a half hour I see it's not going to work. Now I opt to head south for our casita, our little house on the creek, partly because it's downhill and I judge we are equidistant from house and vehicle. Suddenly, it's nearly dark and I hear Rose's beeper. She's on point, but it's too dark to see her as the birds flush. It looks like we're going to spend the night where we are.

Caputo is a Pulitzer Prize winner and an ex–Marine officer, but he doesn't have any matches. As a steadfast smoker I have three lighters and we soon have a roaring fire in the cold night. It occurs to me that this happened nearly fifty years ago when I was fourteen and got lost deer hunting in northern Michigan. I managed to set a big old white pine stump on fire and was quite cozy. After a scant few minutes staring at our bonfire we note that both Rose and Sage are sniffing the area nervously. This is mountain lion country and Rose has the same aversion to this scent as she does to bears in Michigan's Upper Peninsula. Caputo and I talk about lions, but in the back of my mind I'm thinking that a couple of jaguars have been seen near here in recent years. Jaguars are dog killers while mountain lions tend to avoid dogs over about forty pounds. I decide not to bring up the subject of jaguars.

After a couple of hours a rescue chopper called by my wife finds us, but I know my Rose won't board a helicopter. We refuse their assistance, having decided it would be more pleasant to spend the night, but then a ground contingent finds us and we make our way out, avoiding precipitous hundred-foot-deep gullies as we go. Phil is embarrassed but not me because I was never a Marine. Things will look better with a quart of water, a quart of wine, and a midnight dinner.

A decade later I don't like to think of this scenario without the cigarette lighters and the bonfire that led to our discovery. It was nineteen degrees that night, not fatal but uncomfortable. I felt no fear like I have experienced several times at sea. In well over two hundred days of saltwater fly-fishing in the Florida Keys I never boarded the skiff in the morning without looking askance at the outboard motor. This is because I come from the days when it might take fifty pulls to start a five-horse Scott-Atwater so that sweat is flying out of your hair and your arm aches.

May 3, 1984
Adrift in the Marquesas

It's a fair but muggy day when we set off from Garrison Bight for the hour-long run to the Marquesas. We're (I'm with Guy de la Valdène) slightly hungover but this is Key West, where hangovers are freely given out. I decide to ignore the weather news that something is brewing for midafternoon, though this prediction does tend to itch in the back of my mind. We jump a few tarpon at Platform Point off Boca Grande Key, nothing large, about eighty pounds, then have a smooth twelve-mile crossing to the southeast bank of the Marquesas. The fishing is grand, though we can't reach the huge females in the middle of the school. Suddenly there's a depth charge at the reef line and our fishing is ruined by a truly huge hammerhead out of the Gulf Stream. It bobbles a tarpon on its nose, then *crunch*, *crunch*, *crunch*, as it were. The shark throws a rooster tail of mud as it chases a school into shallow water. When it passes the boat I think that it makes *Jaws* look like *Mary Poppins*.

We've been distracted, and finally notice a front closing in from Cuba, to the south. The wind picks up quickly and is opposing the outgoing tide, which makes for choppy water. To be frank, it becomes horrifying. The crossing to the shelter on lee of Boca Grande is interminable because Guy has to run the skiff slowly through the wave troughs, a hand constantly adjusting the throttle. We're both thinking that this will exhaust the full tank of gas we started with. It does and now we're adrift near the spoil bank in clear sight of the longed-for saloons of Key West. We barely miss tying off to a buoy and start drifting out toward Sand Key in the Gulf Stream. We have a CB but the Coast Guard only monitors VHF. Finally we raise a trucker on the Keys Highway and he calls the marina. After much confusion about the nearest marker we are brought gas after a very long hour and a half. Back at the Chart Room in Key West I have a triple martini, which doesn't help me forget the shark's big horned eyeballs.

*Perhaps we weren't in true danger, but it felt like it. So much can happen
out there, like reading a chart and thinking you have three feet of water,
which means you can still slam the bottom between big waves and break
your lower unit. Once we seriously broached while crossing the often-nasty
Northwest Channel to Mule and Archer Keys. We almost made it with
a boat full of water, and luckily reached a sandbar. We bailed and bailed
and I got under the console and dried off a nest of inscrutable wires after
finally noting the connections were color-coded. Guy is as dumb as I am
with mechanical things and was quite impressed. I dread to think of the
days the weather told me we shouldn't leave the dock but we did anyway.*

July 19, 1987
Portage Hell

My brook trout fishing partner Mike was once a timber cruiser.
Last night at his bar, the Dunes Saloon, we made a plan to take his
small Sportspal canoe across a couple of miles of uncharted marsh
and swamp on the East Branch of the Fox on the Upper Peninsula.
We figure it'll take a couple of hours at most. Brook trout lack intelligence and the chance of getting the dreamed-about five-pounder
depends on unfished waters. The "couple of hours" turned into eight.
The day was a literal mud bath because we ended up portaging
thirty-seven beaver dams. We looked tarred and feathered without
the feathers. We caught some brookies and Mike lost a large one,
but I wouldn't return to this place at gunpoint.

*The sense of comedy only comes afterward with a shower and a drink while
scratching the black- and deerfly bites on your scalp. I have visual images
of a man struggling waist-deep in the brush of a collapsed beaver dam.
Once while fishing with Tom McGuane in a johnboat on the Yellowstone
River, before either of us could afford a proper drift boat, a violent line
squall attacked us. We sought shelter with our precious bamboo rods on
an island, but the horrendous wind started somersaulting the johnboat
and McGuane had to run in front of it, dodging the boat like a halfback.*

Another day, fishing with Dan Lahren near Big Timber, Montana, a thunderstorm blindsided us from behind the foothills to the south. You could tell it was close by the way the lightning struck a cottonwood fifty yards away. Suddenly the wind was gusting at close to ninety knots. I'm good at wind, having spent twenty-five summers close to Lake Superior. Luckily, our takeout and vehicle were only a quarter mile downstream. Unluckily, the wind was pushing the high-bowed drift boat uncontrollably fast. As we went whipping past the takeout place Danny flung himself out of the boat with the anchor in his arms. It was fortunate the water was waist-deep because he can't swim. After being dragged fifty yards as if he had roped a bull, he finally swung the boat to shore. It was all dumb but effective.

Of course sometimes our foolishness is irrelevant and chance or fate victimizes us. When I was in Montana last November, an elk hunter got his face swiped off by a blow from a sow grizzly. I shot my fifteenth rattler in our yard in the past five years because it was threatening our old cat Warren a foot from the front doorstep. I'm a bit snake leery and will never forget how uncomfortable I felt back in 1972 when our boat broke down out of sight of land off Ecuador. There were dozens of extremely venomous sea snakes swimming around the boat and the fact that I had caught five striped marlin that day did not allay my nervousness. Years later in the Yucatán, while swimming in a cenote—a rock pool in the jungle connected to the ocean—a friend told me not to be upset if an anaconda approached because the snake would catch my scent and turn away. How comforting. Up to that point I was only concerned about the fer-de-lance.

Your dogs can also get you in trouble. In Arizona, my setter Tess once went on point at the bottom of a very steep arroyo, a bad situation because I had never been able to get her to break point. I threw rocks but failed to flush the covey, so I made my way down like an overweight rock climber, losing my grasp and sliding while feeling my back lose a lot of skin. My fall flushed the covey, and as I lay there Tess was kind enough to lick my face. The real possible danger, however, is other people.

Only recently a friend told me about a disaster that made mine look puny. About thirty years ago, at nineteen, he worked for a hunting outfitter, and they had gone into the Brooks Range of Alaska with a dozen horses. The outfitter and clients had flown out after the hunt, leaving my friend and another young man. The outfitter evidently then got drunk for two weeks and the pickup was ill-organized and missed. Winter was closing in and my friend and the other Montanan hiked out 120 miles. All of the horses died on the way except one, and then it fell through the ice of a river, scrambled out, and died on the spot. It was carrying their last food, moose meat, but they were afraid to retrieve the meat because it would have been fatal to get wet. When they finally reached an oil camp, my friend found he had dropped from 155 pounds to 115. Tough boys. "If I hadn't grown up fishing and hunting I would have died," he told me.

About a month ago in Patagonia, Arizona, I was having a good-bye drink with Phil Caputo. He was leaving for Connecticut and I was headed back to Montana. While laughing about our past long evening in the cold canyon, he said that he would never again go hunting without matches. Good idea. Nothing gets you in trouble more than enthusiasm not tempered by good sense. Now that it's May in Montana I've decided not to hunt morel mushrooms in the vicinity of recent grizzly reports. I love a pan of fried mushrooms, but I'd like to keep my homely face.

(*Field & Stream*)

HUNTING WITH A FRIEND:
ON GOOD FRIENDS
AND FOUL WEATHER
(1995)

I've begun to believe that some of us are not as evolved as we may think. Up in the country, in my prolonged childhood, I liked best to walk, fish, and hunt where there were few, if any, people. After a ten-year hiatus for college and trying to be Rimbaud, Dostoyevsky, and James Joyce, not to speak of William Faulkner, in New York, Boston, and San Francisco, I found myself back in northern Michigan walking, fishing, and hunting. There are a lot more people now, but there are still plenty of places where they aren't. Tennis, golf, and drugs didn't work for me, so for the past thirty years my abiding passions are still centered on upland game birds, fish, and idling around fields, mountains, and the woods on foot, studying habitat but mostly wandering and looking things over.

On the surface, and maybe underneath, this may be regarded by some as an idiot's life. In the very long struggle to find out your own true character there is the real possibility you'll discover a simpleton beneath the skin, or at least something deeply peculiar. But then you slowly arrive at a point where you accept your comfortable idiosyncrasies, aided in part by a study of your sporting friends, who are capable of behavior that is no less strange. A few years back I tried to explain to a long table of studio executives the pleasures of walking around wild country in the moonlight. They nodded but I could tell they thought I was daft. The same tale told to two or three of my favorite hunting or fishing companions would be received as utterly ordinary, say, on the level of drinking too much good wine. It's simply the kind of thing you do when your curiosity arouses you.

Curiosity is what got my friend Guy de la Valdène started. There is a great body of information I didn't know about in his splendid and compelling book about quail, and I certainly had no idea he knew about it. It occurred to me after reading it that one reason you stick with a friend is because they are able to surprise and enliven you. In some respects *For a Handful of Feathers* is a nineteenth-century rather than twentieth-century book; in it you will find none of the shrill gunslinging, the otiose "how to do it to get the most out of it" attitudes of the contemporary hunting mainstream, an arena that has become so mechanized that you may as well stay home and fiddle with the Internet for all the good it does your soul. Instead Guy has come up with an exhaustive sporting coda that doesn't presume that we hunt in a vacuum, as if we could separate the land from the creatures that live there. The death of hunting will come not from the largely imagined forces of anti-hunting but from the death of habitat, the continuing disregard for the land in the manner of a psychopath burning down a house and then wondering why he can't still live there. This illusion of separateness is maddening. We are nature, too, surely as a chimp or trout.

I first met Guy back in the late sixties through Tom McGuane. McGuane was living in the Florida Keys and I had come down from

Michigan to explore the fishing, which we attempted to do on the severest budget with his old Roberts skiff and a malfunctioning twenty-horse outboard, none of which vitiated the pleasures of our first trips out on the flats. At the Sea Center, a hangout for the saltwater guides, I met this oddly formal Frenchman who was in the middle of a sixty-day booking with Woody Sexton, the preeminent Keys guide of the time. I thought this a little strange, not to say expensive, though later it occurred to me that after this first learning foray Guy was able to buy a skiff and guide himself.

The next spring and the four of us, including Russell Chatham, fished in tandem for thirty days and we have continued to do so for years, barring occasional absences for poverty, mental problems, divorce. McGuane threw in the towel first, recognizing the attritional factors of Key West before the rest of us were ready to, for all the various reasons of foolhardiness. Key West, before its gradual and inevitable gentrification, was a nexus, particularly in the seventies, for crazed and random hormones, free-flowing alcohol and pharmaceuticals, the kind of behavioral skew that requires some time to effect recovery, a euphemism for cold sweat and prayer. But the fishing was wonderful.

After that first full spring of fishing in 1970 Guy came to northern Michigan to hunt woodcock and grouse with me, and he has done so ever since, missing only two years out of twenty-five. The first time out seemed a little awkward, with Guy appearing in European hunting clothes, but he allayed the suspicions of two of my local friends by bagging fifteen of the sixteen birds he shot at, filling out the limits for the rest of us, who got only one or two. When you are younger you waste a great deal of time figuring out whether you are good or not. Later on you *know* perfectly well, good or bad or indifferent, and the problem drifts away. Guy is the best shot, and also the best saltwater flycaster, I know, but I should add that this apparently isn't very important to him. It may have been once, but hasn't been for a long time. He tends to think of such discussions as tasteless or impolite. When we both shoot at a particular bird at once he invariably says, "Your bird." This would get irritating if it weren't sincere, though it is a decided improvement over those who claim every bird.

In the ensuing years we made a number of trips, including early ones when I was still a working journalist and Guy a photographer: the southern coast of Ecuador, where we first fished billfish on flies in the early seventies and Guy took the first underwater photos of fighting billfish (a bit perilous); and his home area of Normandy, where we followed a stag hunt. Later came Costa Rican fishing, but we mostly stayed in the States, fishing in the Florida Keys, fishing and hunting in Montana, and trading visits to our own locales for grouse and woodcock in Michigan and quail in North Florida.

Strangely, as you grow older, if you can't hunt with any of two or three friends, you'd rather hunt alone. Newcomers make the grievous error of talking to your dogs—which are confused by such breaches in taste—or they whine about the weather. Admittedly there are the odd miseries of the season, such as when one hunts on days where normally the idea of a mere short walk would be repellent.

Once, in the Upper Peninsula, it began to snow so hard in the middle of a woodcock flight we couldn't see each other more than ten feet away, but my bitch Tess continued to point. Guy laughed at each flush while I began to brood about finding the car. He had on rubber boots and I didn't, so he offered to carry me across a wide slough with at least a foot of water. He's rather sturdy and didn't seem to mind my two hundred pounds (a bit upwards of that), so we set off toward the car with me holding on like ivy. It was even funny when we pitched forward, with the floundering and splashing at least getting the dog's attention off the birds. She was very young then and you don't want to call a young dog off active scent even if it means freezing to death. Afterward, it was one of those rare occasions when a glass of whiskey actually tasted delicious.

Most of our hunting days are relatively wordless, a testament to the quality of attention the sport requires, the absolute absorption in the day itself. By midafternoon, however, the limited talk tends to direct itself toward what we're going to cook for dinner. Since Guy is French and my tastes run in that direction too, we never settle for something simple. A couple of hours of cooking relieves the bone-weariness rather than adding to it. In hundreds of meals we try to avoid repetition, so the imagination is fully engaged, even during the onerous chore of plucking birds (it is a sin against God to skin them). Another boon is that we are able, during bird season, despite up to six hours of walking a day, to gain weight. This cannot be humanly accomplished without night after night of eating multiple courses of quail, wild piglet, venison, mallards, sweetbreads, grouse, woodcock, lobsters, oysters, and crab. Out of respect for my gout we rarely eat beef during bird season. Over the years Guy has nobly and politely tried to adjust to American wines but prefers French, which is now about all we drink, even if it is simple Côtes du Rhône, but there are quirky side roads into Tuscany and Australia.

Ultimately, *For a Handful of Feathers* is a portrait of a hunter and reminiscent of Turgenev's *A Sportman's Sketches*. It is the effort of one man to totally understand the section of land on which he lives. Nothing is left out that should be there. Hunting can be a good experience for your soul, to the degree that you refuse to exclude none of the realities of the natural world, including a meditation on why you hunt, perhaps an ultimately unanswerable question. I have often thought the urge to hunt to be genetic rather than manly or heroic, whatever those characteristics mean in a world where the word "honor" itself is a joke. Unlike our forefathers or Native Americans, we don't have to do it, but then I suspect they also hunted when they didn't have to, for the sheer joy of it. *For a Handful of Feathers* addresses these questions, but more so, it concerns itself with how we use our land, what we can and can't do for the creature life upon it.

(*Sports Afield*/*For a Handful of Feathers*)

MARCHING TO
A DIFFERENT DRUMMER
(1974)

Tonight it is March, a very long way from bird season. In the middle of a Michigan winter it is hard to believe that there ever was an October, with her violent colors, or mornings when you pulled on your boots and walked into some Renaissance painting: blood red to a dusky, muted red, burnt-sienna hills, umber grass, and the waves from a bluff far above Lake Michigan so green and tossed that it was not inconceivable Botticelli's maiden would step out of a shell. This is only to say that you favor autumn, and winter up here looks like nothing so much as a giant marshmallow factory. On long walks when snowmobiles pass, you think that the only virtue of these machines is that they smell like motorboats, and motorboats remind you of the fishing you're going to do in the Florida Keys in a few weeks. There is a ski resort half a dozen miles south, but your boredom with that sport has reached such a point that you avoid driving past the slopes where all those people are actually having fun with winter.

So you take walks. And hope to see a grouse, though the terrain around your small farm is favored with few of them. The snowmobiles pack a trail, and you offer them grudging thanks for making the far reaches of winter accessible. It's no fun to flounder in drifts, and most of my friends who brag about their snowshoes never use them. Often you stand on a trail and wish that yesterday's snowmobile had headed down through that swale. You want to go there, but it is impossible. You think of maybe drawing a map for the neighbor boy so he can cut some new areas for you on his Arctic Cat. You have agreed to buy one when they make less noise than a dripping spigot, a sleeping gerbil, an oak leaf falling on wet ground, a morel growing.

But the occasional grouse. Its thundering flush in the cold air. The involuntary lifting of your arms as if they cradled a shotgun, the noticeable pounding in your chest. Grouse are always a shock, as if you brushed the electric fence while throwing hay to your daughter's horses. A subtle, aerial shock not to be confused with seeing a grizzly while backpacking. That is like grabbing the fence with a wet hand. The grouse are a hundred yards away before you actually think, beginning with a low dodging flight through the trees, then often they hook like an inept golf shot. Why the hook? I don't know. They have to go somewhere.

Ruffed grouse have become to you the ultimate in shooting. You still hunt woodcock, but mostly because you stumble upon them in the search for grouse. You can tell you don't prize them nearly as much because when you miss, you don't feel very bad. For ducks you have to get up at dawn and the beauty of your last teal four years back spoiled it. You might deer hunt a single afternoon but, to be truthful, it has brought no real excitement for more than a decade.

But grouse. Grouse are the trout of the woods. Flushing a grouse is like seeing a good brown trout rising to a mayfly. And the first days of trout season in Michigan invariably coincide with the drumming sound of male grouse in the swamp calling up their harems.

The speed of their flight can be understood by the energy of their drumming. In your winter walks you see few of them because the snow is deep in the swamps where they stay for shelter, and there is thin ice on the water. But each one you do see brings the memory of past seasons, and though you have hunted seriously only for seven years, these seasons are confused with each other. The event is more interesting than the year. All of the seasons merged together would not be an idealization but an intensification. And that is the way you remember them anyway. The seasons are too heavy with failure and the comic to make the stuff of dreams. Sport, when honestly rendered, is scarcely ever dreamlike. If it is a string of unremittent successes, it isn't sporting. Here, then, is a season, concentrated; add six parts water.

The first day is uncomfortably warm: mid-September, and it looks like July with the greenery heavy on the trees. We've had no kill frost and the ferns form a waist-deep layer over the floor of the woods. It is absolutely obnoxious to walk through the ferns because I can't see my feet, and I stumble over the rotting deadfall poplar.

Pat Paton and his son Shaun are thirty yards to my right just across East Creek. We heard a lot of drumming in this area while trout fishing in the spring, and since grouse tend to spend their lives in a comparatively small area, we thought we'd try hunting the creek bottom. We kick up half a dozen birds but have no shots. The brush gets thicker and the tag alder branches whip against our faces. When we pause, mosquitoes and blackflies cloud around our heads. This isn't grouse hunting, it's a jungle movie called *Green Hell*. A woodcock flushes, and I snapshoot at the sound, seeing the brown blur disappear into the foliage.

"Get him?" Pat yells.

"Nope."

You hate to hunt with people who are always insisting that they "might" have got a bird. This is a neophyte's trick, and it causes a lot of aimless poking in the shrubbery. And it is bad for a dog to look for nothing. Dogs get discouraged when their credulity is pushed. Their noses tell them that the dead bird isn't there. It's bad as a general rule to hunt with anyone you wouldn't camp with or introduce to a secret trout-fishing spot. You remember the time you hunted with a dolt who shot a porcupine and the spirit went out of the day.

The jungle walk becomes preposterous. I can't even see Pat's dog, a springer spaniel named Tammy. A dumb name, but a good dog. I know where the dog is only by the waving of fern tips. We've had enough of our swamp trek and emerge into a wide pasture for an easy walk back to the car. Out in the middle of the pasture is a huge lone cow. A Holstein. The cow watches us as we walk and Pat studies the cow. "We've got a problem," he says in a near whisper.

The cow is a bull. The bull begins to toss his head and paw the ground like his brothers do in cartoons. I slide into the brush in order to cross the creek before I realize that a creek does not offer a formidable barrier to a bull. So we stand there listening to some awesome bellowing, with the animal's neck craning up and outward so that we may better hear its warnings. The music stops and the bull begins a classic trot toward us, gradually picking up speed. Maybe it thinks it's a Cape buffalo. Pat fires two warning shots in the air. The bull picks up speed. Pat lightly rakes the animal with No. 9 skeet shot. The bull does a wonderful rodeo buck, then turns and trots in the other direction.

Late in the afternoon Pat picks off a single bird that separated from a brood and flew across a clearing. We go to a bar and over many glasses of beer agree that early grouse season is as bad as early trout season, when you might very well tear your waders on ice. Maybe you think you have to go through it to deserve the rest of the season.

Still no frost as September wanes with the heat of summer. No one wants to go hunting. They are waiting to concentrate on a few weekends in October. So I hunt alone in a four-section swamp and blueberry marsh. I am careful because I've found it easy to get lost within these four square miles. Again, I've been here in the spring. My mother wanted to see warblers and she woke me before dawn thinking I shared her interest in these wee birds. I do love warblers, though I prefer to see them out the window at lunch. Anyway, we heard grouse drumming and I have high hopes while walking along the pulp trails. There is also a bear in this swamp, though I'd prefer not to see him for reasons of cowardice.

I round a bend and begin to descend deeper into the swamp. I see something in the middle of the trail. It is the very rare sight of a grouse simply sitting there looking at the hunter. I raise my gun but pause, deciding to be fair. The grouse flushes, and for a millisecond I regret my generosity, but the bird falls with the shot.

At our last Grouse Society meeting Doc Hall impishly asked us to raise a hand if we had never shot a sitting bird. No one did. If you have a bad streak, say, of missing fifteen birds in a row, it is easy to see a sitting bird as a boon, a gift from Mother Nature as a reward for your sweat, the countless miles of walking and anger and frustration.

You have to hunt a long time to fully understand the degree of difficulty involved. This is especially true of bad years when the bird population, which is cyclical, is down very low. The worst year in my memory was 1967, at least locally. I hunted for a week that November, though mostly I looked for my bird dogs. In the absence of birds they chased leaves and snowflakes and each other. Late on a particularly cold and blank day a friend and I shot at the same bird simultaneously, and both instantly yelled, "I got him." Our friendship was maintained by finding two different-sized pellets in the grouse when we cleaned it—my 16-gauge and his 20. The bird looked meager on the platter at dinner with six adults trying to act offhand about eating it.

The first week in October we had a hard frost, then rain and a strong wind, which made the leaves begin to fall. I certainly haven't waited for the weather but it is appreciated: I've averaged less than a bird a day, though most often I only hunt a few hours. When you hunt alone and are not distracted by others, the time moves more slowly.

You are more totally aware of what you are doing, and the experience becomes much more intense.

Pat calls, and we decide to spend a day hitting favorite places. Some of them were discovered in 1965 when the grouse were at the top of their population curve and birds could have been found almost anywhere. Certain spots are chosen for strictly aesthetic reasons, though few grouse hunters would admit it. We begin the day in an area along the Manistee River that is redolent with memories. I shot the first grouse of my adult life here. (In my boyhood I potted a fair number by sitting in a swamp until they came clucking out of the cover, no doubt mistaking me for a stump.) The place, though, has an unpleasant aspect. I slipped on the wet clay of a cliff overlooking the river and spent a month in the hospital in traction. Some fun.

Crossing the pasture we hunt a bog and pick up two snipe. Then we head for the series of gullies choked with thorn apple and cedar that abut the river. You have to snapshoot in these gullies or the grouse get above the water, and it's pointless to shoot. It would be monstrous to see a bird wasted in the river. Perhaps a hundred yards away we see a brood sitting under a thorn apple tree. This has never happened before, and we immediately have a strategy session. We painfully sneak through the brush along the river and up the hill through the briars. We burst from the cover with our shotguns ready. No grouse. We comb the immediate location in widening circles, without luck. We didn't hear them flush. It is the stuff of a sporting nightmare.

We drive several miles to another spot along a defunct railroad and quickly pick up three birds, all within sight of a general store. But we are still wondering what the hell happened to all those birds under the tree. Grouse have an uncanny ability to keep a tree between themselves and a shooter after the flush. In one particular thicket I have flushed grouse on a dozen occasions and seen them only twice. I keep going back, trying to figure out a way to outwit them. Sometimes a bird will break directly at you, sailing over your head, then turning. I've never made one of those twisting shots.

*   *   *

Now the season is in full stride. My shooting has even improved. Last weekend I got two grouse and a woodcock in a hundred-yard stretch and without a miss. Unfortunately, the next day I missed seven in a row, so my glory was short-lived. I've estimated my success rate at about one out of seven, while a truly superb wing shot like Doc Hall will get one out of three. But he has a marvelous English setter named Heidi and another named Judge that is well above average. Heidi is somehow the most graceful dog I've ever met, extremely feminine and a hard worker.

Since I usually hunt without a dog and without the splendid early-warning system they provide, I become lazy hunting behind a good dog. With them I don't need the continuous state of readiness that I own when hunting alone.

If you are walking through the woods thinking about pretty girls or maybe an argument you had with your wife or, more likely, how you will cook the two grouse in your bag, you are going to miss every shot. If Zen monks had any predilection for the sport they would clean up.

After a fine start with a bird apiece we entered an area that had been pulped over the winter before. It was an unbelievable tangle of poplar tops but we had a honey bucket location to hit on our circular swing. Two hours later we emerged exhausted from the tangle. Each of us had fallen three times and Pat had a sprained finger and cut hand. Pulping is good for grouse because it allows new growth, but terrible for a hunter when the tops are left in disarray. Since this is state land on timber lease you wonder why the yo-yos can't be forced to bulldoze the waste into piles. Though we flushed ten birds I wouldn't walk back into that place at gunpoint.

The other day I talked to Doc Hall about seeing his log, the record of his hunting since 1946. It contains daily accounts of birds flushed, birds shot at, birds bagged, and general remarks on habitat, weather, and dog work. The locations are given code names. Here we encounter the same secrecy found in the trout or tarpon fisherman. You will not exchange secret places with someone who will abuse the area by overhunting or divulging it to others. Doc Hall has so many places that he can afford to be a little careless. Last year we traded spots, though I suspect he already knew about mine.

We got lost in one of his favorites, but only because the shooting was so interesting that we hunted past twilight. So we floundered around in the dark with Doc lighting matches to see the compass mounted in his gunstock. We kept reassuring each other that we weren't lost, but we couldn't find the car.

Getting lost lacks humor. I once spent an entire afternoon trying to get off a hairpin flat in the Manistee River. First the river was on my left, then, fifteen minutes later, it was on my right. It was very warm and I was wearing chest-high waders and carrying a bamboo rod. Michigan's swamps and flat pine barrens are comparatively small, but it's best to have your wits about you. I flushed a lot of birds, aimlessly pointing my fly rod at them and yelling, "Bang!"

A hunting friend arrived from Florida today, hoping to catch the woodcock migratory flights and shoot grouse for two weeks. There's something fascinating about introducing a person to the sport. It is partly finding out what you know, having to be precise in your information. Though my friend has done a great deal of quail and pheasant hunting, ruffed grouse and their heavy cover are new to him. The similarity to teaching someone trout fishing is striking, where the ability to cast competently can be learned in short order and still produce no results. You could shoot a 98 in skeet and flunk miserably in the woods unless you had taken the trouble to find out how grouse live.

Since most Michigan terrain lacks drama you concentrate on particularities. For grouse you look for thorn apple, abandoned orchards, wild grape, wintergreen, budding poplar, chokecherries, all preferred foods. If it has been especially dry you hunt along creeks.

Late in the afternoon you check the sunny sides of hills and along logging trails where the birds come to gravel.

Setting out the next morning, we miss the first dozen birds. It is maddening for my friend, who is the best shot I know. Much of our grief is caused by the fact that we are both piggies, and much of our gunning talk centers on food. We have many recipes on tap, have purchased wines to go with them, and our clumsiness is depressing.

The guilt, not really severe, attached to spending so much time at play can be absurd. If I'm skunked I come home with an involved speech in my head to convince my wife that I really hunted hard and didn't spend the afternoon at the bar. Since she and my daughter love to eat grouse, there is no interest in excuses. I can see the hurt look in their eyes, maybe a trace of disrespect. It's fun to bring in five lake trout with an aggregate weight of fifty pounds and nonchalantly drop them in the sink. But it is not nearly as effective in my home as a grouse or two.

The first ten days will have to be graded as a C minus. Michigan's vaunted October Indian summer is on the verge of a heat wave. We hunt without coats and are without the transfusions of energy cold autumn days give. We get moderately lost in a local swamp, thrash through the deadfalls kicking up seventeen grouse, and not one ends in the bag. Back in the car I can't meet my friend's eyes so I take him to a high bluff along Lake Michigan that always wows visitors. It is a stupendous view with four islands far out in the lake and the promontory of Pyramid Point to the south. At the bottom of the cliff we see a flock of ducks, but they are too far away to identify. Near this bluff my pointer once swam out into heavy seas beyond sight for several hours. Neat dog. We called the sheriff and Coast Guard, but they weren't interested. She finally returned and had a nice nap on the beach.

Surprisingly, my scenic tour yields two birds. I decide not to admit that they are the first two birds I've ever taken here. We have a full dinner with yesterday's two grouse and three woodcock. The woodcock are stuffed with pâté, the grouse with aromatic green grapes that are pulled after twenty minutes and replaced with a bread stuffing. After browning the birds we usually steam them in a closed dish in a cup or two of white wine. Woodcock are especially good for breakfast on toast with scrambled eggs. And a glass of wine. We experiment without being too decorative, as grouse are so delicious they don't need help. The only way to ruin their sharp gamey flavor is by overcooking, which tends to parch their already dry flesh.

We have a fine, though melancholy, day's hunt with Doc Hall. Heidi is dead from the same type of cancer that destroyed my own dog. Good dogs have an uncanny ability to become another person in the family and their absence is deeply felt.

We have lunch sitting on the bank of the Manistee. It is so warm that trout are rising. The dogs are fatigued from the heat and wallow at the river's edge. Judge, Heidi's hunting mate, has given us a number of flawless points, including one in a clearing that imitated all of those make-believe hunting stories. Doc Hall says that woodcock tend to congregate on the south edge of any clearing, simply because they come in from the north and only decide on the clearing after they have begun to cross it. This is not a simple piece of information. It will save a lot of dead hours for me. Though Doc Hall is retired, he sprints through the woods like a kangaroo, cross-country skis all winter, and fishes in the summers. He even soothes my hypochondria free of charge.

It is the first of November and the weather finally breaks at midday with the temperature dropping twenty degrees and the wind wheeling around to the northwest, the prevailing pattern. It is my friend's last day, and starts badly with his Labrador eating our lunch. And we're late, out of the general tiredness that two weeks of walking brings on.

But we are to have an afternoon that is magical, the best afternoon of my hunting life. And this despite a hesitant beginning, some sleet, and a howling wind. We see a dozen birds and take eight. We keep looking at each other through the trees, now barren of leaves, in disbelief. Seven seasons to have one truly perfect day. And two of the shots were among the most difficult of the year. On the long drive home we are reverent rather than talkative.

Falling asleep that night, I remember several years back in the Upper Peninsula when a gas station operator told me that grouse could not be hit on the wing. You had to sit on the car hood with a buddy driving and shoot them on the trails at dusk. As sport, grouse hunting has often seemed ill advised to me in terms of the hours spent. But that is John Calvin creeping up again with all of his boring, utilitarian advice. Grouse hunting is so precious because it is so difficult. There are, no doubt, great shots who don't feel this respect, but my very average skills bow to this creature.

It is December and we have the fillip tossed by the Michigan legislature called the December grouse season. The weather is so foul it is largely a joke except to the hardiest. I've never seen another hunter in December. But then I rarely see other grouse hunters in October. The sport doesn't have the popularity of pheasant or duck hunting. You wonder why, but hesitate to proselytize.

The last day is frantic and silly. I hunt with Alan Lee, a banjo player, and his German shorthair with the unlikely name of Moxie. The name should have been a tip-off, as we spend the afternoon searching for the dog in a snowstorm. Alan finally puts out his coat for the dog to scent, and we go to a local bar. When we return we find the coat in the snow with some difficulty. I tease Alan about the time he missed a grouse sitting in a tree. He's normally a good shot and insists that he didn't want to spoil the meat by a direct hit. The meat is still flying around, a warm, feathered universe.

In a few hours it will be New Year's Eve. We drive the seven miles back to Alan's house afraid to mention the lost dog in the blizzard. But Moxie has a fine sense of direction and meets us eagerly in the driveway.

(*Sports Illustrated*)

MEDITATIONS ON HUNTING
(2006)

Up here on the 45th parallel in Montana the seasons are as well defined as they were in northern Michigan where I spent sixty years. One day in mid-September you are fishing and wondering if the immense local forest fires, about 250,000 acres, have pushed more eagles to the river because you count thirteen, a mixture of balds and goldens. The next morning it is cold and rainy and you watch the snow descending in altitude on the Absaroka mountains across the Yellowstone River from your home. As if cued by an ancient pull you can't comprehend, the heart and mind turn to hunting. Of course the seasons bleed into one another but when it becomes warm again the warmth will be tentative. Bird hunting has been open for two weeks but it's been hot and I haven't wanted to expose my dog to the ample local supply of prairie rattlers.

Hunting and fishing have been a very large part of my life for about sixty years. They are what I do when I'm not writing poems and novels. And when not actually fishing and hunting I am running our dogs, bird-watching, mushrooming, looking for wildflowers, or idly searching for berries that I eat as I go. These were all family routines since I can remember and I merely took them several steps further in the degree of intensity. The natural world is an enormous mystery and I married her very early. In retrospect this now seems an aesthetic decision. I hunt and fish because hunting and fishing take place in beautiful places.

In hunting, my fullest obsession is game birds rather than what is known as "big game," or mammals. This might be because as a literary writer, poet, and novelist, I have a mind that is a bit suggestive and vulnerable to the idea that we are humans trapped in our mammalian skins. Having read widely in the discipline of anthropology I was never completely comfortable watching *Planet of the Apes*, no matter how comic the experience. I have thought for a long time that if anthropology were taught in secondary school, say in the seventh grade, we would have a much better idea who we once were and what we are now. For obvious religious reasons this is not possible. When you gut a deer it is unnerving to see that the organs are located like your own.

I've mostly hunted ruffed grouse, woodcock, snipe, Hungarian partridge, sharptail grouse, doves, and the various quail—bobwhite, Mearns, scaled, and Gambel's—in Michigan, Montana, Florida, Arizona, and New Mexico. I used to hunt ducks occasionally but this was not a happy experience. Hunters tend to be species specific —there are very few generic hunters—and ducks presented problems. I shot a blue-winged teal once when in a questionable mood and that was that. The same thing happened with wood ducks when we flipped a coin to see who had to shoot three of them for dinner. They are delicious but their beauty caused bad dreams. The only duck exception happened on Lake Okeechobee on a day when we must have seen ten thousand bluebills. In addition, I wouldn't shoot a bear for a million dollars. In the twenty-five years we owned a cabin in the Upper Peninsula in Michigan I was in fairly close contact with bears and I developed a pleasantly complicated relationship with them to the degree that I couldn't eat the gift of bear meat without bear nightmares. The wolf has also been a totemic creature to me since childhood though when my immediate neighbor in Montana lost forty-four sheep to wolves I could scarcely have blamed him for shooting them. But he said he couldn't because he can't see in the dark. The problem was brought home to me when I was in France on a book tour and my wife called before dawn (her time) to say that wolves were eating sheep right under our bedroom window and the dogs were frightened. She could hear the crunching of bones.

It is easy to forget that we are humans trapped in mammalian skins, and vice versa, mammals trapped in human skins. We can't escape each other and this makes our approach to the natural world somewhat schizophrenic. Shakespeare said, "We are nature, too," but we have done everything we can to ignore this obvious fact. It is also true in futuristic terms that hunting will become an archaism indulged in only by the eccentric wealthy when the press of population becomes too immense on an exhausted and crowded country. This process is especially visible now in Britain, Ireland, and the rest of Europe.

Bird hunting is easily misunderstood by the neophyte who tends to think of it in terms of the ability to shoot. In reality shooting talent is only the third most important factor, coming after dog work and the knowledge of habitat. To become an adequate shot is merely a matter of practice and exposure. A good coach helps and so does time spent at the skeet range, though it is hard to find a bird that flies with the predictable pattern of a clay pigeon. Because of the blindness in my left eye I have always been what could be classified as "high mediocre" but have made up for it by working my dogs frequently until they are very good indeed.

The best shot and most successful hunter I know, a northern Michigan hunter and friend named Nick Reens, often works four big-running English setters. Once in New Mexico I saw him hit fifteen quail in a row. It is his exhaustive knowledge of habitat, a thing little understood by envious outsiders.

The first principle of habitat is that game birds are as naturally obsessed with filling their tummies as the house finches that flood your bird feeder. Over a number of years of experience and with a modest amount of research you learn their eating habits, their preferred flora. With a single ruffed grouse in Michigan's Upper Peninsula you can open a crop and identify poplar leaves, choke-cherries, desiccated blueberries, thorn apples, varieties of viburnum, and dogwood. You take your dogs to areas that have coverts where the preferred foods are available. Since game birds also need shelter from the frequently nasty weather during the fall in the Great North you hope to find preferred food coverts near stands of conifers or pine plantations, which offer little food but splendid escapes from storms. Another aspect of weather is available moisture. I recall an early fall when the Department of Natural Resources in Michigan announced that woodcock numbers appeared to be low. The late summer had been brutally hot and dry, which had hardened the ground for their tender beaks. I took my setter Rose to a river flat dense with alder thickets and she pointed thirty woodcock in a little more than an hour. The birds needed moist earth their long beaks could penetrate for their worm feasts. The catch was that it is nearly impossible to shoot a bird in such an area. Rose would point and I'd hear the flush but not see the bird rising up through the alder leaves. Another catch was that Rose was frantic with the joy of finding so many birds and ever after wanted to return to such cover. Since I loved her I'd occasionally give in and later emerge totally caked with mud and soaked with swamp water, which meant nothing to her. Neither of my setters, Tess or Rose, cared whether I hit a bird. They only wanted to find birds and point them. The Labs in my life, Sand and Zilpha, have been upset when I miss, giving me that "How could you?" look. They want to carry the birds around in their eternally hungry mouths.

Unfortunately, some men want to make hunting, or fishing, for that matter, a terribly serious activity. Such men hunt as if they were Rommel invading Egypt during World War II. They tend to be elaborately equipped, almost in a parody of the idea of uniforms. In the early years of my hunting I would attempt to be sociable and cooperative but then fairly early learned to reserve my hunting activity for a few friends whom I know well, including their dogs. You don't want to hunt with someone as humorless as Ernest Hemingway in the Serengeti, and even less so with someone who is careless with a shotgun. On my dozens of weeklong hunting trips to the cabin in the Upper Peninsula I tended to stick with friends who were also helpful in the kitchen.

At present I am hunting with a two-year-old Scottish Labrador named Zilpha. Last year as a youngster she was excellent, retrieving at least a hundred Gambel's, scaled, and Mearns quail, plus doves. She also ate a lot of pocket gophers. It is a little discouraging to call in your dog only to find that there is a mortally squeaking gopher head peeking out of her mouth. Gophers and green apples give her frequent tummy aches. This year, however, she has been treating life as a wonderful joke and we are hard into retraining. Both dog trainers and mothers refer to this phenomenon as the "terrible twos." Zilpha is also a wonderful coward. Last winter near Patagonia, Arizona, where we spend the cold months in a little casita, Zilpha pretended she wanted to chase a boar javelina but managed to run strenuously while somehow staying in the same place.

I believe dogs are the reason that I'm a bird hunter, a wing shooter rather than a big game hunter, which would include the local Montana deer, elk, and antelope, though I do go out for ungulates now and then mostly for a share of the meat. Last October I hunted with Danny Lahren to fill our tags but mostly to give the meat to my son-in-law, who was too busy to hunt. We put the sneak on a group of antelope and slowly crawled up a hill. When I peeked over the crest a large female was within thirty yards. Danny

said "shoot" and I said, "I don't feel up to it today," so he shot and
filled his license. I felt ever so slightly embarrassed over the matter
though the meat was delicious indeed. The experience reminded me
of forty years before in northern Michigan when on a cold snowy
November morning a friend and I had shot a whitetail buck running slowly across a marsh. When we reached the deer, however,
we discovered that it was a very old bag of bones with the grayest
muzzle I had ever seen. The Department of Natural Resources told
us it was one of the oldest bucks that they had ever examined. I
was sad about shooting this great-grandpa, partly because we were
very poor at the time and I was tired of meatless meals and the
upshot was that there still was no meat on the table. I have read
that when the Aztecs sacrificed virgins to the gods the bodies were
also meant for the priestly dinner table. The obvious reason for
sacrificing the young was discovered when we tried to roast a leg
of our great-grandpa whitetail. Serving my hunting boots would
have been preferable.

   Hunting appears to be in decline in terms of numbers of hunters. The most obvious reason seems to be continuity of habitat. My
father and my uncles hunted and taught me, and with the exception of a half dozen years my entire life has been spent in rural areas
where I could hunt out the back door if I chose. This was common
in the days before urbanization, but this way of life is passing from
us. Hunting has shifted to being a project or expedition and most
often requires travel.

   Another possibility is that we are now seeing fewer well-
educated hunters because hunting has fallen into disfavor among
upwardly mobile people in suburban parts of our country where
there tends to be a "monoethic," a putative "right way of living"
that excludes hunting. For unclear reasons there is a corrosive
parsimony of spirit among such people, an "in your face" political correctness that puts hunting in the same category as chain-
smoking, fundamentalist religions, and *Playboy* magazine. Another
possible factor is that hunting is real hard work. We are now largely

a desk-bound population. Bird shooting occasionally involves ten miles a day on foot, which is decidedly unlike thirty minutes on a treadmill.

A few weeks ago I took a drive in a remote area of central Montana. At one point I saw no other vehicle for two hours. I counted over a hundred antelope, fifty whitetails and mule deer, three golden eagles, two coveys of Hungarian partridge crossing the road, a few sharptail grouse, not to speak of a small group of yellowlegs along a creek. Last winter my son-in-law counted four hundred elk in the vicinity of our summer house where my neighbor lost forty-four sheep to wolves. We've shot many rattlesnakes in the yard. It's hard to imagine or extrapolate the grandeur or brutality of empty country when living in densely populated areas.

The poet Gary Snyder has written about the presumed virtue of remaining distant from the sources of our food. The United States is not all that "united" in terms of shared experience. It occurred to me that we have come to the point in our history where most of us who eat lamb, chicken, pork, and beef have never known individual lambs, thrown scratch to chickens, slopped the hogs or held a piglet, or brushed down a 4-H heifer for the county fair. Meat has become a packaged abstraction at the supermarket. Perhaps to truly understand hunting we must read widely in the field of anthropology. I've long been addicted to the work of Loren Eiseley, who said in *The Star Thrower*, "We can go down through the layers of dead cities until the gold becomes stone, until the jewels become skulls, until the palace is a hovel, until the hovel becomes a heap of gnawed bones." Of course hunting is as old as man is for the simple reason that we either eat or die. Late last October on a trip to northern Italy during the white truffle season we visited the ruins of the castle of Matilda of Canossa, who virtually owned northern Italy in the eleventh century and while ruling it managed to save the Catholic Church from ruin. A brochure at the castle entrance said that Matilda wrote poetry and loved to hunt with dogs and falcons. Here was a kindred soul from over a great span of centuries.

For some reason five chickens from a nearby coop decided to walk me up the steep path from which I could see the glories of the local forest where Matilda once hunted.

I've been asked many times during public appearances if I must hunt. I've found that the question starts pointless arguments and gave up taking it seriously years ago. I usually answer, "Perhaps I'm less evolved than you are," and let it go at that. Or I might say, "Hunting is my sleep substitute," which means that hunting like fishing banishes all other mental considerations during the activity. In fact I hunt because I've done so since my childhood in northern Michigan. I can still see those arrows aimed harmlessly toward distant deer from my little bow. The main problem was finding the arrows in the tall ferns. After a couple of summers of extreme effort I bagged a ruffed grouse in an alder swamp and started a campfire. Rare but burned ruffed grouse without salt and pepper wasn't tasty, but it led to things that were.

The other morning in the middle of a grotesque Montana heat wave I got up at 4:30 a.m. to go trout fishing as I had done a dozen times during the six-week-long session of extreme heat with the temperature hitting the midnineties by midafternoon. I am not by nature an early riser and, in fact, love sleep to the extent that I take two daily naps. Laurens van der Post said, "We live not only our own lives but, whether we know it or not, also the life of our time." I am not a fan of our time, thus sleep is an attractive alternative to consciousness. But on this particular muggy predawn I was drawn back over coffee to the hundreds of early August mornings I had worked my bird dogs at my cabin in the Upper Peninsula of Michigan, ostensibly to tune them up for the bird season starting September 15, but in reality these dawn forays had become an end in themselves. The dogs didn't need any more training nor did I need to locate any good coverts for grouse and woodcock because over the years I had collected forty-seven good locations. I was merely hunting without a gun and the pleasure of this grew as I became older and less obsessed with shooting and eating the kill, an apparently normal process for the aging hunter.

For a more immediate taste of the experience, here is an abbreviated version of a journal I kept on a recent trip from Montana back to Michigan with Dan Lahren, and his little French Brittany Jacques, and my Scottish Lab Zilpha. The dogs have been friends since infancy which presented a few problems. I was tempted to think of this as a "last hunt" in Michigan but then I fish every September in Montana with Peter Matthiessen, the author of the monumental and melancholy *Wildlife in America*. Peter at seventy-eight is a decade older than me and shows no sign of slowing down.

October 7. Pulled into Grand Marais, a small harbor town on Lake Superior, around noon. Seventy degrees and a rare and grotesque south wind gusting to 40–50 knots. In the field the dogs were unsure of themselves, never having hunted a woodcock. Flushed four and two grouse but no shooting as the wind overrode the sound of the flush, the cue for shooting. Exhausted because of heat. Made chili from three pounds of elk we brought along plus ground Chimayó and guajillo peppers.

October 8. Winds somewhat subsided though occasional gusts sent my hat flying. Still quite warm and dry with moss crunchy underfoot. Finally shot a few woodcock and a grouse, quite critical to Jacques and Zilpha in order to learn this new scent. Zilpha retrieved the woodcock while Jacques ignored them other than looking for more, a frequent thing for pointing dogs, this distaste for woodcock in the mouth. Helped a couple of old men (my age) change a tire far from civilization, about five miles. Heard from them that three locals out fishing in the big south winds drowned in Lake Superior late yesterday. Scattered the ashes of my setter Rose in the local river where she loved to swim.

October 9. Difficult morning. The temperature dropped
to the pleasant forties but we could only find woodcock
in the densest cover, shooting one bird in eight flushes.
Zilpha turns into a beige rocket after retrieving this bird
for me. She's impossible to handle. Jacques is also having
difficulties as if he's still looking for Montana's Hungarian
partridge. We move to more open cover and he becomes
splendid, with Danny shooting a limit. At lunch found
out more about boating accident. The craft was only four
miles out when it became disabled but the huge southern
wind pushed it twelve miles out into heavy water where
it tipped over. One man lashed himself to the boat and
survived while three couldn't hold on. Unlikely the bodies
will be recovered due to coldness of Lake Superior. The
bell was rung three times in the tavern.

October 10. Victory in our time. A blank hard morning
with not a bird raised but then in the afternoon many
grouse and woodcock in a truly remote spot. Both dogs
strutted as if aware that they are the keys to the kingdom
of hunting.

October 11. A truly bum day that for some reason filled
me with pleasure. Intermittent cold hard rain. We were
shivering and utterly soaked before we had sense enough
to give up. A fine dinner of grouse and woodcock, acorn
squash, and French wine.

October 12. Surprise. All night I heard a big northwester
and the thunder of waves from the harbor breakwall. At
dawn I looked out the window and couldn't see my car,
covered as it was by a foot of wind-driven snow. Amazingly
beautiful with patches of blue sky between snow squalls.
Tried to hunt but the woodcock have sensibly fled south
except for a few hiding out beneath low-hanging branches

of fir trees. Leave them alone, I say to myself. A fine day for reading. We drive south to Seney so I can show Danny my old bird-watching haunt, the Seney National Wildlife Refuge, a hundred-thousand-acre wetland. Oddly enough I have hunted with three ornithologists in my life.

October 13. A glorious drive south and across the Mackinac Bridge. There's bound to be some more good weather but now the landscape is doing calisthenics getting ready for winter. Lake Michigan looks as tormented as Lake Superior. Danny will take the dogs back to Montana while I appear at Grand Valley State University in Grand Rapids for five days. I will stay in a fine hotel suite but as always prefer a cabin in the forest.

I have doubts whether hunting should be thought of as a sport. The idea of sport seems to presume spectators and I've been quite unable to watch a current program called *Cast and Blast*. The spirit of mortality does not adapt itself comfortably to the media. I readily admit that during hunting I often sense a shadowy question mark off to the side. I'm certainly at the age of an Elder, not a Hunter, but then our Elders are regularly shuffled off to Managed Care. I still recall the glory of a beautiful autumn day in 1966 when I shot my first grouse on the fly. I had quite a good job in Boston and we had returned to northern Michigan on the suspicious promise of my first book of poems, *Plain Song*, published by W. W. Norton. That autumn day I borrowed an erratic little beagle from a retired railroad worker, Verl McManus. I was a little lost on a deer trail when the beagle began its sharp bark and up flew a grouse, a big mature bird which I bagged. My wife and five-year-old daughter were delighted with this roasted alternative to all of the macaroni we had been eating in our cold house.

SPRING CODA
(1993)

*"Most things come and go, however good to watch;
a few things stay and matter to the end. Rain, for instance."*
—Reynolds Price

Long before I understood what it meant, the vernal equinox was
my most important annual holiday. I think I was fourteen when I
realized that I tended to go haywire—the current term is "depression"
—during the dark winter months in northern Michigan. But around
the middle of March and onward, the sap began to rise again. What is
now called "seasonal affective disorder" is so widespread in northern
climes that only the severest cases are recognizable. Sigurd begins to
sob and rams his head through the glass of the jukebox to get closer
to the music. That sort of thing.

Survival arrives in the new quality of light, even beneath close cloud cover. I have been reminded countless times that my home area receives less sunlight than any other place in the United States except a specific part of the Pacific Northwest. All of us think our weather is unique, but some of it actually is.

By late March, spring fever is palpable as a barn fire, a kind of interior mange, whose itch is forever out of reach of any salve except physical exhaustion. I have long since stopped sorting my fishing tackle a month before the trout opener, as my father did. It only makes things worse. My father would meticulously tie up a season's worth of tapered leaders and groom his trout flies and bass plugs, keeping his 6-12 mosquito repellent separate, under the notion that such an extreme odor would also repel fish.

The equinox is nature's New Year and probably more our own than the one we have, deep in winter and offering only a minute or two of extra daylight. In March the ears perk up instinctively for new bird arrivals, and the somewhat pathetic crocuses and skunk cabbage are a welcome sight. It doesn't matter that it snows on trout opener in late April or that the streams are turbid from the runoff. Even the whine of the first mosquito makes the heart glad.

It is also the time to address certain criminal activities, of which I also am guilty. Put aside this book. Go to your freezer. How much and what kind of fish and game do you have left in there from last summer and fall getting freezer burn? Write it down and subtract it as penance from your bag limit this coming summer and fall.

If you're not going to prepare the game properly and eat it, don't shoot it. The bird carcasses and fish fillets you take to the dump during spring cleaning represent an unnatural act against the natural world. Pluck your birds, don't skin them. Don't breast ducks, use the whole bird. Otherwise, let it fly on. Our imagined dominion over the natural world, an offshoot of our illusions about Manifest Destiny, is exhausting our wild lands to the degree that our grandchildren will be stuck with only Nintendo and spectator sports. If you insist on going for numbers, stick to the skeet range or commercial trout ponds, or play the state lottery, or play with yourself.

See how much you can do on foot. The sharp reductions of fish and game populations through hunting and fishing are invariably related to mechanization. ORVs are little more than chain saws on wheels. When possible, store the boat motors, and crank up the paddles and oars. Unfortunately, our government, when it offers up timber leases, does not demand that log roads be destroyed after cutting. Easy access means diminished quality, even in love.

Don't leave a trace of yourself in the wilds, whether on water or in the forest. The shores of the Great Lakes are lined with detritus on which perch cormorants whose beaks have been distorted grotesquely by chemical pollution. Strangely, even the fitness-buff sportsmen I know who have cross-trained themselves to a frazzle like to drive the last foot to their destination. I have noticed on my own property that if there's a branch on the road, no one hesitates to expand the road. Traces you shouldn't leave behind also include the piles of bait and garbage that lure mammals into shooting range.

Outdoors writers are fond of prating that "a few bad apples spoil it for the rest of us." Perhaps—if 10 percent comprise "a few"; that is roughly the same percentage of malevolently incompetent doctors and lawyers. We have discovered a principle here. Sadly, with writers, outdoors or otherwise, it's closer to 90 percent. If the writer of the outdoors column in your local newspaper betrays real ignorance of botany, forestry, ornithology, game biology, and riverine morphology, holler until the paper hires a better one. It no longer suits our survival as sportsmen to indulge those bumbling sentimentalists and their tales of the old man and the boy and the dog and the ten-point swamp buck that gored the ten-pound brown trout while the American eagle hovered over the ten thousand dollars' worth of Japanese equipment the writer got as freebies for touting the junk.

Another part of your spring coda might be to get involved—no matter your political leanings—in local environmental groups. It doesn't matter if you are far to the right of that round mound of bilge, Rush Limbaugh. It is in your interest as an outdoorsman to defend the integrity of your own bioregion, your prized watersheds. It's unfair to let the environmentalists do all the work and pay for all the benefits you reap hunting and fishing. It would be good to sit down with the woods hippies who are saving your future asses. It will also serve to defuse the anti-hunting faction, real and imagined.

Remember that the land-rapers of a dozen varieties are always waving their American flags to get themselves off the hook. The sacred cow rancher overgrazing public lands is no more the last bastion of the real America than the Chicano lettuce picker, the Haitian busboy in Miami, the Russian émigré drop forger in Detroit. This sort of patriotism is always the last refuge of scoundrels, as Samuel Johnson pointed out. A couple of thousand wolves roam freely in Minnesota, but to date not a single one has been reintroduced into Yellowstone Park for fear it might nail a cow or two on the surrounding, largely public grazing lands. You can pay a couple hundred grand in federal taxes, but if you offer a modest suggestion, these entitled freeloaders will call you a tree hugger. The whole notion of "multiuse" public lands will continue to be a scandal as long as the policy is directed by cows and chain saws. I have no objection to grazing on public lands as long as the notorious abuses the government freely permits are corrected. In the end, if sportsmen don't firmly align themselves with centrist environmentalists, they'd better raise a big kitty and buy Siberia.

Meanwhile, back to spring. Last May, on a long, circular walk (destinations aggravate the brain), I was caught miles from my car by the first thunderstorm of the year. This made me truly happy, as it hadn't rained in the month since the last of the snow had melted, and the woods were tinder-dry. If it didn't rain, the morel mushroom season would be a bust and my brook trout beaver ponds would further atrophy.

The rain caught me out in a large barren area with only a few sparse thickets dotting the sandy subsoil. I had been looking at a set of rather large black-bear tracks in a blowout, a shallow sand pit, but

I was mostly hoping to see a goshawk, the only explanation for the two breastless red-tailed hawks I had found in the past week. I was happy that I had a Hefty garbage bag in my pocket—a twenty-cent technique I learned from an old Ottawa. (Rain gear is an obnoxious thing to cart along, and I try to limit myself to my monocular, a pocketknife, and a compass.)

As the storm gathered around me, I stepped into the garbage bag, stooped and drew it up around my shoulders, lay down in the sand pit, and watched the rain wash away the bear prints. Maybe the first thunderstorm of spring is the best smell in the world. I recalled again the words of a 1692 Baltimore church bulletin: "Do not distress yourself with imaginings. Many fears are born of fatigue and loneliness. You are a child of the universe, no less than the trees and stars; you have a right to be here."

Just don't make a mess of it.

(Esquire Sportsman)

MICHIGAN, MONTANA, AND OTHER SACRED PLACES

A Prairie Prologue
in Nebraska
(2015)

In 1954, as an impetuous, irascible sixteen-year-old, I got my first view quite by accident of Nebraska's Sandhills. In my sophomore year of high school it had occurred to me that the lakes and forests of Michigan were too small for my burgeoning personality. I was an athlete of sorts, a student leader, but also an addict of Faulkner and James Joyce. Throw in Rimbaud and Dostoyevsky and I was an absurdly premature powder keg and felt I should look in a far field.

With the help of the only teacher who didn't think I was nuts, I wangled a job at a resort in Colorado by saying I was a college student, a small fib. My mother gave a resounding "no" to my trip. My father, however, said yes, and that was my trump card. He was a government agronomist but had a somewhat shaky youth. At my age he was working as a shovel man on a cross-Michigan pipeline, camping out even in winter. I often think of this hardship compared with my own rather flimsy problems.

Over an arduously goofy summer in which I discovered that college girls necked more intensely than the high school girls back home, the most memorable event was slopping coffee all over the saucer of Earl Warren, the chief justice of the Supreme Court at the time. I was embarrassed, but then I had never seen a famous person in real life.

To the despair of my parents I decided to hitchhike home from Colorado in hopes of an adventure of some sort. I shipped my trunk ahead with my $1,200 in tip change inside. Leaving town at dawn, I went to a truck stop and asked for directions. Route 30 across Nebraska sounded best. In hitchhiking it is best to keep to your general direction, even though going the other way to California seemed attractive; maybe I could go swimming with the bathing beauty Esther Williams.

A long day of short rides brought me outside Ogallala on the south end of the Sandhills, a National Natural Landmark in north central Nebraska. The name would make most people think they were going to see sand dunes rather than lush, green rolling hills that cover more than a quarter of the state. But sand dunes in fact are what they are, stabilized by tall and short grass that grows from them.

The impact of some twenty thousand square miles of these hills unsettled me completely. It is without a doubt the most mysterious landscape in the United States. You begin to doubt your sensibilities, and if your car doesn't have a compass, carry one along for the detours you'll take to resolve your overwhelming visual curiosity.

There had been no more intelligence to my stop in Ogallala than liking the name because of my study of American Indian cultures and history. To the north I saw a long row of cottonwoods, and I guessed they lined the North Platte River. It was now evening, and I decided to sleep near the river in my minimal bedroll, an army blanket wrapping a sheet. I climbed a fence, a simple act that

I recognized later predestined the writing of twelve hundred pages of fiction in my novels *Dalva* and *The Road Home*. There was no blast of light, and I wasn't hearing Beethoven in my head, but I was feeling giddy and overly dramatic and far too brave to walk back to Ogallala and check into a motel. The Platte was wide, shallow, and sandy, certainly not the trout river it was up near its beginning in Colorado.

I found a patch of bare, sandy ground, unlikely cover for rattle-snakes, and smoothed out a spot for my bedroll. I wanted a campfire, but I was already trespassing and feared starting a grass fire like those used to drive the buffalo hither and yon. I was cold and damp all night and got up several times to exercise my way back into warmth. There was a lovely half-moon that was strong enough to make the landscape glow. That and the sound of the running Platte were enough to allay my discomfort. The moon buried itself in the river as it does in Chinese poems.

I was fine as long as I didn't think about the future and my unrealistic ambition to become a poet and novelist. When the moon set in the predawn hours, it became truly dark, and I was at first frightened by the sound of heavy breathing. But then, as an ex–farm boy, I recognized the odor of cattle. It was OK as long as it wasn't an unruly bull, who would have been snorting immediately. In the first dim light from the east I could see a circle of curious calves sur-rounding me. I muttered good morning and several ran for it.

That was the night I fell in love with the Sandhills. I cel-ebrated by carving the mold off a piece of cheddar and opened a can of nineteen-cent Boothbay sardines, a standby on my youthful hikes. There were severe thundershowers early but that helped get me a long day's ride all the way to Brainerd, Minnesota, where I spent the night trying to sleep on a picnic table in a park while a number of stray dogs growled at me. Finally, a spaniel with a good heart jumped up on the table and cuddled with me, helping to raise the frigid temperature. I had been accepted and the growling dogs departed.

One more awkward moment occurred a scant three-hour hitch-hike from Brainerd, when a car dropped me in Duluth, Minnesota, the next day. (There was no trouble getting rides with my blue Air Force suitcase.) Duluth is a wonderful city on the west end of Lake Superior and is worthy of a few days of any traveler's time. I had stopped in a pawnshop and bought a blackjack on display, a weapon any boy needs. Not twenty feet down the street, two cops grabbed me and took the blackjack. They said they were charging me with carrying a concealed weapon. Since I was a minor, they called my home, then took me to the bus station and shipped me out of town toward Michigan.

In the ensuing years, in honor of my Nebraska baptism, I read widely on the state and its environs and our great prairie from Conrad Richter's *Sea of Grass* to all the novels of Wright Morris and Willa Cather, and all the work of Mari Sandoz. I had already written three novels and wanted to start something ambitious. I was living with my wife and daughters on a small farm in northern Michigan, where we had spent so many of what we called "macaroni years" to describe our small budget, though I often stayed in Santa Monica, California, when working on screenplays.

One important night on the farm, I dreamed of an attractive woman in her thirties sitting on the balcony of an apartment in Santa Monica, thinking of her childhood back in Nebraska. I dreamed about her several nights in a row, and the die was cast. However, my dream heroine was a stern muse, and I spent several years writing *Dalva* and the sequel, *The Road Home*. When I invented the character Dalva, I was at a point in my career when I was much criticized for my limitations on writing about women, for being sexist and macho, so I wanted to create a character who was not only beautiful but very complicated and intelligent. She is as mysterious as the landscape from which she emerges. The name Dalva came through the character's uncle, who had traveled in Brazil, where I once spent a month and learned about samba. "Dalva," I was told, is from perhaps the most haunting of all sambas and means "O morning star"—*estrela d'alva*.

First of all, to write in the voice of my heroine, I had to familiarize myself with her homeland. Research and reading also played a part in getting to know the landscape. Photographs even more so. In the photography section of the Nebraska State Historical Society, I was also able to study the history of the Sandhills, largely family photographs assembled over the years. It's one thing to be reading about a place in 1913, but for a novelist it means a great deal to see it all in photographs, with their fidelity to the texture of life itself.

But an equally important entry point was going there. All told I made at least a dozen trips to the Sandhills while writing the two novels. I was utterly dumbfounded by the tens of thousands of miles I drove there. Never used for farmland, the Sandhills are said to be one of the most unique grasslands in the world and the largest intact native grasslands in North America.

There are a number of good ways to enter the Sandhills. I usually drove from northern Michigan and could make it in a day and a half, but then I'm fond of road trips. I liked entering Nebraska up west of Sioux City, Iowa, and taking Route 12 across the top of Nebraska with my destination being Valentine, in Cherry County. I have friends there, and it has a very good steakhouse, the Peppermill, and a number of decent motels. The route is good for what ails you. There is relatively no traffic, and you can stop on a high hill between Verdel and Niobrara, where there is a fantastic view of the Niobrara River emptying into the Missouri River in a grand marsh. The whole road is sparsely settled and a specific relief from our crowded areas. This is true of Nebraska in general. It reminds you of a place we like to think we used to be, and even of a place we'd all like to live in now. Over the years the Sandhills have become a state of mind when I don't want to be where I am, like London or Los Angeles. I have entered Nebraska from all four directions and they all work.

If you're in a hurry or live distantly, you can fly into Omaha or the state capital, Lincoln, where you must stop and visit the notable

State Capitol, the first in the United States to incorporate a soaring tower rather than the classic dome. The four-hundred-foot tower has an observation deck from which you can look out over Lincoln and the surrounding plains. The building is a true architectural adventure; I've spent a full day wandering within it.

The drive from Lincoln or Omaha into the Sandhills is pleasant and easy. Another good way is to fly into Rapid City, South Dakota, and take Route 79 and 385 south to Chadron, Nebraska. It is a beautiful road from which you can see the Black Hills mountain range. About halfway down you can detour and drive east to visit Wounded Knee, the site of the shameful massacre of the Sioux. When you reach Chadron, rather than driving immediately for Valentine, detour west a short ways to Fort Robinson, a grand old fort and an Army remount station that once held as many as five thousand horses for the United States Cavalry. The fort is the site of the death of Crazy Horse. It has been restored and there are even a limited number of rooms for rent for tourists.

There aren't all that many roads in the Sandhills so it is easy to crisscross them all. There are five hundred thousand cattle, far more cattle than people.

The Sandhills area is our last great prairie. Your trip will be elevating, taking you into an unmarred part of our past.

All of what I've offered sounds quite idyllic, but then the subject is deserving. I've traveled there at all times of the year with no real weather problems. Of course, I was coming from northern Michigan, beside which any other area's weather seems easy. For all the talk about winter weather, which I largely ignore in my travels, there have been only a couple of real whopper blizzards in Nebraska in the past fifty years.

My feeling for the Sandhills competes with that for the magnificent Pacific Ocean. The vastness and waving of the hilly grasslands in the wind make you smell salt.

(New York Times)

NOT QUITE
LEAVING MICHIGAN
(2003)

Years ago a friend told me that when he first drove his young wife from Flint, Michigan, down to the Florida coast she said on seeing the Atlantic, "I thought it would be bigger." In other words, just because you go someplace doesn't mean you're actually "there." The traveler, the visitor, the transient businessman spin their fragile mental wheels, almost prayer wheels, trying to truly locate themselves in alien cities and countrysides. A few years back I wrote an essay on "dislocation" for the *Psychoanalytic Quarterly* in which the subject nearly exfoliated itself into the arena of the somewhat surreal maps we make of the terrain in which we live, which are finally less consoling than the Teutonic *Rand McNally*, the topographical renditions known mostly to pilots and birds.

You're also not quite "there" when you're living in a place you no longer wish to be. This is a metaphysical step well behind Dōgen's admonition that we must "find ourselves where we already are." I effortlessly agree with this thirteenth-century Zen genius and have agreed with him for as long as we've owned our farm in northern Michigan, thirty-three years, but I still found myself where I no longer wished to stay. Leelanau County was changing faster than I wanted it to change. I didn't want to become a powerless whiner talking about the "old days" in a county that had gone in thirty years from a basically agrarian and commercial fishing enclave to an elaborate playground for the Republican rich. My farm was no longer a farm but a "property" and the fact that it had vastly multiplied in value was more melancholy than comforting. We disposed of the home place and set out for the west in the spirit of nineteenth-century yokels.

When someone from Michigan wishes to tell the curious where they live, they hold up their right hand and repeat the saw that Michigan is shaped like a mitten, and then they point out with their left hand where they live. Leelanau County is the little finger. Our local American Legion is called the Little Finger Post. We are a peninsula surrounded by the waters of Lake Michigan and Grand Traverse Bay, a hilly country of surpassing beauty with a large stretch of waterfront protected by a national lakeshore. When we moved to Leelanau County in the late sixties, vacant waterfront was sold for about three hundred dollars a foot. Recently a two-hundred-foot lot sold for twelve thousand a foot, bringing the total to well over two million dollars. Many of the hills I roamed and hunted, or lower areas where I followed paths to the lake to fish, are now occupied by McMansions in which the often retired wealthy couples race between their seven bathrooms to make full use of their considerable investment. Thorstein Veblen's "conspicuous consumption" has become a euphemism.

Still, we might have stayed on in the considerable remaining beauty if both of our daughters weren't in Montana, along with two grandchildren who are easier, moment by moment, to adore because they are being raised by someone else. Having grandchildren is a beloved spectator sport in which you are a viewer rather than a referee.

The southern third of Michigan is heavily industrialized, though the population concentrations are surrounded by verdant farmland. The biggest cities, Detroit, Flint, and Grand Rapids, were always a bit muddy and confusing to an outlander, but nevertheless fascinating. When I was growing up in the north, the rumors of wages to be earned in these big cities were a magnet to country folk. When migrants from home returned from these cities on vacation they wore spiffy clothes and drove new cars. Back in the forties and fifties factory workers earned enough to send their children to college, something that hasn't been possible for decades. For those who stayed back home, the consolations of countryside, with forests, rivers, and lakes, seemed insufficient when you couldn't decently support your family. They still do.

The north—say, the country above the base of the fingers within the mitten—had its own economic burgeoning in the seventies, eighties, and nineties, much of it fueled by tourism, small factories, workers retiring from the immense industries of the south. The only thing that prevented the sprawl from becoming uglier than it did was the presence of state and federal land, which makes up nearly half of Michigan's total acreage.

The problem with our instructive mitten is that it leaves out the Upper Peninsula, a grand stretch of land nearly three hundred miles long measured laterally, bordered on the south by the top of Lake Michigan, and on the north by the somewhat foreboding Lake Superior. This area is commonly left out of the mitten analogy because it has always been rather remote (a sign in the far west of the UP says DETROIT 600 MILES) and sparsely populated and it is rare indeed to meet someone from the Upper Peninsula in, say, New York or Los Angeles. I love this area and have had a cabin on a river near Lake Superior for more than twenty years, and as these years passed I began to spend so much time up there that my wife decided we had to find a more favorable area for a main residence. It has become gradually obvious to me that I favor the Upper Peninsula because the area replicates the atmosphere of my youth, before the population of the county more than doubled. Where else can I live where I can see a large timber wolf on the two-track leading to my cabin?

On the morning of May 17, however, I'm as petulant as a ten-year-old who can't go to the county fair this year because he has broken two dozen fresh eggs by throwing them against the silo. At midmorning it is thirty-five degrees and the air is full of drizzle and snowflakes. Yesterday I found a patch of snow in a gully in the woods, which means it has been a cold spring indeed. How can I as an adult take weather personally? Easy. After an arduous week in New York on publishing business, plus several days in Ohio lecturing, I'm stopping at the cabin for a week on the way back to our new home state, Montana. I never miss this time of year, when I go into a large vacant area and walk among thousands of acres of flowering sugar plum, chokecherry, and dogwood, watch the arriving warblers, hawks, sandhill cranes, catch a few fish to eat.

This year there is not a single flower to be seen and yesterday the cold wind off Lake Superior was gusting to fifty knots, all of which serves to remind me that there are disadvantages to love. You also have to pack in any interesting groceries, as the closest good market is over a hundred miles distant. You end up with five jars of capers on the shelf for fear of being without. I highly value being lost in the woods, though not overnight, and there is ample opportunity for that. Being lost brings you to vivid attention and the imagination comes into full play when it seeks to view the terrain as a bird does. However, being lost is nearly unbearable in June, at the height of bug season—mosquitoes, deerflies, blackflies, and others—when no amount of bug repellent will hold the insects fully at bay. I'm blind in my left eye and once had to stumble out of the woods holding the lid of my right eye open, so swollen was my face from insect bites. I shed my clothes and swam in the river that flows by the cabin, the cold water allowing my pretty face to recover.

The politics of Michigan as a whole are, like the politics of many states, a microcosm of the national arena, which is to say a mixture of Sunset Strip and the boxing world. In the past, of course, we were relentlessly warned against disproportionate power being held by corporations and the rich, but now they both are totally shielded by a national ethic of greed for its own sake. Our governor of eight years, John Engler, has effectively destroyed the Department of Natural Resources, the only barrier to the pervasive theocracy of land rape more often found in western states. It is interesting that the worst malefactors nowadays make much of the hokum of patriotism, religion, and family, whereas the robber barons of old didn't bother with costumery. In the history of Michigan in particular, those who gave their working lives to the extractive businesses of logging and mining were allowed and encouraged to have full mythologies of conquest—to the point of heroism—having committed the often destructive work of the owners. Songs were sung but the money went elsewhere, especially in the Upper Peninsula. Oddly, it was a moderate Republican, William Milliken, who built up a magnificent Department of Natural Resources, only to see his wisdom cast aside with a boggling cynicism.

I am a left-winger from essentially populist farm families on both sides, and my somewhat jaded anger has had a contemporary rejuvenescence in terms of my own geezer land ethic. I'm less likely to blame John Engler, who is a mini-Bush, or Bush, who is a mini-Reagan. The earth itself is only an abstraction these men stride along on their way to a permanent top, wherever that might be. They both remind one of mean-minded fraternity boys who will never get closer to nature than the usual denatured golf course. They are less men than emblematic clones of the culture that produced them. Neither of them as yet has grandchildren to whom they owe a future beyond a stock portfolio, though their ignorance of history reflects itself against a future in which they hope only to grease the wheels of the class for whom they toady themselves.

Of late I've been studying a relatively new academic discipline, called "Human Geography," for a new novel. Other recent works have entailed the study of anthropology and of the nature of the human brain. In contrast my application of this modest new knowledge has been immediate. I would doubtlessly receive a low grade if tested on any subject other than my own imagination, though not lower than those that members of Congress would receive if given a diagnostic test on American history. (Knowledge of world history is as out of the question as simple honesty.)

I immediately seized on the term "geopiety," which is used in Human Geography. It is easy enough to witness how people frame the reality of where they live—whether townships, counties, or states—in the most pleasant light to justify to themselves why they live there. I wish I had put in my journals the number of times on my travels I have heard locals describe their areas as "God's country," which is to suggest that he is likely not present in other areas.

Much is clearer to us when we watch the Republican or Democratic conventions, when state delegate votes are announced and the speakers extol their home states in that peculiar stentorian manner that politicians are so fond of. Often we receive the state mottoes or even the mention of the state bird, and all states are invariably described as "great." Politics is, above all else, the art, theory, and practice of xenophobia. The occasional and apparent loathing of one state or region for another can be both amusing and appalling. Sometimes this is personal and nearly subconscious—say, in the irrational antipathy many northern journalists felt for Jimmy Carter and Bill Clinton, as if all reason were abandoned when the target of inquest came from south of the Mason-Dixon Line. Xenophobia is often implausibly simian, and rather than reading political texts we might do better to look for explanations in the work of Jane Goodall or in the more recent *In My Family Tree*, by Sheila Siddle.

To witness someone transcending xenophobia we must listen again to Woody Guthrie's "This Land Is Your Land."

Michigan, my Michigan, the "winter-water-wonderland," as we call it. The paths of where we have lived our lives are ineradicable. The forests and lakes absorb the boy and vice versa. Creatures are like that. The dozens of Michigan rivers I have fished continue to flow in my brain during a month in Paris, and I will doubtless hear the sounds of these beloved rivers on my deathbed. As a boy I was convinced that dogs, cats, cows, pigs, and horses were my true friends, and a love of Shakespeare and Dostoyevsky, Mozart and Caravaggio does not replace this early companionship. The large black bear that visits my cabin bird feeder for a snack raised its own image in Arles last November when I followed a black dog past Roman ruins.

Meanwhile the paths that dominate our lives are the roads that lead out of and back to our livelihoods. Recently I dreaded a trip to New York but ended up having the best visit in decades because I stayed downtown rather than at the Carlyle, which had been my expense-account habit for twenty-five years. Earlier in life I had lived in the city as a woebegone beatnik, and there were my brief two years at Stony Brook. We landed at LaGuardia on a clear, sunny May morning and I had the unexpected gut jolt, seeing the missing Twin Towers. On early mornings, I walked out to my old haunts in the Village, which were no more the same as they were in the early sixties than my own home county in Michigan is. For reasons not clear to me there was not a trace of unpleasantness. The world won't stay the same for me. Heraclitus notwithstanding, you can't even step into the same river once. Poor young poets can no longer rent a place in the Village for forty bucks a month, but then, as my younger daughter, Anna, crossly reminded me, she and her schoolmates will never be able to live in the county they were raised in. I agreed, but then why can't they discover the Upper Peninsula? Nearly everyone is ground down by the same economic boot.

I'm keeping the cabin, though it will involve a 3,600-mile round trip from Montana several times a year. I am quite unable to totally leave my home state. I asked Tom McGuane, a novelist and Montana rancher and friend since college, if I would hear our dreaded eastern monoethic catchwords—"healing," "caregiver," "closure"—in Montana. He thought not, but I would certainly hear "sustainable" and "megafauna." I sort of knew this, having fished in Montana nearly every year since 1968. When a newspaper reporter asked me why I'd made the move, I said it was because I liked "dirty cars, fat cows, and trains." Livingston owns a large railroad-repair shop and switchyard. Rich and poor live within blocks of each other and even greet each other on the street.

On a sunny Sunday morning in New York, I walked around Brooklyn with two novelist friends, Colum McCann and Jeffrey Lent, then we proceeded on foot across the Brooklyn Bridge, the first time for me since I was nineteen and paying homage to Walt Whitman and Hart Crane. I could live here, I thought, swept away by the splendor of it all, though for reasons of claustrophobia it would have to be in a one-room cabin in the middle of the bridge.

(*These United States*)

OLD, FAITHFUL,
AND MYSTERIOUS
(1972)

Yellowstone is indisputably America's No. 1 travel cliché. But this doesn't seem to diminish its magnificence. One would have to be fabulously jaundiced not to be overwhelmed, assuming that time is taken to walk at least a quarter of a mile away from the traffic arteries that carve the land into seven pieces. If you do not do that, and sad to say not very many people do, you come away having seen only a very frayed rendition of the real park, like hearing a high school band of no distinction whatever play Beethoven's *Ninth Symphony*. Of course this rendition is acceptable to some, perhaps most. It is still vaguely Beethoven. Enjoyable, a catchy tune. But if you walk that minimal quarter of a mile you gain a sense of splendor; before you is a mountain vastness not diminished since Jim Bridger or John Colter or the Indians hundreds of years before Bridger and Colter. You will

lose your niggling sense that "everything" is spoiled. For as long as
you want to stay you won't have to think of the word "ecology" in
its negative sense, a natural chain we have inordinately violated.
Yellowstone is 95 percent wilderness. It is possible to be justly and
intensely critical of what we have done to the remaining 5 percent,
but other than this minuscule lump or series of lumps of land, the
park is still out there, awesome and unsullied.

In mid-July, driving—say, from Gardiner at the historic north
entrance to Old Faithful—can be vexing beyond belief. Traffic jams!
Wilfred and Myrna and the kids have stopped to feed a black bear
a Hostess Twinkie. They think it might be old Smokey himself and
half expect that quavering baritone that warns us against carelessness
with matches. Traffic backs up for a mile. Horns beep, and throughout
the line there is a certain seepage of adrenaline. Whining children
are clouted about head and shoulders, and Dad's lips curl in anger.
Even though the maximum speed limit is forty-five, a safe margin for
the twisting roads and animal life, no one wants a traffic jam when
they're looking at Nature. The upcoming sights will partially quell
the tempers. When you reach Old Faithful you can have a Coke
at the lodge, surely one of the most incredible pieces of American
architecture. And then you can go out and stand on the boardwalk
behind a string of girls in hot pants and wait for the geyser to erupt.
When Old Faithful goes off (every thirty-five to ninety minutes) the
roar of water is accompanied by the clicking shutters of a thousand
Instamatics. Deafening. It would be even more wonderful if you didn't
have to go out into that hot parking lot and get back into the car.
But the Upper Falls way over at the canyon are next on the itinerary.

We got up before dawn and drove in Chico's pickup down through
the park and out through West Yellowstone, across the Henry's
Fork to Ashton, Idaho, where we doubled back east on a small road
through the Targhee National Forest into the southwest corner of
Yellowstone. There were four of us uncomfortably stuffed into the

front seat as Dick Lemuth, who had been dozing in the camper, claimed he was quickly dying from an exhaust leak. He did look a trifle pale, and Chico admitted to bad mufflers. We wanted to enter the park near the Bechler Ranger Station and hike in about six miles, where we would meet the Bechler River, then move along the river until we found good fishing. The night before, when the equipment and food were divided up, I had felt very unsure of myself. Any backcountry trip is strong medicine, though this notion is scorned by those who do it often. Both Lemuth and Tom McGuane will take off alone into the woods, sometimes for days on end. But when I am alone in some comparative wilderness area I have often fallen into an utter, petulant snit of loneliness. A near hysteria over the nonhuman silence. No arrangements have been made for me! One can get lost enough to panic on a hundred-acre woodlot, let alone in the 3,500 square *miles* of Yellowstone. Teddy Roosevelt, in some respects the father of the National Park System, once said that you don't really know a man until you have camped with him. This bit of information is posted on the wall at Charley O's bar and restaurant in New York City, a place I immoderately longed for while stuffing my pack with the rather arcane-looking equipment.

It is a matter of supreme irritation to find out that the most pressing problems in the park now are litter and traffic. Looming rather large behind is the general dispute in conservation circles between the hyperthyroid protectionists and those who favor "land use," a concept that has served so often as a euphemism for land abuse. The point is really that the flora and fauna can't talk other than in very subtle ways and must be defended. The original intent in making Yellowstone our first national park back in 1872 was to maintain the area in a "pristine" condition for the enjoyment of the people, to protect and preserve the area as it was found. The irony in the notion of enjoyment and preservation has been continuously evident, but never so much as in recent years. One grievously feels that the intent in administering the park should be to allow as many people as possible to enjoy it without overwhelming it or turning it into a geographical extension of society's ills: waste, traffic, overcrowding, and the destruction of the environment.

Some of the lesser problems are more immediately fascinating. How does the staff of rangers protect the people from their aggressive stupidities toward the animals? In the hundred-year history of the park only four deaths can be attributed to animals. This is an absolute triumph of brute patience if one thinks of the endless ways the animals are harried and abused. Extreme cases are the rule: parents spread jam on a child's face to get a photo of a bear licking the jam off; another photographing father attempts to put his daughter piggyback on a bear; a man coaxes a bear into the front seat of the car with his wife, again for a picture; and early in this century a death was the result of a quaint tourist poking a treed grizzly cub with the point of his umbrella.

In June of last year a park visitor from Spokane, Marvin Schrader, was taking snapshots of his wife, using as a backdrop a prone bull bison. Then Schrader attempted to walk around close behind the bison for reasons that will remain unknown. The animal charged, knocking Schrader through the air for a good distance, a horn catching him in the abdomen and disemboweling him. The signs, plus the warnings in the park literature handed out at every entrance, make it hard to understand how this pathetic accident could have happened. Nearly every fisherman or hunter knows that you don't walk up and kick a domestic bull or walk between a range cow and her calf, let alone treat truly wild creatures this way. But people who wouldn't dream of trying to pet a stray German shepherd or a Doberman don't hesitate to try it with a bear.

Recently there has been a controversy of some magnitude over the management of grizzly bears at Yellowstone. Within the last three years most of the dumps have been removed or sanitized in favor of incinerators in the hope of weaning bears away from garbage and back to natural food. In 1970 a dozen grizzlies had to be destroyed and eight were shipped to zoos, a tragic 10 percent of the total number in the park. John and Frank Craighead, the well-publicized grizzly experts, have been extremely critical of the program and have gained support in the press. Glen Cole, who is the resident research biologist at Yellowstone and appears no less brilliant than the Craigheads, has insisted the plan will work in time. It seems it might, and after a relatively short interval. Last year the rangers had to destroy only six grizzlies, and none were sent to zoos.

It is important to understand that the number of people who are injured by grizzlies is statistically insignificant, the odds running at around one injury per million visitors for the past forty years. But a certain wild-eyed melodrama gathers around any incident in which an animal injures a human, whether it is a bear, elk, or bison, and no matter how explicable the situation. Wolves have been much maligned despite the fact that there is not a single validated case in the history of the United States of a wolf attacking a human. The park has an estimated fifteen wolves within its boundaries. For a while it was thought that these animals were extinct in Yellowstone, which would be understandable in that 134 were killed between 1916 and 1926 in a misguided predator-control program.

Finally, now that the bears seem to have returned to natural feeding habits, one would prefer to have visitors told to "proceed at your own risk" rather than killing any more of the dwindling number of grizzlies. One senses a great distaste on the part of the rangers and naturalists for killing anything; each troublesome bear has a "rap sheet" and is given several chances. But this in itself doesn't seem fair in a place specifically set aside for the bear to be a "natural" beast. Despite all of its inherent drama, troublesome bears are one of the least of the problems in running Yellowstone.

We helped each other strap on the packs and started out immediately using our encased fly rods as walking sticks. I had been given the lightest pack, about thirty-five pounds, in deference to my shabby physical appearance. I admit to overemphasizing health difficulties. Within the first mile or so I managed to sweat through several layers of clothing and deeply regretted my succession of nightcaps the evening before. McGuane was leading at what is best described as a dogtrot. He wanted to go fishing. After another mile of physical torment I gathered courage and shrieked, "Slow down!" This tactic worked momentarily, but then the pace quickened again. *Fake a fall*, I thought to myself, *and cover your body with catsup as if wounded on a field of battle*. No handy catsup. "My feet hurt," I yelled, and they stopped. My feet actually did hurt. I was sure my right heel had turned to grape jelly and gristle. The three of them stood there impatiently as I applied medication and a bandage. I tried to light a cigarette, but my matches were wet with sweat. Chico offered me some raisins. Raisins! Later when we made camp I discovered that we had walked the first six miles in less than an hour and a half, sort of a hideous Grand Prix of hiking. My legs trembled, but I was happy. With the pack off my back I felt I could jump lodgepole pines in a single bound. We ate some rotten-tasting dehydrated stew quickly and headed for the river, Chico and Lemuth upstream, and McGuane and I a mile farther down.

Walking to the river in silence I thought of some of the grizzly stories the rangers had told me in the past few days and felt a slight tightening of the spine. But bears are seen infrequently in this area, and only three people in the history of Yellowstone have been injured while backpacking. Grizzlies are so implacably grand and can run as fast as a racehorse for a few hundred yards. Silvertip overtakes Cañonero on the first turn. In a Glen Cole monograph there is a description of how a grizzly takes an elk, jumping up against the elk's hindquarters until the legs buckle, then to the nape which it shakes like a terrier, down to the stomach which it tears open. Mostly the older or infirm elk are taken, and it keeps the herd clean. Like Cyrano, I would parry and thrust with my three-ounce fly rod. You are much more likely to be struck by lightning, but then, after all, I know three people who have been struck by lightning.

We walked through a mucky swale and another half mile over a ridge, picking our way over fallen trees. There was the river, and so much larger than I had expected. In Michigan it would be one of the biggest, with numerous pop cans strewn on the bottom and a steady obnoxious flow of hollering canoeists. Here there was only a green quietness and water that was very cold and eerily crystalline, so clear in fact that it was difficult for me when wading to judge the depth. The tops of my cheap lightweight waders were immediately a foot shy of the surface, and the wrong way. Ouch.

Tired legs were benumbed but soon forgotten as fish rose to a hatch of small white moths. I flogged away for an hour with nothing grand to my credit, then walked along the bank on a game trail for a mile, looking down into each pool. It was all so strangely beautiful that I lost my violent desire to fish. Where were all the tourists? Around a bend McGuane was casting to a rising fish, and the scene looked like some ultrarealistic nineteenth-century sporting painting done all in primary colors. We talked for a while but were interrupted by an osprey that appeared directly overhead. Then another, perhaps the mate, joined the first, and they wheeled above us with cries that were nearly human. We assumed they were warning us away from their nest as they were no higher than the treetops, which is a rare lack of distance for a bird of prey that survives not by our generosity but by its own immutable wariness.

We decided to leave them in peace and moved off upstream to where the Bechler is joined by Boundary Creek. We took a number of fish, and I gradually became uncomfortable with the darkening sky and woods. There was no sense of fear, but I had a total feeling of not belonging. Only a few days before, I had experienced the same sensation at a Crow Indian powwow well after midnight with few white people around when the dancing had become what we wrongly call "frenzied," and I felt I had no act that I could commit with an equal cultural validity. No chance. People think they love the wilderness but very few do at close range. We walked back to camp in the gathering dark through rough clots of saw grass and small swamps that were sweet to the nose. I asked McGuane if he felt genetically at home in this bog. Then we saw from the edge of the Bechler meadows three great blue herons moving along in flight very low, three or four feet above the grass, with somnambulistic movements of their vast wings. They didn't appear distressed that we were there. It seemed only they had someplace to go.

Yellowstone's centennial is a good time in history for those who direct the National Park Service to count their options, and it appears they are doing so. You won't meet a single administrator at Yellowstone who favors any more development of the area. Short bypasses have been built or are being built around Old Faithful, West Thumb, and Lake Village, but these are already tremendously over-developed locales, and the building of the bypasses only simplifies a traffic problem. One would prefer to see a council of naturalists with veto power over any development for safety's sake. They seem to be less lenient with the public, less in favor of the constant balancing act that is required to please the body politic. Enough balancing has been done at this point to last out this century and all of the next if there is to be one; now we need to go overboard in the direction of hardline checks. It is not very amusing to find out that a great battle was fought by the protectionists in the past to keep the railroads out of the park, and those poor souls didn't even use the word "ecology." A few railroads now would be a blessed thing as a substitute for cars. Intelligent public sentiment is building to the extent that any additions to Yellowstone's three-hundred-mile road system would be little short of a justification for sabotage.

Something very much on the plus side at Yellowstone is the apparent quality of the professional personnel. Everyone has been stuffed to the gills with bad experiences with civil servants. This is not the case at Yellowstone, whether with ranger or naturalist or administrator. Everyone is so straightforward and healthy-looking and almost jolly that it is easy to forget other, more careworn government employees. One finds little buck passing, and actual mistakes on the management level are admitted; these people simply have a charming sort of zeal for what they are doing. Vernon Hennesay, one of Superintendent Jack Anderson's assistants, is a good example. Now in his early forties, Hennesay has been with the park service in six different states. Enduring this kind of transferring without the profit motive available in other lines of work is admirable. Of course, in the urbanized seventies a national park would be a splendid place to live.

Another plus factor is the proposed Absaroka-Beartooth Wilderness area, which would abut much of the park's northern and eastern borders and would provide a fine ecological buffer zone. (It would also wipe out some 1,080 poison stations not far from park boundaries which, unfortunately, bears and wolves and eagles aren't aware of as legal barriers.) But passage is at best uncertain due to the usual developer-miner-rancher power combination. The tourist industry in the Rockies is surprisingly not very vocal. Such an area would certainly ensure prosperity in decades to come as other less protected and developed areas in the country become inevitably less beautiful.

But back to the traffic, the single most boggling problem. What to do with it? It is not in our nature to unbuild roads. Couldn't we make an exception for a national park? Whatever else it does, a car exercises in its structure total environmental control. And the most eager vehicular tourist becomes bored with mere scenery. That we are not a nation of walkers is not less true for being so blatantly obvious. It is here that one begins to doubt some of the promotional ambitions of the National Park Service and its commercial adjunct in the park, the Yellowstone Company. The park simply cannot continue to endure the drive-through-in-half-a-day visitors, a group that represents 53 percent of the 2.5 million people who visit the park annually. Looking over a map, one speculates on which of the five entrances could be closed to discourage this traffic that is only trying to get someplace else in a hurry, perhaps down to the Tetons for an hour, then to Estes Park for another hour, then a quick three-hundred-mile swing over to the Black Hills. And at last to rest for a full week at Uncle Ted's Flamingo Spa & Bombazine Snake and Curio Palace. Overheard at Mammoth Hot Springs was the head of a large family from Saint Louis saying that "the little ones and the wife" were disappointed not to see any animals "to speak of" and they all were heading right on up to Glacier (six hours away) to try their "luck." This can be translated into "We didn't see any bears along the road's shoulder, so we're getting the hell out of here." None of Yellowstone's literature should be permitted to emphasize this roadside or drive-in zoo aspect, however underplayed. We have to get away from the car seat as a couch and the car windows as a television, a dimensionless screen on which wonders are expected to take place in quick succession. In cars people only "see" to the exclusion of the other four senses.

There is another troublesome cliché that all American vacationists are morons. An amazing number of Yellowstone visitors attend the lectures and take the modest nature walks. Here is where one finds the ardent partisans of Yellowstone, the army of repeaters who return year after year, the unhurried ones. Something should be done to protect them from the irritations caused by that other half, the frenetic voyeurs. But still a great amount of the park is largely unseen except by the ambitious backpackers, the rangers, and the naturalists. Maybe this isn't a bad thing in itself. Wilderness is mainly wilderness because it's hard to get to and rough to travel through, and the particularities of nature have to be known to enjoy it in any viable way. There is a secretive melancholy among those who love and know the wilderness. It is an experience like religious conversion that has to be undergone to be understood.

It is the radical, visionary ecologist Edward Abbey who seems to have the best idea to ensure that our children's children will have places of beauty left to them: close the parks to public motor traffic. Let people walk or ride bicycles and horses. A few buses will be available for the elderly and infirm. Park personnel in trucks can carry the camping equipment on ahead to the different sites. A quiet park without gas fumes or horns. A true retreat into natural wonder. And by this relatively simple act you enlarge the boundaries tenfold, for distance and space are functions of speed and time. Take the motorboats off Yellowstone Lake and it enlarges. Nearly everyone can row or ride a bike or a horse. Let people play cowboy since it looms anyway so large as a national myth. Surely the quantity of the visitors will drop, but the quality of the experience will increase immeasurably.

Any number of people would love this backcountry but have been put off by tales of crowds. But there are no people out here. You can strike out anywhere and by day's end you will long for some company. The roads are only very thin strips of civility. We ate a breakfast of dehydrated eggs with hot-pepper sauce and set off for the day's fishing, walking upstream several miles to where the Bechler emerged from a faintly foreboding canyon. It was interesting though arduous fishing. The weather was as bright and clear as the water, and the fish were wary. Chico, with his manic intensity for fly-fishing, was the most successful. Lemuth the purist insisted on using only dry flies. Some of my specialized lust for angling was stolen by the beauty around me. Several times I caught myself acting out John Colter in buckskins, one of the very first white men to see the area after he left Lewis and Clark out of curiosity about the territory to the south of that expedition's course. I knew I was surrounded by a splendid "nothing." Late in the afternoon McGuane and I hurried back to camp and ate a packet of chili, thinking the stew of the night before to be at best unfortunate. We had released all of our fish, knowing that a fly-caught fish has an excellent chance of survival. Lemuth and Chico had the sense to keep four. They were baked in foil with lemon and slices of onion. Around the small campfire the usual extended fibs about adventure and sex and fishing were rife.

We went to bed early, and though exhausted I had terminal insomnia; my civilized body is acclimated to staying up until 3:00 a.m. I again felt alternately a joy at being there and, as with all my wilderness trips, a vague paranoia about the dangers my imagination seemed to want to create. Are there rattlesnakes at this altitude? Outside the tent it was cold and dark, full of mad croaking noises. It is only the language of herons, and how can that be mad? Then if not mad, a noise strangest to the ear. I could almost see them out there in the black marsh calling out to the others, waiting for an answer, calling again. Once on the Escanaba River I called to a heron who flew so startlingly close his wing flaps were audible and his shadow crossed my fly line. "Didn't you see me?" He turned around upstream and came back, perching in a white pine across the river until some while later his curiosity was settled, and he flew away.

Animal noises. At Apollinaris Spring the other day a crowd with cameras approached a cow and calf and bull elk too closely. The bull lifted his neck and bugled, and there was a definite retreat by all, though perhaps he was only bugling for the pleasure of it. Twice in my life I've heard a mountain lion in the woods; the quality of the sound differs from that cougar in the car advertisement who sits on a hood or a block Styrofoam sign. A naturalist I know said he approached a feeding grizzly too closely out of eagerness, and the warning sounded like a diesel truck revving up behind teeth.

I reached around in the dark for a bottle of codeine pills—a toothache had heated up the side of my face and it pulsed as if the tooth had a heartbeat of its own. Pain is usually a very shabby thing, but my mind was drawn elsewhere. I lay there thinking of the last desperate plunge of the Nez Percé Indians through the wilderness, and how they struggled to be free together like some giant tormented game fish. The Nez Percé had among them a small group of dreamers and mystics who held a doctrine that the Creative Power had made the earth with no marks or boundaries or unnatural divisions. No land could be owned, and submission to our government was bad. They shared the general park area with the Crow and Blackfoot, the Bannock and Shoshone, plus the impoverished aborigines the Tukuarika. The land wasn't ours before we were the land's. Anyway, a little less than one hundred years ago, after many of our grandfathers were born and the park was established by an act of Congress, the Nez Percé passed some twenty miles north of the Bechler in their doomed flight from the United States Cavalry. They happened to kill a few tourists in their passage—when we won a battle it was called a victory, and when they won a battle it was called a massacre. All of this less than a century ago. Our truncated history. Chief Joseph worried about his children as any father might, and Looking Glass died from a stray bullet after the final battle was over. Satanta, the Kiowa chief, committed suicide rather than remain imprisoned.

Maybe we do honor to the memory of such people only in our parks, where we have left at least some of the land as it once was and as the Nez Percé dreamers wanted it: wild, untrammeled, free, and communally owned.

(*Sports Illustrated*)

SAFELY WITHOUT
PORTFOLIO IN KEY WEST
(1977)

There is a wonderful dread at sea. It cleanses and numbs. As if we were animals our eyes begin to turn outward again, and the edge of weather on the horizon is more interesting than our garden-variety neuroses.

I am far out of whack, out on a big skiff called the *Sweat Hawg*, some twenty miles west of the Marquesas, and a total of fifty miles at sea from Key West. I am talking about the fragility of human relationships with a fishing guide and friend, Bob Hall. He is somewhat of an expert in such matters, having been married six times. Rather than simply live, Hall *propels* himself willy-nilly through life. In his midfifties, burly, insistent, wonderfully opinionated, Hall is totally without fashionable concerns of any sort and, in this way, totally unlike the hundreds of twilit Key West zombies on voyages of self-discovery, chemical and otherwise.

Bob Hall is a former Seabee out of World War II, a former car salesman, tuna-boat skipper, boat captain for an idle-rich restaurant operator. He worked out of Ensenada and knew the Baja, Mexico, of the fifties. In a curious way he is the most existential man I've ever known—flip about the past in a Bogartian way, with all of his energies directed to the present tense. You scarcely think of a man as rebellious if it has never occurred to him to think about the rules, much less obey them. The Latin, sluggishly tropical atmosphere of Key West is perfect for Hall, a laissez-faire melancholy in the streets at dusk when you are on your fifth drink after fishing that tells you that you are safe, that no one has the inclination to hassle you. Key West—where you can be safely without portfolio.

The truth is, Key West isn't what it used to be. But then nothing is. Wanting a place to be like it used to be is the most boring of all human preoccupations. I lived in both Greenwich Village and North Beach in the fifties. They are, gladly, not like they were. Neither is Spain any longer an economic time warp for the children of dentists.

Key West. Called by the Spanish *Cayo Hueso*, or "island of bones." There is a precise sort of offbeat, vaguely down-at-the-heels charm to the place; an island ringed by reefs, with the Gulf Stream nearby, itself part of a reef, stuffed now with marinas, honky-tonks, violently independent ladies. You can't say the charm is faded because that would assume golden years that, in fact, never existed. I've met any number of people who despise the place. Key West, for so small an island, has a strangely notorious reputation. It's not a place for Mom and Dad from Ohio to go. They might better stop way up in Orlando. Hemingway lived a decade in Key West, and luminaries such as Wallace Stevens, John Dos Passos, and Harry Truman were visitors. It is not kind and warm. Tennessee Williams makes his home here now. Truman Capote visits, somehow closer to the other Truman than anyone thinks. I scarcely ever recommend Key

West to anyone. It is, like San Francisco, for bright but tired people who want to get tireder, for alcoholics who want to get drunker. Or for fishermen.

I often doubt that I'd come to Key West at all if it weren't for the ocean; but then I've been coming here for eight years now, and water and land have inextricably married. I fish, mostly for tarpon, every day that I'm here, but there are lots of better and cheaper places to fish for tarpon these days. This comes under the heading of "illusion of purity in sport."

The notion of purity in sport is a peculiar one. Most of the outdoor sporting magazines are full of all this wretched fodder of man slugging it out with the elements using his dick as a weapon, for which we may read—on the surface—gun or fishing rod. Actually, the intelligent people I know use sport as a total wipeout of the mind, whether it is tennis, fishing, or hunting. But without the loony macho pretenses.

In Key West you can fish wisely and well all day in a true wilderness of water, then be dumb enough to blow out your brains with street coke in the evening, say, in the toilet stall of a bar, thinking, "This might turn out to be good." So enervation enters paradise. In the morning one boot is wet, the other dry. How did it happen? A sliver of mystery. But within an hour you're in a skiff and the island has dropped from sight. It's hot and there's a tidal gurgle coming out of Mooney Harbor in the Marquesas. The brain is clear and empty again.

Meanwhile, even farther out in the ocean with Bob Hall in an area known as the Quicksands. There are a fair number of shipwrecks in the Quicksands, in water ranging from fifteen to thirty feet. The Quicksands are also used by the Navy for aerial-bombing practice, and in the clear water the craters are evidence of our defense effort. I mostly think about how many fish the repeated concussions kill.

The Florida Keys are the remnants of a great ocean-reef line still surrounded by subreefs, tidal flats, tidal estuaries, a profligate number of small mangrove islets, islands, atolls, and hidden tide pools.

Shipwrecks quickly become extensions of these reefs. Marine life is drawn to obstacles in the water; the whole predatory cycle of smaller being hunted by larger, larger being devoured by the huge. You see it clearly in miniature on a wreck: the blue runner, yellowtail, permit, bar jack, snapper, jack crevalle, amberjack, cobia, barracuda. Some of the barracuda are huge—gluttons in an untended supermarket. But they are not the end of the chain. Tiger sharks weighing a half ton or more swim by on occasion, also the hammerhead, which of all sharks in the evolutionary chain most resembles a nightmare. Despite all current nonsense, sharks are gorgeous predators and I would no more kill one than I'd kill an eagle or a crow or a coyote. They have a spectacular talent for killing. How can one be critical of a leopard? And to extend the chain, there are marlin and swordfish nearby in the Gulf Stream.

Quicksands. Shipwrecks. The sea is foreign, and a trip to a foreign land is a succession of strangely durable perceptions. It strikes you that you are floating over a graveyard. You have never checked out the numbers but, peering down in the waters, the ancient ribs of the wrecked ships serve as grave markers as surely as the simple mounds of overgrown earth in an Indian cemetery.

Some of these wrecks, in fact the best of them, have been saved from predatory guides and scuba divers by the complications of finding them. Bob Hall is an expert. It might involve running a course off the last point of land which quickly becomes invisible: say, 223 points on the compass, at 3300 rpm on the engines, for 21 minutes and 30 seconds. Then you are close and you turn on the depth recorder.

It is a shared and secret knowledge and you could spend years looking on your own and come up with nothing. On this particular day we look over three wrecks and decide to take a cobia late in the afternoon for the smoker. Like certain kinds of meat, cobia is especially delicious when smoked overnight. We watch another guide, Ralph Delph, help his client boat the new amberjack record on fly rod, over a hundred pounds, beating the old record by thirty. There is a curious pleasure in taking a large game fish on fly rod once you have paid the obnoxious dues of years of learning how, fishing every day, all day, a month at a time.

Fly-fishing for saltwater fish is patently electric for those used to fishing for trout that usually weigh a pound or less. A tarpon over a hundred pounds will take a fly the size of a goldfish in a dime-store bowl. It makes a succession of awesome jumps and the fly rod seems to turn into a cattle prod. It is out of control. It takes forever to learn properly: a knowledge of tides, hundreds of square miles of territory, the skills of the stalk, the skill of throwing a fly from a moving boat at a moving fish on a windy day. It's utterly eccentric, at some nether end of fishing, just as a fighter pilot is tempted to fly under a bridge upside down.

We always let the fish go. Once in a while we save something to eat. I like the feeling of some men I once saw fishing off the coast of Ecuador. They knew nothing of our exhaustions in all that trackless ocean. Shore was a few huts and a tin-roofed honky-tonk. But no use following what you aren't, flowers for a simpler void. Perhaps it's that I think that in a particular kind of sport, in particular places, given the skill, you can reclaim a remnant of a heritage the tide of history has swept away.

And best of all there is the ocean, where there are "none of us" if you know where to go. Back in the late thirties, Hemingway knew it was the last true wilderness. Anything left on land, save the Arctic and Antarctic wastes, exists only by our permission. We despoil it, but the ocean does not exist by our permission. You can still discover a hidden place, or far out on the face of the ocean you can find that nothingness that wounds by a sort of elemental fear and heals at the same time.

(*Outside*)

PIE IN THE SKY
(1993)

"Only connect."
—*E. M. Forster*

Midwesterners, myself in the main, are overfond of nostrums, no matter how pathetic. Even when we are knee-jerk liberals (people responsive to more than their own bank account), we are chin-up George Babbitts with hope ringing clearly in our hearts on a daily basis. Or nightly, as many of my most radiant plots hatch themselves after midnight, perhaps fueled by VO or Cabernet. There is the possibility that we let the field corn grow too close to the house. I think of it as the Bill Moyers syndrome, wherein the most brutish massacre may be thought to show a certain "creativity." If Bill Moyers isn't from the Midwest, he should be. In favor of this soft-edged optimism is the idea that if Abe Lincoln had been from New Jersey

or Connecticut, we'd never have heard of him. Cynicism breeds
wealth and anonymity.

So here comes the latest of hundreds of these nostrums. I want
to send each member of Congress four books: Aldo Leopold's *Sand
County Almanac*, Edward Abbey's *Desert Solitaire*, Gary Snyder's
Practice of the Wild, and Peter Matthiessen's *Wildlife in America*. If all
the members of Congress actually read these four books the entire
environmental movement could dissolve because it would no longer
be needed. For the first time since we entered World War II Congress
would glow with high intent and clear purpose. The restorative
powers of knowledge in these books would be so instantaneous that
workers could immediately begin removing the hog troughs from
the House and Senate.

I have to attribute the giddiness of this past-midnight thinking to the full moon and the fact that I had spent the entire day
rereading *Wildlife in America*, surely among the early and signal
books that prodded our consciences into action in the form of the
now somewhat bifurcated environmental movement, the current
disarray being caused by the same sort of tribalism that has become
a murderous curse throughout the world. We have a hundred fully
staffed organizations with full "agendas" (a ghastly word), but next
to nothing is being done in the area where everything must begin,
habitat restoration. In their defense, there is the modest point that all
the good energy is exhausted in trying to attract the attention of the
shills who govern us. In fact most of the twenty million environmentalists, including the portion of hunters and fishermen who are actually conscious, are unaware that they lack the political clout of, say,
the top twenty men in mining, timber, ranching, and agribusiness.

Wildlife in America is a history of what we have done with our
fauna since we got off a succession of rickety craft in the seven-
teenth century. It is so gorgeously written that it is best read as a
bedside book at a chapter a day. A couple of years ago while we
were fly-fishing in Costa Rica, Russell Chatham said to me, "There's
nothing quite like consciousness," readily admitting that there's a

preposterous downside to this condition. Matthiessen's book is an intensely rough ride for lovers of the outdoors, shimmering with impermanence, but ultimately a grace note in that it confirms what we have always known: we trashed a virtual paradise. It occurred to me that if we collapse earth's history into twenty hours, we have destroyed most of her bounty in the last few minutes. That admitted, what is the process of redemption?

I would suggest that we should all be allowed five minutes of breast-beating after reading *Wildlife in America*, then all our options should be considered. There has been a terrifying surge of breast-beating in America of late, almost a lust to be a victim of some sort in order to avoid what we have individually and collectively become (Robert Hughes's recent book *Culture of Complaint* will give you an electric perm on this score), but the most severe case of abuse in childhood is the countryside itself.

The most difficult thing to get over, perhaps more so for a sportsman who has reached middle age, is the myth of plenitude. When I was very young my father and I were somewhat embarrassed when we didn't "limit out" on trout, bass, or bluegills. At least that's the way I remember it, and this memory has probably neglected many ghastly days. It is the myth that fortified our western movement, the idea that in the territory ahead there were endless fish and game. It was easy to forget that our first closed deer season due to a shortage of the animal was in 1696 in Massachusetts. The bison disappeared from West Virginia in 1825, the elk from Pennsylvania in 1867, the caribou from Maine in 1905, not to speak of the usual seventy million buffalo, or the perhaps billion passenger pigeons, the very last of which, named Martha, died in 1914 in the Cincinnati Zoo. The ready assumption with migratory game birds was, "They must have gone somewhere else this year." Matthiessen quotes William Beebe, who wrote in 1906, "The beauty and genius of a work of art may be reconceived, though its first material expression be destroyed; a vanished harmony may yet again inspire the composer; but when the last individual of a race of living things breathes no more, another

heaven and another earth must pass before such a one can be again."
This includes the spotted owl, the object of so much ridicule in the
timber industry.

In our favor, consciousness did arrive, and particularly since
the 1940s we have done more than perhaps any other industrialized country in the world to protect our fish and game populations.
The judicial tolerance for rube violations is largely a thing of the
past. However, and this is a big one, the game and fish we no longer
destroy with careless abandon are still losing ground on a level as
grandiose as with earlier depredations. It is as if our judicial system
no longer punishes anyone directly, it merely burns down or bulldozes
their houses, sterilizes them, and poisons their water supply.

The first step in the sportsman's specific penance for having
blown it for three hundred years is habitat sensitivity and reconstruc-
tion, and any sportsman who isn't an environmentalist is morally
deeding his grandchildren a Ruhr valley for a happy hunting ground.
We should continue to have faith in favorite organizations whether
it be Trout Unlimited, Greenpeace, the Nature Conservancy, or
Earth First!, but we must bring it closer to home. Sacrificing an
expensive sporting trip to Belize, Christmas Island, Argentina, or
wherever in favor of restoring a desecrated local watershed is a good
idea. Farmers might think of replanting torn-out hedgerows, oil men
of restoring those scalped drilling sites; county road commissions
could stop silting up creeks, and suburbanites could examine their
shrubbery and see if it's good for the creature world rather than being
merely pretty. And remind the ranchers that surround the wolfless
Yellowstone that even Italy tolerates three hundred wolves in areas
that are also grazed on. The business of public land should not be
primarily business. There is nothing more destructive to the quality
of sport than its mechanization.

The real tonic in these suggestions is that you get to feel something other than frustration over the shabbiness of the political
process. There is a real pleasure in getting your hands dirty in your
own locale, your own bioregion. When you send a check to your

environmental organization, add a note to the effect that you wish they'd all get together before Christmas every year and come up with a common wish list of, say, seven items. It has been said that if the feminists had stuck together in the seventies, by now they'd have their equal pay for equal work. We desperately need more cohesion in the environmental movement and a great deal less theater, tribalism, and self-aggrandizement.

Meanwhile, back to my plot to send Congress the four key books mentioned earlier. When I awoke at dawn, or maybe it was midmorning, I remembered a similar project ten years before: three essential books on the history of Central America, as our behavior down there had been totally misinformed. At the time, I told a prominent senator about the scheme, and he quipped that he was unaware that anyone in Congress read books. There was also the cost estimate of $25,000. A better idea would be to find a relatively barren forty, what Faulkner called "the lightless and gutted and empty land," and restore it as much as possible. I called my handy realtor, and, as of press time, I'm on the verge of closing the deal and am plotting out what I'm going to plant in my thickets. It will be a twenty-year-long welcome party as the land gradually fills with its proper inhabitants. In case you don't know, they belong here as much as we do.

(*Esquire Sportsman*)

THE BEGINNER'S MIND
(1994)

At the onset it has occurred to me as a novelist and poet that I could not write a legitimate natural history essay at gunpoint. As indicated earlier in my life by my grades in high school and college in the life sciences and geology, my mind was either elsewhere or nowhere in particular. After I set a new record for a low grade in the hundred-rock identification test in the natural sciences department at Michigan State University the professor gazed at me with the intense curiosity owned by the man who discovered the duckbill platypus. At the time, when I was nineteen, my mind had been diverted by Rimbaud and Dostoyevsky, Mozart and Stravinsky, and if Rilke had said in his *Letters to a Young Poet* to study invertebrate zoology I would have done so, only he never broached the subject.

Curiously, I'm still trying. There's an old wooden Burgundy crate in my four-wheel drive that contains a dozen or so natural history guidebooks that I use frequently. Once in the Sandhills of

Nebraska I sat on a knoll on a June afternoon and identified all the weeds and grasses around me using Van Bruggen's *Wildflowers, Grasses and Other Plants of the Northern Plains and Black Hills*. I also fell asleep and saw Crazy Horse, who helped me dream up the heroine for my then unwritten novel *Dalva*. On waking, it dawned on me as it had dozens of times before that everything goes together or we're in real trouble. Mozart and the loon belong to the same nature, as does the mind of Lorca and the gray hawk I'm lucky to have nesting near our adobe in Patagonia, Arizona. The coyote's voice and the petroglyph of the lizard king near Baboquivari marry in a purer voice than any of our current machineries of joy. The elf owls that flocked into the black oak above our campfire on the Gray Ranch made me feel more at home on earth than my farmhouse of twenty-five years. That many owls in one tree lifts your skull so you may see them with another eye that more closely resembles their own. William Blake's line is appropriate: "How do you know but ev'ry Bird that cuts the airy way, / Is an immense world of delight, clos'd to our senses five?" This is the opposite of the anthropomorphism so properly scorned in literary types of scientists. I simply agree with the visionary notion that reality is the aggregate of the perceptions of all creatures.

But back to the not-so-ordinary earth and the Gray Ranch. On my first trip there a few years ago I realized it takes a golden eagle or a bush pilot to make a quick read of five hundred square miles. I was thrown directly back into the dozens of Zane Grey novels I had read in my youth, which was not a bad place to be, considering the direction of current events toward chaos and fungoid tribalism. There was an urge to yodel "purple mountain's majesty," or re-concoct that Rousseauian fantasy that far up some distant arroyo in the Animas, now shrouded in January shadows, all the local creatures were drinking milk from the same golden bowl. It was, and is, that kind of place. Of course I wondered why Dad didn't own this rather than the three-acre Michigan swamp which, nonetheless, was good birding. My science aversion did not include the birds that were introduced in the third grade by Audubon cards, which had a specific leg up on baseball cards.

The fact is the Gray Ranch is breathtaking—that is, you forget to breathe, the vision before you when you come over the back road from Douglas is vertiginous, surreal, the vast expanse of valley before you not quite convincingly real. Frankly, the only thing that could improve on it would be an Apache village, but that one has been kissed permanently good-bye. I have never quite understood why much of our Bureau of Land Management and Forest Service land could not be returned to its original owners. There is firm evidence that they would do a better job of managing it.

From painful experience I mentally rattled off a number of cautionary notes. There is a wonderful quote in Huanchu Daoren's reflections on the Tao, *Back to Beginnings*. "Mountain forests are beautiful places, but once you become attached to them, they become cities." What is meant by "attached" here is a desperate clinging, an obsessiveness that finally blinds you to the wilderness before you, at which point you may as well be in Times Square or touring the Pentagon. More importantly, in this state of mind you cannot competently defend the wilderness you presume to love.

On the first trip my camping partner, Doug Peacock of grizzly bear renown, was intent on sleeping out in the really high lonesome despite the warnings at ranch headquarters that it was going to be "mighty cool" in the high country. This turned out to be a cowboy euphemism for a temperature of fifteen degrees. The tip-off about the cold front had actually come the day before when we were looking for waterbirds out on the Wilcox Playa in a snowstorm. The bedrooms at ranch headquarters looked rather attractive and so did the idea of central heating, but then I had just come down from northern Michigan where it is truly frigid in January and it was unseemly for me to hedge. That night when the temperature plummeted it occurred to me I hadn't slept outside in Michigan during the winter since I won my Polar Bear merit badge in the Boy Scouts, after which I was booted out as a malcontent.

Peacock, however, is the ultimate camper, in some years spending over half his nights under the stars. We simply used two sleeping bags apiece, one stuffed in another, and wore stocking caps. I had been having the most intense of Hollywood screenplay problems but they drifted away in the face of stars that glittered barely above the treetops and sycamores so burnished by the moonglow they kept rearranging themselves as if their roots were underground legs. Our only real problem was that the olive oil congealed around the edges of the frying pan and the Bordeaux was overchilled in our gloved hands. There was a mighty chorus from a nearby bobcat who was treating the new odors of garlic and Italian sausage with noisy surprise. The most recurrent thought during those two days was wishing for a seven-year vacation so I could adequately walk out the ranch, slowly identifying everything that wasn't underground. I might even memorize the clouds.

Two years later on the eve of our return a specific freight of confusion had accumulated about the Gray Ranch. In the interim I had been assured in both Montana and Michigan that the ranch had been sold to Ted Turner. Since I'm quite a fibber myself, what with being a novelist, I tend to believe other fibbers unquestioningly. I fully understood that the Nature Conservancy might not wish to keep that much capital in one basket, the mildest of understatements, and though Turner is indeed an environmentalist, I feared his interest in buffalo that do not belong in the area.

Another, rather astounding, rumor arose that Drum Hadley was buying the ranch through his Animas Foundation, with the Conservancy retaining large easements in the higher altitudes. Rather than sitting around in a dither, I checked the rumor out and found it was true. "Astounding" is not too strong a word, as I knew of Hadley only through his poetry which had been recommended to me by Charles Olson one sunny spring afternoon in Gloucester, Massachusetts, long ago, and later by Gary Snyder. In the religious world this would be similar to being lauded by Pope John XXIII and Gandhi. I had always thought of Hadley as a Black Mountain populist who had holed up on a ranch in a canyon near Douglas, Arizona, and certainly hadn't guessed that he could muster the wherewithal to buy a ranch of this awesome proportion.

I recalled a quote from Hadley's mentor, Olson, in his book on Melville, *Call Me Ishmael*: "I take SPACE to be the central fact to man born in America, from Folsom cave to now." This, whether illusion or reality, is a whopper of a statement, but it was truer when Olson wrote the book forty years ago, and certainly purer truth in Melville's time.

Why, then, should I be such an ardent claustrophobe, despite the fact that I spend nine months of the year in Michigan's Upper Peninsula and Patagonia, Arizona, the shared habitat of bear, mountain lion, all sorts of creatures, and in each place, the stray wolf still passes by? It wasn't just the hearing of the dark wings of the madness of overpopulation in the future. More real is the prospect that developers buy wild regions and dice them into parcels for us who love the outdoors and have the cash to buy them. The Forbes ranch in northern New Mexico was a dire portent, and one could, properly informed, add a thousand other places this was happening. There is a nearly spiritual truth in Edward Abbey's comment, "It's not the beer cans I mind, it's the roads." With Hadley's purchase and the Conservancy's easements, this immense ranch would remain intact, and I could stop mentally turning it into a city.

Late on an April afternoon we set up camp, with Peacock in a hurry to take a walk for another look at some petroglyphs he had noted two years before. What he thinks of as a stroll is an aerobic nightmare for the less hardy. Ten miles is not improbable for this geezer in the Michigan woods, but in the rumpled West I go my own slower way when camping with my partner who is thought by many to be the world's largest billy goat. I also fall with some frequency, my feet refusing to acknowledge a terrain where you have to watch where your feet are stepping. The tendinitis in my bursae was throbbing, the result of doing the splits in a fifty-yard skid down an arroyo near Patagonia, so I made my way slowly up a creek bed that owned an aura of mystery. The notion arose that I was a flatlander down to my very zygotes, my feet requiring moss, ferns, deadfalls, tamarack bogs, and osier-choked gullies.

Not so long ago, only a few minutes in geologic time, we attacked the wilds with implements of greed and domination. Now, or so it appears, we are having a run at it with sporting equipment, none of it as friendly to the earth as the human foot or the hooves of horses. Walking makes the world its own size and a scant hour in a forty-acre woodlot is liable to dissipate the worst case of claustrophobia. The same hour in the high country of the Gray Ranch and you're ready to levitate. I remind myself again not to burden the air with requests from the wild but to see what I can see with the attentiveness of the creature world. I scout the creek canyon just far enough to see an enormous opening which I'll save for the morning.

We had our customary first-night camping dinner of thick, rare Delmonicos wrapped in tortillas, accompanied by Bordeaux, which increases goodwill as proven by the French, those kindly souls. It was that first night that the curious elf owls gathered in the black oak branches above us. Doug had seen them grouped this way only once before down in the remotest Pinacates. Such splendor is humbling and properly so. It was the equivalent of wandering the Upper Peninsula for twenty years hoping to see a wolf and then seeing one a scant hundred yards from my cabin. When the owls left, there were the nightjars, whose song is closest to the loon's in the resonance of the memories it evokes. We were camped in the same place that we had been on that cold night two years before, but now the dark was soft and dulcet and I watched the entire arc of the moon until it burst against Animas Peak, the last golden light shedding down the talus.

At dawn, for eccentric reasons, I scoured my guidebooks for something odd to look for on my walk, deciding on the rare night-blooming cereus. My hip pain was a torment, so every hundred yards or so I'd go blank and lay down like a tired deer. There was a wan hope of seeing the enormous male mountain lion that was said to live in the area. He kept himself as hidden as the night-blooming cereus though at one point I had the feeling I was being observed. Since I'm a somewhat goofy poet, I do not feel obligated like the scientist to regard these intuitions as nonsense. It is easy to forget that we are, above all else, mammals. An anthropology text has curled the hair of many an aesthete.

I mostly crawled up a steep hill that would have been regarded as Michigan's only mountain. It was rocky but in the crevices wildflowers bloomed and far above was a bona fide golden eagle. Two years before we had seen several at once in the area called the "flats," which is a single seventy-square-mile pasture, sort of an Ur-pasture still in the condition in which pioneers had found it, along with the Apache. I'm not cattle shy as most amateur environmentalists are, but my father was an agronomist and soil conservationist and I know overgrazing when I see it. You don't look sideways at grass, you look down. Cattle exposure that precipitates erosion is a good start.

Any sort of contentiousness was far from my mind, though, when I reached the mountaintop. One boulder was smooth and I imagined it was a habitual sitting spot for those of the Casas Grandes culture who had preceded me there by nearly a thousand years. The area is visited by violent thunderstorms and I could see lightning had struck the place numerous times, shattering boulders into small chunks of crystal. The place would be a New Ager fantasy but then I was not in the mood to dislike anyone. Back home the Anishinabe (Ojibwe Indians) favor lightning trees and this place had endured godly punishment way beyond trees which burn and half-explode. It would be a good place, finally, to die, and we don't find many such locations in a lifetime. This is an utterly normal thought rather than a sad one. I'm unaware of anyone who has gotten off this beauteous earth alive save the Lord, and that is disputed by many.

The natural world had so grasped me that morning that I forgot lunch, but far up the draw I could smell it on my way back with an ursine wag to my head and a crinkled nose. I share with Peacock a love for all the simple pleasures, not just a few of them, and that dawn we had put together lamb shanks, a few heads of garlic, casca-bels, and a pound of white tepary beans from Gary Nabhan's Native Seeds/SEARCH. We had heaped coals around the Dutch oven, and I judged by the odor a quarter mile distant that it was ready. This kind of lunch is necessary if you are to take a nap, and if you don't take a nap you are not fresh for the day's second half. You become a conniving eco–ward heeler with fatigued ideas about how you would run the West if you were king of the cordillera. By taking a nap I stay put as plain old Jim, who occasionally has something fit for the collective suggestion box. A nap can give you an hour's break from needing to be right all the time, an affliction leading to blindness to the natural world, not to speak of your wife and children.

Late that afternoon, after studying petroglyphs and flycatchers, we had a long jouncing drive to ranch headquarters to meet Mr. Hadley for dinner. I had prepared a list of questions about every-thing from the Bureau of Land Management to the Savory grazing methods, Wes Jackson, Bruce Babbitt (hooray, at last), the Gray Ranch's carrying capacity, methane, and the flavor of local beef (excellent), none of which I asked because we started talking about twentieth-century poetry. All told, your putative reporter did not put forward a single germane question about the ranch, somewhat in the manner of my beloved Omaha Indians among whom it is impolite to ask questions of anyone about anything, so they don't. There is also a specific ranch etiquette I learned in the Sandhills, certainly the best-managed grazing area in the United States, where information is volunteered rather than extracted.

After dinner we took a walk down a moonlit road and Hadley quoted the third of Rilke's *Duino Elegies* in its entirety in German,

the sort of act that raised his credibility in my belief system up there
with Thomas Jefferson's, whether he likes the comparison or not.
Though I was modestly groggy at the time, it seemed reasonable that
a poet could run a huge ranch better than anyone else, especially if,
as in Hadley's case, he had thirty years of experience.

On the slow ride back, which was much shortened by Peacock's
braying of every blues tune in his head, the moon lit up Animas
Peak so it looked a short trot away, and as we gained altitude the
wind stiffened. The sand and grit in the air yellowed the moon and
the landscape. I guessed the wind by my Great Lakes standards to
be about forty knots and we secured our campsite with difficulty. I
turned my sleeping bag so that it would stop billowing like a wind
sock, and looked out from our grassy bench at the landscape, which
now was shimmering and haunted. Spirits were afoot. First came the
Natives, then the turn-of-the-century cowboys, the night and day
laborers of the cattle empires. A hundred years ago, or thereabouts,
four hundred thousand cattle perished from starvation in this two-
hundred-mile-wide neighborhood between Cloverdale (population
none) and Nogales on the Mexican border of Arizona. Despite the
legion of naysayers, we're doing much better now. In fact, the land I
was sleeping on was a heretofore improbable experiment on whether
the natural and the man-organized communities could not only
coexist but thrive to the mutual benefit of both. This was the teeter-
totter that needed to be balanced between radical environmentalists
and the stock associations, neither of which was going to go away.
I was pretty much in the camp of the former and retained the right
to shoot off my mouth about public grazing, but it was a splendid
tonic that night to see what the private initiative that surrounded
me with sure and certain hope had accomplished. The Gray Ranch
was still here, big as all outdoors.

(*Heart of the Land*)

LEARNING MONTANA, OR TURN ME LOOSE
(2006)

To show my NASCAR roots, earlier in my life when trapped in one of the claustrophobic capitals of the world, I would sing a line from an old Merle Haggard song: "Turn me loose, set me free / Somewhere in the middle of Montana." I only sing when I'm alone because no one except a politician deserves the punishment of my voice.

Now I live in the center of Montana for half of the year, and the other half in the mountains near the Mexican border. Both of these are car-punishing places, partly because I fish sixty days a year and bird hunt nearly that much. In other words I use an SUV for purposes for which it was hopefully designed. I am a specialist in hard rather than soft miles, a sucker for what Robert Frost called the road less traveled. Ever since my youth in northern Michigan I've known that it is the gravel roads that lead to the good places. During my recent trip in the 2007 Suburban I put at least a thousand miles of gravel roads on the odometer, all without butt pain.

When we migrated to Livingston I measured the newness of it all by our dogs Mary, an English cocker, and Rose, an English setter. We hadn't lived in an urban area since the midsixties when I taught briefly at Stony Brook. Rose had never walked in a town before and would sit down in the park and look at me for an explanation for activities such as tennis, soccer, horseshoes. The odors in alleys especially fascinated her so that the walking was slow and decidedly non-aerobic. As a country girl her hackles rose on seeing other dogs though within a month she was eager to greet dozens of other dogs while being walked along the Yellowstone River that passes through Livingston. I admit my claustrophobia was tenuous in our rental as we waited for our purchased house, well outside of town, to be remodeled. I could, however, see out the window of the upstairs bathroom Wineglass Mountain a few miles to the southwest where a pack of timber wolves is in residence, and from the front bedroom the Absaroka mountains, the home of grizzly bears. At night I was consoled by the sound of freight trains, the idea that the locals rarely washed their pickup trucks, pastured cows were fat, haystacks were high, and the Livingston citizenry acted like they still wanted to vote for Eisenhower.

For those not familiar with Montana it is a little hard to comprehend its size and the dimensions of its empty areas. Montana is three times the size of Michigan with one-tenth the population. The drawback here is that Montana ranks dead last among the fifty states in the wages category so it's clearly not a place to come if you're looking for work. In our time here I've been fishing sixty days a year between May and October which, along with writing novels, doesn't leave a lot of time for exploring a state that I thought I knew quite well though it turned out I didn't.

On an earlier Montana driving trip in 1970 I was with McGuane in his new Porsche, not a good car for lumpy back roads. The problem with the Porsche was that it wouldn't start without manual pushing. I recall a morning in Browning on the Blackfeet Reservation gathering some kids together in the motel parking lot to give us a push. We paid a buck apiece, finished drinking our strawberry Maalox, and headed for Choteau and Fort Benton. We weren't behaving well but the trip had a wonderful yield in that it gave me the idea for my novella "Legends of the Fall," and its consequent movie, and McGuane had the first inkling for a screenplay which later became a movie starring Marlon Brando and Jack Nicholson, *Missouri Breaks*. For unclear reasons I've gotten most of my ideas for my novels while driving and walking in unfamiliar areas of the United States. The mind is opened and freshened by the oxygen of new landscapes. There's a bit of that feeling we all remember when we got our first driver's license and drove off in the country alone. Our spirits elevated into new possibilities. When you're an outdoorsman it's even more meaningful when you're not limited to serviceable roads. I started in 1954 with a 1929 Model A (for fifty bucks) with which I could putt-putt down the worst two-tracks to hunt birds and deer. Since I finally became solvent in my late thirties I've always owned SUVs—three Subarus, three Toyota Land Cruisers, and, more lately, a succession of three Tahoes.

The recent Tahoes certainly predisposed me to the 2007 Suburban. I had felt a little guilty buying the Subarus and Toyotas at the time because my dad had always been a "GM man." People used to be brand-faithful but at the time the Subarus and Toyotas seemed the best option for a backwoods sportsman. The succession of Tahoes, however, has been wonderful for hauling bird dogs, and with plenty of power to tow boats. And you needn't lose speed on the hundreds of mountain roads where a big engine is an advantage.

I had looked at new Suburbans but never had driven one. They seemed a little large and ungainly, especially when I was still in Michigan's Upper Peninsula and the log roads in dense forest could make turning around dicey. This is no longer a problem in the Southwest and Montana. In fact one ranch I regularly hunt on in New Mexico has five hundred thousand acres to turn around in.

Still, when I first drove the Suburban I had a little of the feeling I had when piloting a Hatteras between the Tortugas and Key West. I quickly got used to it though I doubt I'd want to own one in New York City what with my less than stellar depth perception from having only one workable eye. Outside collapsible side mirrors have saved me repair money in my woods adventures. It used to be expensive to tear off these mirrors on trees.

I was lucky to have an old friend and Montana native, Dan Lahren, as a traveling companion. We've hunted and fished together for twenty years and he has a good knowledge of the small roads in empty areas. When an obsessive outdoorsman isn't fishing or hunting he's at least looking for places to do so and there's no better way to find them than wandering for days and examining the landscape. Danny also has the advantage of being a gearhead. He just finished redoing a '53 Pontiac and actually comprehends internal combustion and other mechanical abstrusities like how to detach the spare tire from the undercarriage on the Suburban. As a novelist my only area of true expertise is the imagination.

I actually live on a gravel road that has been brutally washboarded by hay trucks which was an immediate test for the Suburban's fine suspension. You heard the chattering bumps but you didn't feel them. I don't live that remotely but it's amusing to tell city visitors that my neighbor to the north lost forty-four sheep to wolves two years ago and that we've killed a couple dozen rattlesnakes in our yard. We shot three while roasting a wild piglet a friend had FedExed from Florida for our Fourth of July feast. Two of them were either mating or wrestling. I didn't ask which. I'm generally an eco-ninny but with grandchildren and dogs playing in the yard and after losing an English setter who was bitten twice in the face, I now consider rattlesnakes to be terrorists and treat them accordingly.

On the first leg of our trip we headed northwest to a stretch of the Missouri River south of the city of Great Falls. We were towing a high-bowed Lavro drift boat and fished an afternoon and the following morning. We had done very well for years on this section of river but now fishing was painfully slow because we were at the tail end of a nasty five-week heat wave. In fact when I got out of the boat at noon I was sure my head was a poached rutabaga. Normally Danny's birding dog Jacques, a French Brittany, hangs over the gunwale to give the next trout a brief lick (that's what he always does) but on that morning he dozed under the shade of the bow deck.

We drove northwest toward Choteau which is on the edge of the huge Bob Marshall Wilderness. The Suburban is equipped, like my Tahoe, with XM Radio, which I have learned to love dearly, especially the channels "Willie's Place" and "The Blues." For some reason the company took off my all-time favorite, "World Zone." To show that I'm actually, though only occasionally, a high-powered intellectual I also listen to the three classical channels. Of late I've been ignoring CNN because news of car bombs has become mentally fatiguing. Another real boon to XM is that you can get Bob Edwards on New York Public Radio. He was always the voice of my mornings before NPR removed him.

Choteau is an awesome place in the old sense before teenagers demolished the word. I can think of no more impressive landscape in the United States in its utter vastness. We drove up the verdant Teton River wash into the Bob Marshall for a dozen miles and we noted that it was perfect grizzly bear habitat. The locals already know that, as some grizzlies have been noticed traveling down the wooded river bottom until they are uncomfortably close to town. A couple of years ago a rare early June blizzard killed a thousand or so cattle, and grizzlies piled out of the wilderness to haul off the carcasses. A rancher reported seeing twenty at his place. "I didn't get out of the truck," he said.

When we pulled into the Log Cabin for dinner a pretty girl was in the parking lot smoking a cigarette. Danny immediately backed the Suburban toward her because the big GPS screen turns into a video machine when you back up. The girl wasn't GM's motive but it was nice to see her on the screen.

Incidentally, road food in Montana is a horror for sensitive folks like myself and that's why I split the trip into two sections. The Log Cabin Cafe in Choteau, however, is an exception. Twice a week Chef Dan makes seventeen pies and a slice of the gooseberry would have been a triumph in Paris. So would the non-diet sausage soup and fried chicken.

At dawn we headed about a hundred miles down the face of the Bob Marshall, hugging as close to the mountains as possible on small-ranch dirt roads. Some of them were narrow enough that we regretted towing a boat but we made it through. We finally arrived at the little village of Lincoln, home of the infamous Unabomber, for a midmorning breakfast. There is some local regret that the Feds hauled off the Unabomber's cabin to California as it would have made it to "tourist attraction."

We headed south toward Anaconda, a fine old mining town, then toward Melrose, our destination. Unfortunately when we stopped by Georgetown Lake, Jacques rolled on a big dead brook trout and out of respect for GM we shampooed the dog who was consequently pissed off. My editor had told me we couldn't drive with alcohol in our "systems," rather mechanical wording, so it is lucky that the Sportman Motel, where we stay when fishing the Big Hole River in Melrose, is a mere 124 feet from the Hitchin' Post, certainly a walkable distance for a well-earned drink.

We were on the Big Hole River very early and in contrast to the Missouri we had very good luck. There was a major spruce moth hatch, not so good for the spruce trees but wonderful for the fishermen, with larger fish becoming active. When you see a big brown trout come to the surface you have the kind of goose bumps some fools have for actresses.

The second part of our trip began a week later after my digestion had recovered. We had fished the Yellowstone River to fill my three-days-a-week quota so we left the boat home. We became more adventuresome in our choice of roads, heading north to White Sulphur Springs and taking Milligan Road to Cascade south of Great Falls, one of the loveliest stretches of ranch backcountry in America. It's not passable if there's been heavy rain because then the mud, locally called "gumbo," makes the road worse than Midwestern glare ice. Near Cascade we used the GPS to navigate west seventy miles or so on tiny dirt roads to the Shonkin Sag. For anyone with even a minimal interest in geology this is a fascinating area because it was once the path of the Missouri River before the Keewatin Ice Sheet changed the topography during the glacial state of the Pleistocene.

We somehow ended up in Fort Benton which was booked so we drove over to Loma on the Marias River, a stroke of luck as I love the confluence of rivers and the Marias emptied into the Missouri just a mile from our tourist cabin. This was where Lewis and Clark camped a week and made the fortunate decision to stick to the Missouri rather than following the path of the Marias. We had a fine meal that evening at the restored Grand Union Hotel in the old river town of Fort Benton. Our waitress Kelsey even strained the alcohol out of a splendid bottle of Châteauneuf-du-Pape.

The next day was a challenge. We wanted to head along the Missouri Breaks country toward Zortman, another old mining town. We were wary because two weeks before a friend had blown a tire in this area while doing some ill-advised hill climbing, a sport better left to motorcycles.

We took a right turn in Big Sandy and wandered basically by compass and GPS for five hours seeing only two other vehicles. GPS is fine if the roads are on the map and some of ours weren't and more closely resembled cow paths than roads. This is preposterously grand country and bears the same unfriendly look as the Badlands in the Dakotas. I was so pleased to finally see where the Judith River emptied into the Missouri because as a map person I had imagined it so often.

After dinner in Lewistown we took another two-hour drive around the countryside to look at some of Danny's favorite bird-hunting spots. With this Suburban the usual road fatigue is minimal. We parked the car at the motel and walked three strenuous blocks to the Glacier Tavern where the Absolut martinis cost three bucks rather than the twelve to fifteen they charge in Manhattan, another reason to be footloose in the center of Montana other than the mountains and rivers without end.

When I got home the next day I parked the Suburban next to my Tahoe which has a front bumper bound back together with barbed wire after I hit a stump while bird hunting. I suspect I'll buy this great vehicle the next time around partly because you can always sleep in the back if you get stuck in the country I love.

LIFE ON THE BORDER
(2001)

I was driving north on a small gravel road between Portal, Arizona (population 170), and Rodeo, New Mexico (population 250), just east of the Chiricahuas. My son-in-law was with me and we had just spent a couple of days on the kind of hopeless venture I've been attracted to all my life. I wanted to see the eared trogon, a bird related to the quetzal, though at this time, a couple of years ago, eared trogons had rarely been seen in the United States since 1977. Impossible missions are very soothing.

We had just come over a hot and dusty rise in this very empty country when we spotted the four migrants dragging their feet along the road. As we passed, choking them with a cloud of dust, they waved their empty plastic milk jugs, which they use to carry water on their long journeys. Douglas, Arizona, and Agua Prieta, in Mexico, was about seventy miles south, probably a three-day walk in the near-wilderness. I stopped the car, remembering I had a full case of

Evian in the backseat, bottled water I carry because Arizona water tastes terrible compared with that of my farm in Michigan. My son-in-law lined the bottles up neatly on the road's shoulder and gave the Mexicans the peace sign. They waved back. Each bottle cost $1.87, about the average daily wage of 40 percent of Mexicans. That was why they were walking north.

There was a girl of eighteen years, Ana Claudia Villa Herrera, who in 1998 left her home city of Córdoba in the state of Veracruz in eastern Mexico for el norte, as they call it, the promised land of the United States. She was traveling with her brother and a friend, and she carried a baby in her arms. The state of Veracruz is a green and rumpled place of surpassing beauty, the equal of anywhere in North America. From Córdoba to the west you can see Pico de Orizaba, the highest mountain in Mexico at nearly twenty thousand feet, and from the snow-shrouded peak of Orizaba if you were a wayward raven or an angel you could see across the dark forest below and the green plains beyond to the brilliantly blue Caribbean, almost a disturbing blue, which totally befits its marriage to the sky. How could anyone leave such a beautiful place? But that question is from the viewpoint of angels or the rich, and Ana Claudia was a poor girl from Córdoba.

I walked the Nogales border fence this afternoon. We semi-rich liberals simply don't live on the same planet as the people in Nogales, Sonora, and severely fool ourselves if we think we do. The collapse of the tech stocks was pleasant if only because of the fatigue of noting the appearance of yet another multibillionaire who favored American-cheese sandwiches with his spritzers, and who was taking lessons on the use of toilet paper and how to boil water. Up to now even the austere and usually levelheaded *New York Times* over-frothed with tales of new wealth. I took to wearing very old clothes daubed with the tincture of kerosene, recalling those Bible stories describing a rich man as someone with a couple of camels and a granary full of grain. There's nothing quite like sitting in a six-hundred-dollar-a-day hotel room (expense account) in New York City and reading the fabulous *Labyrinth of Solitude*, by Octavio Paz, meditating on the Mexican poor and being kept awake by the twenty-nine-dollar small pot of coffee the room-service waiter (Guatemalan) has brought.

Meanwhile along the monstrous Nogales border fence I am watched by children on the other side. One small boy has a sore under his left eye that looks like a large red tear. Another tells me that I am ugly. They are all amused when I agree. I look above their heads at the hills of Nogales on the Sonoran side. It snowed and rained hard last night, which must have made certain cardboard shacks less-than-effective shelter. Many are heated only by a pot of water boiling on a hot plate. The view reminds me of the favelas in Rio, where some children once threw stones at my limousine as I was on the way back from watching a polo match at a club. The driver was upset with me because I insisted on the route through the favelas. I am a left-wing Democrat, and suffering is a bleakly tantalizing prospect for observation. I rather envied the orthodontist's daughter from Wisconsin who found the abject poverty of New Delhi to be "spiritual." Her religious pilgrimage also took her to the beaches of the Seychelles and Bali.

There are no beaches in Nogales. A Santa Cruz River tributary runs through town in a cement culvert, but it's so virulently polluted that it is guilty of causing the preternaturally high disease rates for everything from lupus to multiple sclerosis among the locals. The purity of the high desert does not include towns and cities. Approaching Tucson on many days, one can see a brackish carapace in the distance like an enormous dead turtle nestled in the mountains. Tucsonan yuppies have effectively banned cigarette smoking in their restaurants but have not managed well with drugs, poverty, or an alarmingly high murder rate. As in so many cities, a freeway, in this case I-10, vaguely separates the town. *North of I-10 is where the good people are and south is where the brown criminals reside.* North of the Catalinas, semi-comic gated communities with faux–Santa Fe stucco grandeur draw on the hearts of monied couples who move to Tucson for the climate, many of them from the East. Since the rich come from an essentially artless culture, the decorative gewgaws are usually from the Mexicans or Pueblo Indians. You see stunningly painted armoires from Michoacán, certainly not from the decidedly English influences of North Carolina furniture destined for Park and Fifth Avenues. In Zihuatanejo down on the Mexican coast, I watched a ragged woman paint a dinner plate that within five minutes became a surpassingly lovely art "object." This is apparently impossible north of the border.

If Ana Claudia skipped school or work with friends, she might have gone to the port city of Veracruz, a scant hour and a half by bus from Córdoba. If it was especially hot, which Veracruz often is, the girls could go into the acuario and watch tarpon, sharks, grouper, and dozens of other species swim in a complete circle around a huge and cool darkened room. Perhaps the fish don't know that they are trapped as they move mostly counterclockwise in a metaphor unconnected to anything but the lives of captive creatures. Another wonderful place where the girls could have sought coolness was an American-type mall a few miles south of Veracruz in the suburb of Boca del Río. Probably the girls preferred the mall to the acuario or the green mountains and the sea. Looking in a window at a gold Rolex, the girls doubtless figured out that it would take years to buy such a watch—so much effort to tell the time, when it is always time to go to work, rest for work, and eat for strength to work.

I've spent eleven winters, usually five months a year, in a casita on a creek near the Mexican border. When I move back north I'm always startled by the nearly total ignorance about Mexico. ("They're dirty!" I heard. No, as a general rule they keep themselves cleaner than the English, the French, or New Yorkers do.) Many of us who are reasonably informed when it comes to so-called Third World cultures are often belittled because we have a "return ticket," but then most of us know nothing at all.

In my youth I spent a couple of years at farm labor, though much of it within the polite confines of a university horticultural-experiment farm. In addition to the "higher" irrigation and tractor work, I also hoed, and picked beans, cucumbers, berries, apples, cherries, peaches, and so on. As a nascent beatnik in San Francisco in the late fifties I'd take a labor truck before dawn out of the Mission District to the fields around Salinas and Modesto.

I recall that one day a teenage girl came by in an old Studebaker pickup loaded with oranges, which she sold to us bean pickers two for a nickel, surely the most delicious oranges in Christendom. I recall she had a Steinbeck novel, *The Pastures of Heaven*, of all things, on the seat beside her. I didn't say anything because she wasn't looking at any of us directly. I think my best day was nine dollars, which would bankroll me for two days in North Beach learning how to smoke dope in an alley beside the Hungry I and eating a thirty-cent plate of macaroni salad at the Co-Existence Bagel Shop, which wasn't nearly as good as the bowl of noodles you could get for the same price at a cheap Chinese workingman's restaurant. When you're nineteen, you can work twelve hours a day in the fields and still have energy to misbehave. Yours is the only mouth you have to feed.

If you clear five bucks a day at a maquiladora factory (GE, Samsonite luggage, etc.) you could climb on the roof and see over to the American side, where a busser at Pizza Hut makes more than five bucks an hour. The official death figure for our entire Mexican border last year was 369 (several sources told me the real number was triple that), in short about four or five average plane wrecks. It is easier for us to take plane wrecks if only brown folks are involved.

I've had a peek or two through the keyhole of brown folks, but I am aware that the dimensions of my experience are narrow indeed compared with the raw meat on the floor that the migrant experiences. It was darkly comic when I was asked to leave a strip club because I was an Indian (I'm not). It was a little less comic when after a minor auto accident the ER staff did a good job checking on my wife but neglected the small shards of glass in my chin and scalp. A year or so later when I met the doctor again on a social occasion, he joked, "Oh my God, I wondered what that lovely woman was doing with a drunk Indian." There have been a number of other experiences when the point has been made to me as a mere tourist in another world.

Despite the fact that the border has largely become a militarized zone with the increasing INS staff, the area is still porous to drug smugglers. The situation reminds one of the political posturing of our leaders during the Vietnam War. It's a no-win situation, what with nearly two thousand miles of contiguity between Mexico and the United States, much of it rough country. There is also the simple fact that dope use in state and federal prisons is exceedingly high, which is logically accompanied by the question that if you can't keep dope out of prisons, how are you going to keep it out of the country?

This becomes more apparent when you survey the seventeen thousand produce trucks per month entering American Nogales in the top winter period for shipment. How can you search that many trucks laden with vegetables? You can't, without an army. Neither can you truly police the marijuana producers in Humboldt County or abolish the use of dope in Detroit.

College boys go into Nogales, Sonora, looking for a puta and to get drunk. Mexicans come into Nogales, Arizona, to hit the Walmart. Drugs and money flip-flop along this somewhat invisible line, which is mostly a cow fence. A girl could easily think, "I'm young and strong, I can make it." She is the mouse and we are the cat, more like the puma and jaguar playing a mortal political game. "Get past us and you're welcome," we say. To do our dirty work. She tried.

When I'm in certain areas with my English setter, Rose, and she decides to point Mearns, scaled, or Gambel's quail across the fence in Mexico, I scan the vicinity, then cross the border and shoot the quail. This is probably a dumb thing to do, but I've never seen another human in the immediate area when I'm there, and besides, Rose won't come off point until I've flushed the birds. Theoretically I could end up in prison, but that's been a possibility for dozens of other things I've done in my life and I've only ever gone to jail for buying a blackjack in Duluth, Minnesota, forty-seven years ago, when I was sixteen. Friends from the East who have hunted with me down here are puzzled by the shabby little barbed wire fence that separates our countries in many places. I explain that anything more than this would still be hopeless. This rumpled, mountainous area would be a perilous place to cross, though young men in good shape could make it. Besides, in the open grasslands you would be noticeable to the INS spotter planes that regularly cover the area. I checked out their efficiency one day as I was working my dog way up a canyon by running under a mesquite tree while an INS plane flew overhead. I took out my pocket watch, and an INS patrol vehicle came roaring up the two-track in less than three minutes. I blew my dog whistle and waved with a merry smile, a little joke in return for how many times they've checked me over the years. I'm dark-complected and spend as much time as possible outdoors because I don't like it indoors. Racial profiling might be frowned upon elsewhere, but it's the only game in town down here.

Far from any border is Xalapa, the capital of the state of Veracruz. The city was founded by the Aztecs in the fourteenth century. Ana Claudia might have remembered from a school trip to Xalapa the stare of a three-thousand-year-old Olmec head in the archaeological museum. The seven recovered stone heads weigh as much as forty tons each. Ana Claudia stares at her ancient ancestor, a Buddha head much less reassuring than the Buddha's. The head stares back, too magnificent for compassion.

About ten years ago I was up a remote canyon hunting just after dawn. This is not a good time to hunt quail, because they haven't yet dispersed from the close-packed coveys in which they spend the night, and it's harder for a dog to pick up their scent. But the weather had been so unnaturally warm in mid-December that some of the seven kinds of local rattlesnakes had begun to emerge in the warm afternoons. I'm not phobic about rattlers, but it isn't out of the question for a bird dog to be dumb enough to point one and be bitten fatally on the nose.

After an hour or so I was ready to give up, but then Tess, my dog at the time, was evidently on point around the next canyon corner because her collar bell had stopped ringing. Instead of a covey of quail, it was two Mexican men leading three mules packed with what I suspected wasn't candy bars or toilet paper. They had rifles strapped around their shoulders. Tess was wagging her tail and one of the men smiled nervously. After all, I had a sixteen-gauge shotgun, very effective at the fifty or so feet that separated us. I gave the peace sign, smiled lavishly with a "*Buenos días*," then scurried up a steep side canyon with a real tight butt.

But there wasn't much shooting around here back then, or now, for that matter. Smugglers tend to cut and run, and this is real hard country to chase and find anything, including your cows. A smuggler also cuts and runs because this is purely a demand economy and there's plenty of supply.

The music of Veracruz is sweetly delirious in a manner resembling the music of Brazil. It is Caribbean in character, much closer to the music of Cuba than to that of Sonora. By ten in the morning there are marimbas near the zócalo, the city square, a music that loves the heat of the air and softens the sound of traffic. Girls dance alone and with other girls, then finally with boys and men. In Ana Claudia's state of Veracruz, women seem to be missing certain bones in their bodies and this allows them to move to salsa music with improbable fluidity and grace, with rhythm that is unknown to us but indigenous to the human body. There is a salsa song that goes, "This world is full of fucking sharks, so we have to learn to swim."

I have no mind for rational solutions to the border problem. Nothing I ever hear from Washington, DC, has any relationship to the reality I know down here.

I'm also wondering if it behooves a writer to try to be right. Yeats warned about cutting off the horse's legs to get it into a box. An economist extols the benefits of cheap undocumented workers to the economy at large, while a labor economist would see a deleterious effect on union wages, and a rare sympathetic right-wing economist might add that the middle class and lower middle class have already lost 20 percent of their position in the last twenty years, mostly for reasons of our technocracy plus the decline of real wages adjusted for inflation.

A historian might very well question the validity of the Gadsden Purchase, in which the US government bought my locale for fifty-two cents an acre from a group of Mexicans that had no right to sell it. The United Nations would question our right to take all of the Colorado River's water, leaving the estuarine area in Mexico as dry as the bones their people leave up here in the desert. A true disciple of Jesus would say that we have to do something about these desperate people, though this is the smallest voice of all. Most politicians have the same moral imperative as a cancer cell: continue what you're up to at all costs. Meanwhile, the xenophobes merely jump up and down on the border screeching, surely a testament to our primate roots. Everyone not already here must be kept out, and anyone here illegally, if not immediately expunged, should be made as uncomfortable as possible. The reality of the border crosser is delirium, hunger, acute suffering. Compassion is a quality that easily runs dry.

Coming south from Xalapa toward Córdoba on mountain roads you see butterflies, songbirds, flowering trees of yellow, red, and violet, sheer cliffs that drop to a green valley holding a turbulent river raising clouds of mist. There are aplomado falcons and also Ana Claudia's unsought totemic bird, the harpy, known locally as the bone-crushing eagle, which feeds on lesser primates, the monkeys that are, like it or not, genetically our close relatives. Perhaps this bone-crushing eagle should be the insignia of the INS that Ana Claudia tried to escape.

Recently, on the way to my studio, I looked off to the south toward Mexico, recalling when I was down there at a "rest" resort for two weeks trying to quit drinking and smoking. One morning I was a bit hysterical and trotted down a road to a construction site and gave a laborer ten bucks for a cigarette. He didn't want to take it, so I stuffed it in the pocket of his soiled T-shirt. A small group of other laborers gathered around, and one of them spoke good English, having learned it in Chicago before he was kicked out of our country. I explained myself, and there were indulgent smiles. The burly gringo with a wallet jammed with credit cards had given their coworker the equivalent of three days' wages for a cigarette. The daffy gringo ate too much, drank too much, and chain-smoked, so he was paying two grand a week to stop doing so, the sum each week exceeding any of the workers' annual wage. The morning was still coolish, but I was suddenly bathed in my own rank sweat, my body drowning in the easily perceivable ironies. I could have said that I had been a construction worker, a hod carrier, had picked beans and done farm labor for a living for a couple of years, but it would have been meaningless. The Mexican who had worked in Chicago regarded my damp, stricken look and said, "Don't worry, this has happened before."

Metaphorically speaking, the grass is definitely greener on this side of the border, though on both sides the ground is usually brown and severely overgrazed. After years as an ex–farm boy eco-moderate, I have finally come to see our Bureau of Land Management, the landlord of so much public land, as the spawn of Satan, rending the surface of the earth, the living garment of God, for the usual reasons of greed and stupidity. If I weren't part owner of some Scottish Highland cattle in Michigan, amply fed on alfalfa, I would pray for la vache folle, mad cow disease.

This area of borderland Arizona is rough country and has nothing to do with the tourist's perception of Arizona, which is replete with pink prickly pear cactus, angular saguaros against the setting sun, cute coyotes on the verge of winking, older folks frolicking on golf courses with almost-smiling mountains in the background. I certainly don't feel threatened by man and nature down here, though I admit that I've killed a rattler in my bedroom (the French door was left open), my wife was bitten on the butt by a scorpion, and I dispatched another rattler after nearly stepping on it while getting out of the car to open our gate. If you discount drug smuggling and the smuggling of "undocumented aliens," there really isn't much of the kind of crime down here that daily challenges city residents.

There is a custom in the city of Veracruz called the danzón: *three nights a week mostly older people dance to an orchestra in the zócalo just past twilight. There are several hundred of these dancers who are well dressed and sedate, and despite their age their dance movements are anything but sedate. The older couples dance as if they are still in love. Maybe Ana Claudia's parents danced here at one time. The music of Veracruz creates children with the certainty of the Caribbean's tide. The tide and the moon are in the music, which is full of humid sea odors and water sounds.*

If you're undocumented coming up from the south in this area, or "sector," your problems are an open book. Highway 19 runs from Nogales to Tucson, and Highway 83 runs from Parker Lake up to Interstate 10 leading to Tucson and El Paso. Both of these routes have additional INS checks, where your vehicle is funneled through curious eyes.

If you wish to chance it on foot you're dealing with mountains: the Pajaritos, the San Cayetanos, the Patagonias, the Santa Ritas, the Empires, the Mustangs, and the Whetstones. They are not green and gentle slopes. I've quail-hunted in all of them and have invariably found empty plastic milk jugs. A migrant found dead in a barrel on the ranch where I keep my studio very probably died from drinking bad water. Except during the rainy season, nearly all of the creeks are dry, and standing water is easily tainted by cattle and wildlife. You're not an effective walker with giardia or other intestinal afflictions. Other than the scarcity of potable water it is the terrain itself that defeats the most. I've had at least one leg injury every year from walking in this sharp, rocky terrain, and most migrants are trying to walk at night, nearly always when the moon is brightest. You're up against hunger, thirst, exhaustion, and likely injury, all for our glorious minimum wage, if that. This condition cannot be extrapolated; it must be seen firsthand. I've known only a few people who night-walk the mountains, and they are well equipped and no one is chasing them. Everyone in an official position is chasing the migrants. Oddly enough I don't know any normal citizens who bother calling the police or the INS when they see migrants scurrying down canyons or through the brush. Perhaps it's sheer boredom with the problem, mixed with a little compassion.

You don't hear anything from politicians and pundits that bears any relationship to what you know from actually living on the border. When Pat Buchanan briefly visited the area he suggested building a border "moat." I was asked by a Chicano in my local bar, the Wagon Wheel, how Buchanan could keep water in his moat when it would have to cross so many mountains in its two-thousand-mile length. This moat would certainly create jobs but was perhaps no more feasible than my own plan for an underground airport. Water runs down a steep hill real fast.

In barrios on warm evenings people gather in the yards of those lucky enough to have a cable television, glowing in a window or doorway. In the city of Veracruz there are sixty-eight channels, many from the United States, though they are dubbed in Spanish. Maybe Ana Claudia made her decision one evening sitting in a warm, moist yard with mosquitoes in the air, watching all the movement on the screen, when her own life seemed sunken and stationary. A baseball player made twenty-five million dollars a year! That was more than twenty-five thousand poor people in Córdoba

made. There were sitcoms with laughter and pretty girls with handsome
men running on beaches, ads with beautiful clothes, food, and cars.

Still, numbers freeze the soul and bring forth cynicism, because
numbers from government employees are invariably spun in a posi-
tive nature. Some yokel's pot patch with a "street value of ten million dollars" is uprooted, and I would think such inflated figures
would only encourage people to enter the business. If even such
fiscal conservatives as William F. Buckley, George Will, and the
Republican governor of New Mexico Gary Johnson are dubious
about our drug war, you wonder why it hasn't slipped more deeply
down the political food chain. Why spend billions unsuccessfully
interdicting marijuana? Since I've had a number of friends die from
combinations of meth, coke, and heroin, it's hard to cast them in
the same innocent light.

But statistics, numbers: If the Tucson sector has more than
six hundred thousand apprehensions on record for last year, how
about the totally unknown number of those who got through? They
disappear into our landscape and are absorbed into our countless
menial jobs in meatpacking and agribusiness, into the cleaning-up
jobs in the cities where if you stay up very late you can see them
floating home in well-intentioned anonymity. A great deal of effort,
anyway, has been spent in the redesigning of America so that the
well-heeled will not have to suffer the irritation of noticing the
poor. Cities have become as gated as wealthy suburbs. Down here
most gated communities just have a fancy entry and a short stretch
of expensive fence. It's the idea of safety in a culture of profitable
and improbable illusions. Oddly, if you want to see the whole social
spectrum in America you have to visit a rural village, where if a rich
man has a house on a hill he still visits the post office, the grocery
store, and the tavern, and knows everyone's name.

At the Kennedy inauguration, Robert Frost was ill-advised when he
spewed the bullshit, "The land was ours before we were the land's." This

is a Wagnerian line, a line of empire, a line that is utterly blind to suffer-
ing. Tell that line to five hundred Native American tribes or anyone on the
over 2.5 million acres of scarcely life-giving land of the Tohono O'odham
(formerly the Papago) reservation, southwest of Tucson. General Philip
Sheridan readily admitted that a reservation was usually a worthless piece
of land surrounded by scoundrels. There is an excruciating poverty here
that contrasts with the austere desert beauty and the sacred mountain,
Baboquivari, looming in the east. Much of this land is sparsely populated,
empty, what cartographers call "sleeping beauties." In the summer in
the desert the temperature is over 100 degrees every day and the ground
temperature reaches 150. Migrants and smugglers try to move at night to
escape the dire heat and the INS spotter planes, scorpions, and various
species of rattlesnakes. Still, it is a better place to cross than farther west
in the immense and desolate Cabeza Prieta. A smuggler pilot told me years
ago that he could navigate the Cabeza on moonlit nights by bone piles and
skulls, as if they were upside-down constellations.

It is an interesting footnote that Mexico has become a pass-
through route for migrants from other countries in the world. Last
year's apprehensions included seven people from Afghanistan, with
appreciable numbers of those arrested coming from El Salvador
(670), Guatemala (586), Honduras (307), Poland (90), Ecuador
(86), the People's Republic of China (71), Brazil (63), Costa Rica
(43), Peru (36), Ukraine (31), India (23), Colombia (21), and Sri
Lanka (11). No one talks about the 200,000 technologically qualified we're inviting in this year because our rather bovine educational
setup can't quite create enough fodder for the system we've devised.
It's not surprising that so many "foreigners" wish to crash our economically superheated party.

There's an old Romani song that goes, "Why do you spit in our
faces with your wicked mouths?" A decade of prosperity run amok
has made us less rather than more interested in the fate of other
nations. In regard to Mexico there's the belief in Washington that
you can close the door despite the fact that the door has no hinges

and is anyway constructed of a couple of centuries of hot air. Those in the border states see the horror no one else sees because it is not a discursive media abstraction, but flesh-and-blood suffering.

So Ana Claudia crossed with her brother and child into Indian country, walking up a dry wash for forty miles, but when she reached the highway she simply dropped dead near the place where recently a nineteen-year-old girl also died from thirst with a baby at her breast. The baby was covered with sun blisters, but lived. So did Ana Claudia's. The particular cruelty of a dry wash is that everywhere there is evidence of the water that once passed this way, with the banks verdant with flora. We don't know how long it took Ana Claudia to walk her mere forty miles in the United States, but we know what her last hours were like. Her body progressed from losing one quart of water onward to losing seven quarts: lethargy, increasing pulse, nausea, dizziness, blue shading of vision, delirium, swelling of the tongue, deafness, dimness of vision, shriveling of skin, and then death, the fallen body wrenched into a question mark. How could we not wish that the politicians on both sides of the border who let her die this way would die in the same manner? But then such people have never missed a single lunch. Ana Claudia Villa Herrera. What a lovely name.

(Men's Journal)

THE BEGINNER
AND OTHER JOURNALISM

THE BEGINNER MEETS
THE EIGHT SAMURAI
(1977)

It was truly a big deal up here in the outback, far up in northern Michigan where the first tentative warm days of the year aided by a spring gale had finally driven the ice out of the bays and the worst winter in the history of this part of the Republic came to a sliding end. On the way in to watch the players of the Almaden Grand Masters the Beginner had stopped by a point of the bay to see a massive ice floe that had come ashore stopping a mere three feet or so from a house. The way the ice towered over the house reminded him that winter could be a serious matter. It took some imagination to think of tennis when the few outdoor courts in the area that weren't still smothered in snow had that raw, gaunt look of early spring.

The Logan Racquet Club in Traverse City is an expensive testament to the tennis boom in the last half decade. Despite an assuredly flippy economy Americans love expensive forms of exercise. A few

months before, the Beginner had arrived at the only other indoor
court in the area, at Sugarloaf Mountain, and announced he was
ready to learn the game. This decision was precipitated by watching
a mixed doubles match at the Everglades Club in Palm Beach in
January. The opposing ladies were predictably young and lissome.
Florida women, especially the Palm Beach species, are fetishists
about health to a degree equaling that of their California counterparts. But the men in this case, Archie Peck and Stanley Rumbaugh,
were older than the Beginner and in magnificent shape. It made
him feel sluggish and ghastly at thirty-nine. There was little point
in announcing to this crowd that he could lift two garbage cans
and ten fence poles at once! You're not supposed to talk during a
match and, anyway, fence poles and garbage cans are not a matter
of preeminent concern in Palm Beach.

So he went back home and brooded about his blood pressure
and weight and his dolefully boring exercises. For days on end he
sat in his terry cloth robe and watched the violence of the winter
which prevented his daily walks. His favorite meadow was chest
high in snow and along its eastern edge a fifteen-foot drift furled for
a hundred yards. The winter was only available to crows. His wife
and sixteen-year-old daughter blathered about tennis incessantly and
spent enough time and money at the tennis barn to make a serious
dent in their income, but he avoided mentioning it for fear of criticism about his far more expensive drinking and poker and fishing
habits. Besides, he had bought a racing quarter horse colt over the
phone one day on impulse and could not get rid of the resulting
knot in his stomach. Then, late one night deep into a mystery novel
and a fresh bottle of bourbon, and after a copious snack when such
resolutions are possible, the Beginner stood in front of the mirror and
said, "I will get in shape or die trying." He had been a poet for some
twenty years and was given to such Byronic postures over relatively
simple matters, somewhat in the manner in which Genghis Khan
might have passed out conquered countries to faithful officers over
a dinner of broiled goat.

Off to the tennis barn eight miles away, assuring himself with each mile that nothing was impossible given the antique virtue of sheer pluck. It looked simple and graceful on television, ignorant as he was of the true nature of the game. For years he had been fascinated by watching matches where the game appeared to be some sort of elegant physical chess and had superseded his interest in pro football. In the locker room his confidence began to go haywire. He was blind in one eye and the dread of failure was not lessened by the fact that he had become a fair wing shot and flycaster. If having a single eye did not prevent him from hitting grouse and woodcock, or from achieving the sort of hand-eye coordination required in tarpon fishing, then tennis wasn't out of the question. Besides the pro was an old and dear friend, Benny Boyd: an arrogant Irishman, former college basketball and baseball player, Michigan straight pool champion at one time. Our Beginner should have been tipped when in reply to a nervous question Boyd said he had learned tennis in his late twenties by playing six hours a day.

Of course, any of the millions who play the game have an inkling of what happened to the Beginner. In three weeks and nine lessons he went more than mildly batty. In short, he really ate it. He couldn't even hit the ball at times. Or muscles trained for strength fired the ball into the ceiling with tremendous force. The ball machine became the stuff of actual nightmares, and his old friend Boyd the object of strangling fantasies. His body was all wrong. When he swung the racquet the muscles of his upper back bunched into knots. When he totally missed three backhands in a row one day he thought he heard a giggle from the lobby door and cocked the racquet to hurl it before he came to his senses. The new blisters seemed to be biting the bone. After the fifth lesson when he began running for the ball he noted a new manifestation of the old Newtonian law: when he ran after a ball and stopped to set up, his belly kept moving for a long split second, throwing him a bit off balance. Not until then had he discovered the extra weight outside the desirable parameters, what was left over outside the inner body that did the work. Naturally he wanted to quit and sulk but had shot off his mouth too much to make quitting graceful. A business trip to Montana brought wonderful relief. He was even a little better when he returned, for no discernible reason. But those first nine lessons had been by far the most miserable experience of his sporting life. He saw himself seeded in the last ten of ten million tennis players. The old palliative "There's nowhere to go but up" has never made any sense, even to a drowning man.

On that last Thursday of March, the day before the Grand Masters tournament was to begin, the Beginner regained his sense of humor in what used to be regarded as a "fell swoop." At the Logan Racquet Club, Torben Ulrich, the number-one-seeded senior in the world, was having a workout with Sven Davidson, the number two seed. Also hitting were Beppe Merlo of Italy and Al Bunis, who had invented the whole idea of a Grand Masters tour. The humor came back after seeing the first strokes between the Dane and the Swede. It was a plainly impossible level of the game, exceeding the best local players as far as the best local players were above the Beginner. It was as distant from televised tennis as the reality of catching a fish is from watching someone catch a fish. Ulrich has a sort of incandescent grace about him and reminded the Beginner of the time he saw another Dane, Erik Bruhn, dance in New York twenty years before. Ulrich's legs also reminded him of his expensive stud colt in Montana. He could not believe that an athlete could have a more flawless body any more than he could believe that Ulrich was forty-eight, until during a break in the workout he saw the lines under the player's eyes.

Then Pancho Gonzales walked into the lobby. Gonzales is feral, haughty, vulpine. Like many other great athletes and men of genius in the arts or politics, he does not assume an environment but creates his own as he goes. He is the central fact of wherever he is and would be so in a bar in Manitoba where no one ever saw a game of tennis. It is difficult to understand just why this is so but there are any number of analogies. In literature Gonzales is Hemingway at his arrogant best while Ulrich is the shy, nearly serene Faulkner, and so on in other areas: Ruth compared to Gehrig, Lyndon Johnson to Adlai Stevenson, Patton to Rommel, Billy Graham to a Zen master. It is not simply a matter of style, but probably a nearly conscious decision on how to achieve one's ends by a particular appropriation of life's energies. Personality brings us close to a balk and we are clearly superstitious about the magic of excellence.

Gonzales pulls a minor prima donna number. He understood it was a four-hour drive from Chicago rather than the nine hours it actually took. Then he flashes a grin as mercurial as his scowl and he is ready for a brief workout with Ulrich. Even in practice Gonzales is the gamesman, swiping his forehand arm around his back and hitting a baseline shot without acknowledging the groans of the spectators. He is class throwing a little trash to the peasants. They love it, including the Beginner, who is so totally released from his dreams of excellence that he has forgotten himself completely. He now loves to see limits of the game, the mere rudiments of which were insufferable the day before. He has been an easy mark for the American nitwittery that it's best to deliquesce if you can't be the champ.

The Friday evening preliminaries are composed of four singles matches—the tour of eight players is designed to resolve itself over a weekend: Beppe Merlo beats Rex Hartwig, the great doubles player from Australia. Merlo is studiously unorthodox, using a racquet that is strung at a boggling twenty-two pounds. Merlo explains this by saying that as a boy in Milan he strung his racquets himself with any material available and grew accustomed to the control of the soft service. In that his credits include wins over a dozen greats the strategy seems believable if limited. Whitney Reed loses as expected to Sven Davidson. Reed, a San Francisco pro, is a replacement for Frank Sedgman, who has snapped his Achilles tendon. For reasons not entirely clear Reed draws the sympathies of the crowd. Perhaps it is easier to empathize with Reed's offhand grace than with Davidson's

Nordic perfection. Ulrich is the star of the evening, beating Luis Ayala of Chile easily, con brio, with the kind of insouciance one identifies with a gazelle at play. The Gonzales–Vic Seixas match is a bit of a disappointment—simply good tennis without the fireworks one had hoped for and which were yet to come.

The Beginner went home with tired eyes and a whirling brain that could be only partly accounted for by the free wine that Almaden, the tournament sponsors, had passed out. But he had little time to digest the evening before it was time to get up on Saturday morning and drive back to Traverse City.

The Saturday session seemed a great deal more serious despite the fact that the eight players seemed to have an easygoing camaraderie off the court. There is the simple brutal fact that it is more fun to win than lose. It would not be much lessened if everyone got the same amount of money. Ulrich defeated Davidson in a long match. Gonzales easily disposed of Merlo. In the second set Gonzales seemed to lose his temper and served four aces in a row. The Beginner had a great deal of difficulty in seeing the serve and the local judges seemed a bit out of their water. The crowd loved it despite Gonzales having all the charm of a shark eating a dory full of kindergartners.

The two doubles matches provided a nice contrast, with the Ulrich-Davidson pair beating Seixas and Reed, and the crowd seemed breathless a number of times during the match. Again, the emotional draw was the play of Whitney Reed. Sven Davidson crushed a ball in his hand, complaining to the judge that it was too soft. A ball boy walked off with the ball attempting the same trick and seemed puzzled that he couldn't make a dent in it.

During the Gonzales-Hartwig versus Ayala-Merlo doubles, which the former pair won relentlessly, the Beginner talked to Seixsas and Davidson. Seixas proved an impeccable gentleman, looking an even decade younger than his actual age of fifty-two. It was mysterious that a man could be so even-tempered and good. Seixas, who retired as a stockbroker and now heads the Greenbrier tennis program, was playing with a strange racquet designed by Acro. With an Allen wrench you could adjust the string tension on the spot. The Beginner, who owned a roomful of fly rods and shotguns, felt his heart soar. He envisioned traveling throughout the world adjusting his tool with an Allen wrench tucked in a leather pouch, estimating the climate, altitude, and opponent. When the Beginner started his lessons begrudgingly with his daughter's cast-off racquet his wife said, "I hope this isn't just another excuse to buy more equipment." It was tough to go off in fishing shorts, deck shoes, and a sweatshirt. The equipment would come later when he proved his faithfulness to the game.

Sven Davidson proved an unlikely sort, all charm in contrast to his drill-sergeant appearance on the court. He reminded the Beginner that he had introduced the motion for open tennis in Paris in 1968. He plainly questioned the credibility of the winner-take-all super matches currently so popular. The Beginner wondered at all the damage done to athletics by the misdirected hacks in the governing bodies.

Hartwig who seemed to begin the tournament as somewhat of a curiosity to the Beginner soon changed the minds of everyone. He and Gonzales easily beat Ulrich-Davidson in the Sunday doubles final. Hartwig is an Australian farmer with the build and tenacity of a pit bull. The Beginner discussed with Hartwig the vagaries of the cattle business and the fact that Hartwig had spent a decade away from tennis. It wasn't visible on the court. At one point Hartwig rallied and went smashing into a wall. He lay splayed on the floor for a moment but still nearly returned Davidson's forehand smash from a prone position. He seemed oblivious to the standing ovation, as if anyone would do the same.

But Sunday, the final day, belonged to Gonzales. The Beginner had bet his pro, Benny Boyd, that Ulrich would beat Gonzales. Ulrich had won the Beginner's heart with his serenity, his aura of total concentration and composure. But then Ulrich, not at all deferentially, had predicted a Gonzales victory though he had beaten Gonzales in their last match the year before. Now Gonzales had fully

recovered from an auto accident and was in first-rate shape having
lost a lot of weight—plus the fast court favored him. In the locker
room before the match he was angry and unapproachable, throwing
off a palpable ozone like the generators under a huge dam. Something
burning with enormous energy though without smoke or fire.

The match didn't bear recounting. Gonzales didn't beat Ulrich,
he flayed him alive, 6–0, 6–2. He was not so much above the crowd
as beyond it in some sphere of total commitment to winning. Ulrich
played well but Gonzales played with heartless perfection and a
power that wasn't totally enjoyable to watch.

After the match Gonzales was pleasant to the Beginner for the
first time of the weekend. He wasn't thinking it out, he was simply
very happy with himself. Outside the locker room and on his way to
catch a flight Al Bunis seemed amazed and delighted. But Gonzales,
who owned his doubles victory with Hartwig and his singles match,
said he had played his best in five or six years.

During a champagne reception the Beginner noticed that the
spirit of identification was gone and the spectators tended to talk
about other matters. As opposed to Connors and Năstase and within
the laws of the conservation of energy, you could at least watch
these matches, but Gonzales and Ulrich had pushed it out of that
realm. Down in the lobby Gonzales, the great hammerhead shark,
was nice to everyone. He fittingly enough works out of Caesars
Palace in Las Vegas. After one especially tiresome spectator left he
quipped to the effect that he had learned from Joe Louis how to
handle such nonsense. The Beginner understood for the first time
how so prescient a soul as Arthur Ashe could list this man among his
heroes. The Beginner wondered also what Gonzales could do with
Connors in a short match. But perhaps this was only the sentiment
of the quickly aging.

A DELICATE CREATURE
(1970S)

Walker's Cay, Bahamas

Sitting on the porch of a villa with a large drink in my hand I am watching beyond the stubby points of my toes the finest rising moon of my life. It is to the east, down here, and coming up apparently just over Abaco and casting a shimmering nimbus on the water all the way to Africa. My casual knowledge of such things leads me to think it's aimed at me. But this is fatigue mixed with a heat so thick that it falls as liquid from the air, even in the middle of night when only the lizards and a few drunken yachtsmen are still awake.

It was our first full day and we had intended to spend it tagging sharks. But there were none. Not a shark in the whole bloody aquamarine splendor of the open ocean. Five boats, a camera crew, six anglers, two shark cages, a full-fledged marine biologist, Jack Casey from Narragansett, and hundreds of pounds of chum—in this case hacked-up bonito. But no sharks. At dinner everyone tried to be nonchalant but there was that air of the boy who lost all of his marbles the very first day of school.

And while we were unloading gear after this day of nothing an aged sybarite had stepped off his $400,000 Bertram yacht complete with exercycle on the deck, Keane paintings of war-torn kittens in the lounge, to ask me what we were doing.

"Sharks," I said.

"O my gawd, hasn't that been done to death?" He had that air of superiority owned by those who only use their immense yachts as floating living rooms.

Of course he had a point in a world that varies its annual entertainments from sharks to man-eating birds, bees, rats, rabbits, earthquakes, burning skyscrapers. No matter that in the case of sharks the information was all the most hopeless Sunset Strip bilge. A few years ago I had the same problem with wanting to study grizzlies when the beast was publicly viewed only as something that ate two girls at Glacier. After he ate the two girls he was no longer interesting fodder even though he had spent millions of years *not* eating two girls. It's a world owned by the hotshots, to be sure, but no one seems to be able to remember who made last week's *Time* cover.

Meanwhile, back out at sea the next morning, one senses from the uneasy vantage point of a tuna tower that a whole universe exists in the three hundred fathoms beneath you that at least on a local basis is not much interfered with. One of the expert anglers, Al Ristori, says to Casey that he thinks we are above "dead bottom," sea bottom without sufficient natural anchors to harbor the whole chain of sea life that might attract predators. The expedition leader, Bill Munro, suggests we try a long line of reefs farther to the east.

The move proves magical. The chum line begins to work almost immediately. With a chum line you accentuate an artificial feeding situation by dribbling chunks of fish and innards over the side of a boat. The current or tide carries the oil and scent for great distances.

Some sharks can evidently pick up a scent or a disturbance in the water up to three miles away.

Casey runs through the tagging procedures with the anglers. Certain aspects are less than simple. As an instance, there are close to 350 species of sharks on earth and tagging as a main source of knowledge is worthless without a great deal of accuracy in regard to size, sex, and particular species.

Jack Casey works for the Department of the Interior but has the sort of vitality I have learned to associate with the field biologist as opposed to the teacher or bureaucrat. They work for peanuts. My own local game warden has a passion and knowledge about nature that would shame any eco-freak I've ever met. They are *exposed*. Over the years Casey has been involved in the tagging of fourteen thousand sharks and confesses that knowledge has only increased his fascination. He is built like a barrel, an ebullient running back, and is unique among our group as one who never tires from the sun and heat and long hours. He's never been in the Bahamas before and he doesn't mean to miss a second. I share a little of his passion remembering when I went to Africa as an amateur bird-watcher and every single bird was a new species for me.

In long evening talk Casey points out mainly what isn't known about sharks. One of the taggings has revealed a blue shark traveling from Long Island to Cape Verde off the coast of Africa within a year. Another traveled from Long Island to Guyana.

Certain mysteries of age and size aren't resolved. A shark tagged off Greenland was discovered sixteen years later to have shrunk. This and similar discoveries have led scientists to question certain assumptions relating to size as a determinant of age. Unlike bony fishes and mammals, the shark has an internal framework that is entirely cartilaginous which requires different techniques to assess its age; some sharks have been proven to have reached thirty years and there is speculation now that some are a great deal older. The only effective research instrument to answer these questions is tagging despite the minimal 3 percent return rate on the tags.

More bad luck: now that we have found sharks and are tagging, the seas have become far too rough to film. Some of us leave the boat to continue tagging in the heavy water and the rest seek the lee afforded by a giant reef. I see three waterspouts on the far horizon but decide no one wants to talk about them. We are in relatively small boats for offshore fishing—twenty-five-foot makos—but they easily make the hundred-mile run from Florida. They also have shallow draft and high maneuverability, without which our reef exploration would be impossible.

We anchor in a calm lagoon among immense conical coral heads. We are at the beginning of the outgoing tide and our chum slick is immediately visible threading its way out through a narrow passage in the coral. The bottom is sixty feet below but clearly visible. A prodigious amount of marine life descends on the chum— grouper, snapper, yellowtail, and two huge barracuda. (Later while snorkeling I counted thirty species in fifteen minutes.) An angler hooks one of the barracuda and the other swiftly bites it in half. I feel a little bad about interrupting the life cycle of these two fish who may have spent years together in this pocket in the reef.

Finally the sharks begin to arrive in numbers and our cameramen-divers quickly stop free swimming and get into the cages. We actually don't expect any problems but feeding sharks occasionally go into what is accurately called a "frenzy" and then you need the safety of a cage to save your skin and all that warm meat beneath it. The anglers are only using shoulder harnesses rather than fighting chairs and it is mildly comical to watch them being yanked around the boats in the brutal heat. Most of the larger sharks make the refuge of the coral heads and break the lines. Oddly, we see none of the vast hammerheads common near the Marquesas off Key West but these hammerheads seem to follow the tarpon migration.

We end up tagging over eighty sharks of fifteen species in five days. Casey is pleased though the rest of us as fellow Americans had rather hoped for something stupendous and awesome. Back to the movies for that.

JIM HARRISON: *The pure research of tagging—what might it lead to, what might you find out if you got enough sharks tagged?*

JACK CASEY: The reason that we tag, that I'm tagging sharks, is primarily to understand their migrations and, hopefully, to get some age and growth data from them, to learn something about their biology. Why they migrate, for example. Fish migrate for basically two reasons: to a feeding ground or for part of the reproductive cycle. Once you know that, once you have some idea of what they do, then it becomes a matter of applying some kind of practical application to this. Whether or not you should be harvesting so many, for example. How many you should take and at what size. And until you have some idea of that phase of their life history, almost anything you want to do to control their numbers or to regulate the catches is not based on scientific fact.

The recapture rate on the fourteen thousand sharks that we've tagged so far is 3 percent. So there's three out of a hundred sharks we expect to recover. And that is a *very good* recapture rate for a noncommercial species. The recapture rate in the early years in tuna fish was less than 1 percent before they had a commercial fishery. When they instituted a commercial fishery, it skyrocketed in some places to 30 percent. But 3 percent is very good.

So how old would a ten-foot mako shark be?

One of the questions often asked about sharks is, how long do they live and how fast do they grow? The Australian school shark lives for sixteen or twenty years, the porbeagle shark, in the western North Atlantic, has lived for twenty or thirty years. But of the several hundred different species of sharks, we know very little about all but half a dozen in terms of age and growth. This is very few. It is an indication, however, that the shark is a very slow-growing and long-lived animal in general. The problem with aging them specifically is that they do not have the scales and ear structures that reflect age rings the way one would expect on a tree and most bony fishes. As a consequence, other, less direct methods have to be used. We, for example, are using the backbone. We have found there are some rings in the vertebrae of the shark and in one species that we've been working on intensively, we are quite convinced the sandbar shark lives for longer than twenty years. Tagging data would support the age and growth studies that we're doing from examining hard parts in the animal.

The sharks that we're dealing with here, are they sharks that have been tagged before? Has there been any kind of work done on these sharks?

No, the sharks of the Bahamas, for example, there are some species that are very difficult to identify. There's a whole group of sharks called the Carcharhinidae or requiem sharks that look very similar. We know very little about them, whether they're resident populations. The Caribbean reef shark, we're not sure if that is resident on reefs such as the whole Bahamas chain, or whether they make long-distance migrations as do some of our pelagic species that we get further north, the blue shark, for example. There's very little known about their migrations and very little known about their food habits and life history in general.

Talking about the uniqueness of sharks, as a group of fishes—is it in any way a leg up?

The fish world in general is divided into two basic groups: the bony fishes and the cartilaginous fishes. This is one of the major things that separates them, morphologically. From a success standpoint, the shark has been very successful in combating the rigors of evolution. So we have sharks that go back 300 million years. They were here long before man appeared on the horizon, and perhaps if evolution works its hand, will be here long after we're gone. They're unique, they've been able to cope and adapt with the changing environment and have been very successful in doing so. Some of the bony fishes have been able to cope also, but the shark is very primitive and it is as well adapted to its environment today as it was several hundred thousand years ago.

What is the process, the physical process involved in tagging?

The tagging process itself is critical in that many people believe that the shark is an indestructible animal. The popular accounts that sharks live on the dock for hours or days are just not true. Perhaps they may live for several hours in that there is some movement involved, but the shark in effect is quite a delicate creature. So the procedures for tagging them are quite specific, both in capturing them [and] hooking up early enough so the shark doesn't swallow the hook, that he's fought for a relatively short time. The longer a fish is on the line, the more traumatic the experience, the more likely he's going to be so tired when he's released that there's less chance for survival. In our personal experience, we try to take the shark as quickly as possible, handle him as little as possible, leave him in the water, tag him, and release him with as little trauma as we can. If he's thrashing wildly on a short leader or being brought into the boat, there's a very good chance he'll be injured internally.

One of the problems is that after someone has captured and tagged several or perhaps a hundred sharks, he tends to become careless, and—this should be emphasized—even the smaller shark can inflict very painful injuries on anyone who is careless with them or treats them as other than a dangerous animal. Even the smaller sharks are fully capable of inflicting serious injuries, and I'm talking about two- or three-footers. We have to balance our appreciation of the animal, our fear of it, if you will, and also a respect for it rather than a familiarity with it, if we're fishermen.

We've not been able to test all the various things we'd like to test on tagging a shark in captivity, for example, but what we've developed from experience is a technique that on several species has lasted one, two, three, up to ten years, and as long as that technique lasts and the tags last, we feel it's the best we can go with. It's tricky, and we look for the experienced sportsman to do it. We're interested in fishermen that know fish and go shark-fishing and are interested in releasing the animal in good condition.

Jack, when you hook a shark, you obviously leave the hook in. Would this hook be digested? Dissolved? Is it dangerous to the shark?

I don't think that it hurts the shark. We've caught sharks that have had three hooks, mako sharks that have had three hooks in the jaw or lip, "lip-hooked," as we say. As long as it's on the outside, it apparently doesn't impair their feeding. It may fall out, depending on the configuration and type of hook, very quickly. Now if it's hooked deep, if the hook is swallowed or deep in the throat or in the stomach, that's another matter. We have tagged quite a few sharks that have had the hook swallowed and we've never had a recovery. With the 3 percent recapture rate, it's possible that maybe some of them will be recovered, but there's no evidence right now that a shark hooked deep in the gut will survive. So we ask our taggers to set up as quickly as they can on the fish rather than let him take the bait for a long period of time and ensure that they get a hook-up and yet kill the fish.

How many species of sharks are there, and is there any knowledge of how many sharks populate the various seas total?

The number of sharks in the world, the number of different species in the world, is estimated at 300 to 350. Why it's "estimated" is because new species are being identified almost every year, and they're a diversified group of animals ranging in size from seven or eight inches, fully mature, up to giant whale sharks. How many sharks populate the world's oceans? I don't think that is really known. Some species are very abundant—the blue shark in the western North Atlantic, for example, is our most abundant pelagic species, and it's probably the most abundant pelagic species throughout the world. It's cosmopolitan in distribution and occurs in all oceans, in the tropics, subtropics, in temperate zones, the world oceans. Other species are so rare as to have been recorded once or twice. It's very dangerous to try to answer a question about sharks in general. At least for the scientist.

We all know that sharks are dangerous. We also know that the percentage of attacks is very, very small compared to practically anything else you can do. You are more likely to be struck by lightning and so forth. Is there a way to educate people to realize that the species could at one point be endangered? To get over their primordial fear of the shark?

It's true that occasional swimmer attacks are such a remote danger—thousands and millions of swimmer-days every year along the coasts and occasionally there's an attack. People are also taking another look at sharks and saying, "They have a place in our environment," and perhaps we should not be too concerned about these large predators since the incidence of attack is so low. But that in itself is a danger because once you become familiar and know something about an animal, you tend to treat it as a pet, if you will. People who are swimming or bathing or skin diving and they see sharks, it's a prudent course of action to leave the water.

A lot of sharks are brought in every year by anglers, sportsmen, and they're not used whatsoever. All they've done is taken the jaw out or whatever. Is there any way that one can educate the anglers, if they're going to bring in a shark, if they can eat it, if they can use the hide, anything to get them out of just towing them out there and dropping them?

The utilization of sharks is an interesting question, particularly from the American standpoint. Shark hides have been used for leather, the meat has been used for food. The Japanese, Europeans, South Americans, all of them utilize sharks. The world landings of sharks are very close to one-third the world landings of tuna, billfish, and swordfish. In other parts of the world, they eat large sharks and use them for salted shark, a form of bacalao. They're using them in sausage and fishcakes and so on. Some sharks are better than others and they have to be treated as almost a delicate food between the time you catch one and cook it. Usually, the smaller the shark, the better eating for American tastes.

Jack, you've been involved in shark research now for fifteen years. Are you as fascinated today as when you started?

Yes. The fascination, of course, transcends different levels. In the beginning I was just fascinated with sharks as a large preda- tor that I hadn't been exposed to, hadn't had the opportunity to see, and so there was that kind of new, bright fascination. And as you learn more about them and get into their life his- tory, what is not known about them, it becomes more and more fascinating in that the more you know, the less you feel you know. And I think this is true of almost any scientist that gets involved in a biological study, that he feels he knows the animal better but he wants to know more, and the real, critical questions keep changing, all the time.

Casey describes sharks as the wolves of the sea. And with wolves they share a low reproductive capacity and an extremely graduated growth rate and sensitivity to the environment. They don't have the intelligence we associate with wolves but then they don't live in our world. Sharks are delicate creatures, a superior biological organism existing virtually unchanged for several hundred million years, and on the evolutionary scale they may be described as a triumph of adaptation.

The psychopathology of hate and apprehension is something we've always dealt with very poorly. If you swim on our Atlantic coast the odds are one in a billion you'll be bothered by a shark. In Paul Budker's *The Life of Sharks* there is a photo of the fossilized jaw of *Otodus megalodon*, the ancient relative of the great white shark, vulgarly known as Jaws. Six men are standing looking out at the photographer from this beast's mouth. But we are Chicken Little ninnies. We have nothing to fear from this world that is as intrinsically beautiful and complicated, and not quite as fearsome, as our own.

REAL BIG BROWN TRUCK
(1990)

The GMC Sierra 4x4 means business. Perhaps too much so. The downside of the business is that it was late at night and I had this very long truck wedged at a gate in the underground parking garage at the Ann Arbor Inn. I was in the process of disassembling the gate when a kindly passerby helped me through, which meant hopping a few cement barriers.

"That sure is a real big brown truck," he said, both of us a tad bleary from whatever. I gave him ten bucks to apply to his next vice, which struck me as imminent, and went to bed after finally locating my room.

Up to that day I had been flats fishing in Key West for two weeks, and my brain was somewhat sunburned. I am also blind in one eye, which tends to delimit my depth perception and peripheral vision, plus sitting way up there in the cab of a big pickup makes barriers and parking gates look like mere toys. It is also a known fact that your emotions affect your driving, and I was in the middle of a month where nine of my books were being reissued, to be followed by the release of two movies I had cowritten. The only reason I didn't have an album coming out was that I only sing to my bird dogs. Now you know why I failed the gauntlet of the parking garage, though other specific victories seemed just up the road.

What was important to me was that the vehicle fulfilled a specific need—I wanted to be a normal, actual person who drives a big pickup, adding that I've eschewed the notion of "macho" in order to be a kinder, gentler guy.

So I headed north, stopping for a few days at my farm, which seemed a great deal more farmlike when I covered the acres in the GMC, beside which my Subaru, my wife's Saab, and my daughter's Mazda appeared effete and trivial. To be frank, I felt like a genuine American, although there was the cautionary note of an old friend who changed identities, wardrobe, sometimes wives or girlfriends with each new vehicle. After he traded in a Jaguar (and a fashion model) for a Dodge van, he brought over a chubby lass in a peasant dress who threw her own pots, as it were. One day on the way home from a coffeehouse, a GTO caught his eye, and the counterculture lady took off for California in the van when she caught him with an ex-cheerleader barmaid. I wasn't going to allow the novelty of a truck to make me abandon a marriage of long standing for a cowgirl type who might howl, "We was great tonight, Jim Bob."

It seemed better to test the GMC's metal—all two and a half tons of it—in the Upper Peninsula rather than in the dulcet, housebroken hills of Leelanau County, where I was liable to run over some brain surgeon's or arbitrageur's peony bed. I called the elderly Finnish gentleman who takes care of my cabin near Grand Marais to see if my two-track was open. It was the third week of April, but then the snow doesn't own a calendar.

"Maybe you can make it. Maybe not," he said. I packed quickly for this challenge, concentrating on the food that boosts morale when the weather is bad, including several magnums of Bordeaux,

a drink not usually favored in the northland. My urge to be normal
has never entered the culinary—on the road, tears have formed
before the spiritual shabbiness represented by salad bars, the decline
of a nation reflected in the beige crust forming on the potato salad.

By the Straits of Mackinac even the vaguest signs of spring
had fled, and much of the normally blue water was still ice white.
The truck was as comfortable as a car, with the advantage of height
for visibility. There was a rare (for me) tendency to speed, as the
weight of the vehicle at seventy miles per hour made it adhere to
the road, unlike my Subaru, which at that speed verges on liftoff.
Even more charming on two-lane Route 2 was the kick-ass passing
gear, which I suspected might be costing a buck's worth of gas per
use. Remembering that I was in the movie business, I stomped the
accelerator at whim, knowing that Ray Stark and Sydney Pollack
would approve.

Heading north out of Seney toward Grand Marais the woods
begin to fill up with snow and I actually regretted not bringing my
cross-country skis. At the same time the previous year, the heat wave
had already begun. The immediate prospects of steelhead fishing
didn't look good, and the remaining drifts on adjoining two-tracks
were over bumper height. I had counted on making it out on a trail
to a rarely visited area of Lake Superior. In twelve years in Grand
Marais, I had found people there only once—curiously enough, a
family from Nebraska who asked me for directions back to town.

My two-tracking was generally thwarted by the depth of snow
though I made it to the lake, unwisely, by the grace of the truck. Low
range on the four-wheel drive is particularly low, so I simply charged
and humped over the soft snowbanks, roaring and spewing a rooster
tail of mud when I hit the ground. The long wheelbase presented
some problems turning around in the woods. At one point I was
clearly trapped until I was bright enough to remember I had a reverse
gear. Another time I was frankly stuck but prayed to the god of food
and wine, because it was an eleven-mile walk to the cabin, and to
my pot of a traditional Mexican stew called posole (pork neck bones,

venison, lamb shanks, dried hominy, three kinds of chili peppers, et cetera). Then I thought of what my friend Hunter Thompson said: "Always teach your kid on a renter." This wasn't my truck! Roger Smith wouldn't want me to go without dinner. Roger would want me to stomp it, which I did, howling and fishtailing for a hundred yards, and utterly alarming my old Labrador on the seat beside me. Later I discovered a few brush scratches on the cab, but I figured Roger wouldn't mind touching those up. The posole was splendid, and I napped long and hard and well, barely waking in time to close my bar, the Dunes Saloon.

The next day, in reaction, I was gentler with the truck. I dragged a couple of brats and left them eating gravel, but nothing more violent. It's curious, but when you drive a pickup, folks in fancy cars ignore you as if you were wearing a janitor's uniform. You discover, however, a whole world of pickup aficionados who want to know far more about the vehicle than you are able to deliver. I concentrated on bluster and ignored technical questions as beneath contempt.

That evening I prepared my annual spring-cleaning rigatoni with thirty-three cloves of garlic, fresh spinach, Italian plum tomatoes, and Parmigiano-Reggiano, with a grilled Summerfield squab on the side basted with lemon, butter, and tarragon. I set the alarm for my nap so I wouldn't miss a shot at smelt fishing that night. The fact that the Sucker River in front of my cabin was up to the level of the fifth stair down to the river made steelheading a glum prospect, and smelt fishing was a lowlife alternative. We left the bar right after midnight—smelt fishing is a middle-of-the-night sport—and made our way down a road that was ruts and mud up to the rocker panels. We made it through only to find Grand Sable Lake was still pretty frozen, and there were only two small smelt to be had. The GMC is wonderful in such situations as you avoid the typical pickup rocking-horse motion and the truck's suspension handles the washboard log roads nearly as well as the Range Rover's.

I went home to Leelanau County, then tried the trip again ten days later. This time I avoided pushing the truck by trading a six-pack for a bag of smelt in the bar. I had lost some of my urge to be normal because I was due in Hollywood in a few days and they apparently aren't hiring me because I'm normal. It was time to become smart. There was the memory of myself as a young poet thumbing my nose at New York by having a book jacket photo of myself in bib overalls leaning against an old pickup, the caption saying that I was an "international white-trash sports fop." It is a tonic to think so. Meanwhile it is late in the afternoon of May 5, and outside the cabin there is what could accurately be described as a blizzard. Normally I would worry about getting out of here in the morning, but out there in the driving wind and snow is a real big brown truck.

(*Automobile*)

FLOATING:
ON FISHING,
AND ON THE WATER

ON THE WATER
(1976)

The Leelanau Peninsula, where I live on a small farm, juts some forty miles into northern Lake Michigan. On certain hilltops on the crown of land that forms the geologic spine of the peninsula, you can see water on three sides. Some eight years ago, after an extended stay in New York, I arrived on the peninsula at dawn after driving straight through. Cresting a hill, I spotted the old stone farmhouse. But beside it lay something far more splendid—the glint of water in the dawn sun. At the foot of a sloping two-mile hill stretched the sixteen-mile length of Lake Leelanau. Then came another long crest of hills with the pastel greens of late spring deepening into the darker greens of June, and beyond that the blue, glittering expanse of Lake Michigan.

There is an excitement to water, and to the multitude of enjoyments it offers, that strikes a deep, resonant chord in all of us. Perhaps it is the sense of freedom in venturing out into what Ernest

Hemingway called the last wild country, a tractless world of our own, in which all of us can plunge into whatever activity or adventure we please. For some people this means skimming across the surface on a pair of water skis in the wake of a towboat at thirty-five miles an hour. To others, it is sliding down a backcountry creek in a canoe, with no sound but the dip of the paddle into the stream and the breeze swaying the evergreen branches overhead. To a man in a kayak, it is the rush of adrenaline that comes as he plunges into the waterspouts, souse holes, and standing waves of a white-water rapid. For the lithe and athletic, the excitement comes from skylarking about a harbor on a contraption called a Windsurfer, which is a kind of surfboard equipped with a bedsheet-sized sail. Or for some fanatical souls, it arrives with winter, when the lake freezes over and they can go clattering across its hardened surface in iceboats at more than a mile a minute.

To me, water means a chance to go fishing.

That morning, on my arrival home, I went over my fishing tackle. Then I spent the rest of the day driving around the country visiting the different marinas to check out the action. Every one was chockablock full of boats of every size and description. There were outriggered sport fishermen, humble fourteen-foot aluminum rowing dinghies, and seventy-foot cabin cruisers that had made the voyage all the way up from Florida. Some of their owners undoubtedly were readying their craft for one of the weekend salmon tournaments that take place all summer long in the small towns along the northeast coast of Lake Michigan. The fish that they pursue are the coho, which runs up to thirty pounds, and the chinook, or king salmon, which reaches sixty. Both of these varieties are pretty tough fighting fish while still green—a local Michigan term that means mature but still prespawning.

One attraction of the tournaments, to be sure, is the chance of hooking a cash prize of as much as $2,600, but the real reason most people go is the opportunity to mix with a host of other anglers in good water. In the old days before the Michigan Department of

Natural Resources installed a dozen or so launching ramps in the area, trailer-borne boats used to be lined up at tournament time for five miles back of the only launching site. I have commonly seen a couple thousand boats churning out of the harbors at the height of the tournament season—some of them bona fide entrants, but most just ordinary people going out for a day's fishing. There are craft under fourteen feet, really too small for safety, and fifty-two-foot, $300,000 Hatteras cruisers. Once clear of the harbor they spread over a ten-by-fifteen-mile stretch of water, exchanging information —and sometimes deliberate and artful misinformation—on their ship-to-shore radios. From the air the scene resembles some sort of comic armada, with a jangle of tangled lines and very bad tempers in the hot spots.

My own lifelong love affair with fishing—and with boats and water—began when I was still a kid, barely out of short pants. I remember standing in a barn with my father, who was the county agricultural agent of Michigan's Osceola County. A farmer was building us a rowboat out of white pine, and I smelled the resinous wood shavings that littered the hay chaff and watched the barn swallows dart around the rafters and ropes and hay pulleys. The half-built boat was a total mystery to a nine-year-old, but nonetheless an exciting promise of vague future delights.

The future began to take more real shape with the delivery of the completed craft at the small lake where my father and his brothers had built the cabin in which we spent our summers. We watched the launching of that heavy, cumbersome skiff, splendid in its fresh gray paint, as if it had been an ocean liner sliding down the bank to float among the lily pads. It had cost the sum of $50, and my brother and I cleansed and cared for it as religiously as if it had cost $50,000. We would wait in frantic competition to be chosen to row my father or mother around the lake in the evening to plug for bass. Some of my happiest memories are bound up with the creak of oars, the cries of herons and loons, the plop of the bass plug on the water, and the hiss of the kerosene lantern, whose mellow glow encircled the delicious aroma of a late-night fish fry. It was years before it occurred to me that being given the honor of cleaning all the fish, or of rowing my Swedish-farmer grandfather around the lake for up to twelve hours at a stretch, was really more in the nature of being a chore than a high privilege.

It has also dawned upon me belatedly that, in its humble way, that first rowboat was the beginning of real knowledge of the water, and of how to move on it. In that boat, my father taught me to row, and to tack in zigzags into the waves rather than to roll sloppily into the troughs. I also learned that driving a boat is not like driving a car. There is far less margin of safety. You don't just pull up to a dock and put on the brakes. And when you start to turn a rowboat, you go sideways for a while. You have to think about all these maneuvers in advance, and you have to really understand them before you ever get into your first powerboat.

I also began to appreciate that easily half of the success of any boat-borne fisherman is due to the skill of the boat handler. Some thirty years after that first rowboat took possession of my soul, I was fighting a big fish—a striped marlin by the feel of it—in the confluence of the Humboldt and El Niño Currents twenty miles off the coast of Ecuador. I was an hour into the fish, and the equatorial heat had pushed me toward terminal fatigue. Worse yet, I was working from a dead boat. Our single engine had quit, and the captain was unable to help me by moving the boat slowly forward to help raise the fish or by making the long, sweeping curves that would temporarily create less tension in the line so that I could take it in. (Such maneuvers had been worked out years before by pioneer deep-sea fishermen like Zane Grey. Once Grey battled for nine hours to bring in a swordfish he had hooked, and then discovered that all that time he had been mostly fighting the tension on his own line while the swordfish had been feeding.) My fish sounded. Without getting any help from the boat, it is almost impossible to haul up from the depths a big fish that is sulking, or one that has died from too rapid a change in water pressure. I was afraid that I'd lost him.

We drifted on the swells in a silence broken only by the soft fluffing sound of the wings of the frigate birds and the staccato Spanish of the mates. We had no radio and no other boat was in sight, not even one of those small skiffs in which Peruvian fishermen venture out to purse seine for small fish. I felt like a boxer nearing the end of a club fight in which his opponent is the referee's brother. My imagination called up visions of a watery demise among the venomous yellow sea snakes that were drifting here and there around us. But after a seemingly endless hour of hammering and tinkering, the captain got the engine started again. And by expertly maneuvering the boat, he helped me to bring up the fish—which proved to be not a marlin but another fine trophy, a 190-pound sailfish.

Fishing the flats off Florida for tarpon and bonefish demands a somewhat different but no less exacting kind of skill, one that nobody practices more deftly than a Florida Keys tarpon guide I know, who fishes out of Little Torch Key. His touch is apparent just in the way that he drives his bonefish skiff to the fishing grounds. An ordinary boatman heads straight for his objective as fast as an 85- to 135-horsepower outboard will push the low-profiled craft; on a rough day, his passenger is apt to arrive soaking wet. My friend zigzags among the keys, plotting his course to keep in the lee of one island after another. He may take an extra fifteen minutes, but the fisherman stays dry.

More marvelous still is to watch him pole a boat. He is a former US Navy physical-training instructor, and he can probably still press 150 pounds. He can pole that boat upwind or uptide, and he can make it go so fast it leaves a wake. But strength is only part of the marvel. To turn a boat while poling, an amateur like me has to twist his body. But my friend does it just by planting the pole exactly where he wants it—to the rear or to one side—with the timing of a pole vaulter, but with greater skill, since he makes his plant behind him, and by touch rather than by sight. He can pole that shallow-draft boat in a dew, as they say in the trade, and so quietly that the spookiest of fish will never hear him coming.

Boat-handling abilities like this are one reason that guides are
not allowed to post international game-fish records. If they were,
they would hold them all. This particular guide recently caught
a tarpon that was about fifty pounds over the saltwater fly-fishing
record—and, being a staunch conservationist, promptly threw it
back.

At the exact opposite end of the scale in maneuverability from a
bonefish skiff is the craft I use for duck hunting on Lake Okeechobee.
This is a large truck inner tube with a sling for a seat. It is unbeliev-
ably awkward, especially when you have a seventy-pound Labrador
retriever sitting in your lap. You cover yourself with camouflage cloth
and wait for the ducks. The recoil of your gun sends you spinning in
half circles. During slow periods you keep an eye out for alligators.
A big one snuck up uncomfortably close one day and stole half our
ducks. My rage over the loss was tempered by relief that the alliga-
tor had preferred the ducks to one—or both—of the legs that I was
trolling so vulnerably in the water.

For fishing backwoods lakes and rivers that are virtually
unreachable overland, I favor a johnboat or a canoe. A johnboat,
flat and boxy, is roomier and infinitely more comfortable to fish
from than a canoe. But it is less maneuverable and far more apt
to slide out from under you when you stand up on the seat to cast.
This happened to me one day when I was fishing around a logjam.
Most Michigan rivers have eddies where fallen trees and branches
and old sawlogs have been gathering into a big knot for who knows
how long. White pine logs, so big that they might have been felled
a hundred years ago when most of the real giants were cut, have
been washed out of some of these jams by storms. When dried out
and sawed up, they are still perfectly usable. A jam is a prime trout
habitat; a brown trout that is seeking food and shelter might take a
station there for life.

I was trying for one of these settlers when the boat took a weird
little turn and I fell into the logjam, catching my jacket on a branch
in a way that held me pinned underwater. The boat handler can't do

much in such a situation except stop the boat—which may take a while in a stiff current. What saved me was the experience of having often gone under in my waders. If you relax when that happens, the river will eventually carry you into an eddy and you can get out. If you thrash about in wild-eyed panic, you can expend so much energy that you move into shock, and if the water is cold, you are subject to hypothermia, a sometimes-fatal lowering of your body temperature. I held my breath and with calm deliberation wriggled around until I could unhook the jacket and scramble onto a log.

Barring such occasional accidents, johnboats make eminently sensible backwoods fishing craft. But to me there is one kind of craft that goes beyond the sensible, a boat that is part magic. Something about a canoe makes it aesthetically unmatchable—particularly the old-fashioned wood-and-canvas type. It melds better into a wilderness setting than a silver aluminum johnboat. I think a common desire to play Indian is part of it. Like thousands of other northern-Michigan youngsters, I destroyed half a dozen birch trees in my youth trying to build a canoe of bark. Hardly anyone paddles around in birchbark, of course, and for my money no vessel on earth compares in grace, beauty, and good handling qualities with, say, a fifteen-foot wood-and-canvas job. It weighs only fifty-eight pounds, and you can get a sense of ease and maneuverability out of it. And it is quiet. While drifting along through cedar swamps, the quietness of a canoe has allowed me to see innumerable ducks, beaver, deer, nesting eagles, and once a bobcat that came down to the water to drink. Bobcats are primarily nocturnal creatures; you almost never see one by daylight, but a canoe is a passport even to a bobcat's world.

The canoe—as well as its Inuit brother the kayak—is also a passport to white-water running, a form of sport that scares the hell out of me. On some western rivers—the middle branch of the Salmon in Idaho, say, or parts of the Yellowstone in Montana—the roar of the water sounds like a freight train. A friend of mine who floated down the Salmon a couple of years ago during the spring runoff says he came around a corner and there, suddenly, was a wave that he *knew* was forty feet high billowing back from the canyon wall. The physics of that are preposterous.

I would sooner trust my luck in a kayak on an Alaskan river, however, than in one of the iceboats I sometimes see flitting along Lake Leelanau on an arctic afternoon. Those of my friends who enjoy the sport tell me it's worth the weeks of watching the weather, the logistical problems involved in rounding up all the other fanatics at a moment's notice when ice and wind are right, the trouble of trekking miles to the nearest available site, and the bother of bundling up in snowsuits that conceal all evidence of age or sex. My own view is that ice belongs in drinks and I belong somewhere other than perched on a fence rail going one hundred miles an hour at twenty below zero. I must admit, though, that it looks like the thrill of a lifetime.

Waterskiing appears to the uninitiated to be even more precarious than iceboating, but with a skilled driver at the helm it can be safer than most downhill runs on snow. With an idiot at the helm, it can be something close to suicide. Ask my brother. He and I took up waterskiing on that same lake where we had learned to row. With unbounded and baseless confidence, we set out in a light but sturdy outboard that our family had lately acquired. I took the helm first and, after a few false starts, got my brother up on top of the water. We were soon roaring around the lake, close enough to the shore that anybody who happened to be about could admire our skill. I was looking back over my shoulder at my brother, who was skiing so close behind the boat that I could read his ecstatic expression. He was, in fact, far too close to the boat. Our hastily chosen towrope was about half the length that it should have been. Suddenly his face registered incredulous dismay. A second later the boat was plowing right through a flimsy wooden dock. Still clinging reflexively to the towrope and leaning back to avoid the flying debris, my brother shot through the path the boat had cleared. On the other side, I cut the motor and we drifted to a stop amid floating remnants of the demolished dock. The boat was intact except for some scratched paint, and our injuries were chiefly to our pride.

But mishaps are the exception in water sports. For the most part, whether you are lazing on a converted lobster boat off Halibut Point near Gloucester, Massachusetts, or casting for brown trout from a johnboat on the Yellowstone, it is all fine. The water is there and we can all own it and there are few reasons to get upset—literally or figuratively. The beauty, the fun, the slight spice of danger in sports afloat offset the troubles, the hardships, the fears. And rightly so, or else we would stay safely tucked in our living rooms with small chance for happiness.

(*Sports Afloat*)

STARTING OVER
(2000)

On the surface fishing is a primitive activity. I mean, in the anthropological sense that fishing is included in the hunting and gathering activities of our remote ancestors. It is all about filling the tummy.

In a decidedly comic sense, it is hard to stay on the surface. Especially in the past two decades, a legion of men (and some women) have been writing about fishing. It's as if since fish spend their entire lives under water, we try to join them by going even deeper. Except in the rarest cases (for instance, Thomas McGuane's *The Longest Silence*) we utterly fail, because it's as hard to write well about fishing as it is about anything else. Shocking as it might seem, we know even less about fish than we do about women. We even talk about the Zen of fishing with a captious banality. As a twenty-five-year student of Zen, I must tell you that fishing is fishing and Zen is Zen. The confusion here is that any activity that requires skill and during which we also manage to keep our mouths shut seems to acquire a touch of the sacred.

Some of us feel particularly good about essentially Pleistocene activities. If I walk a full hour through the woods to a beaver pond and catch a two-pound brook trout on a no. 16 yellow-bellied female Adams, I feel very good. The important thing isn't the technique or the equipment but the totality of the experience, of which the technique and equipment are a very small part. There are the hundred varieties of trees and shrubs you pass through, the dozen different wildflowers, the glacial moraines, the stratocumulus clouds, the four warblers and the brown thrasher, the heron you flushed, the loon near the lake where you parked the car, the Virginia rail you mistook for a cattail, the thumping of your heart when you hook a fish, the very cold beer when you return to the car just before dark, even the onion in the baked-bean sandwich you packed along. But above all it is the mystery of the water itself, in the consciousness, not the skill or the expensive equipment.

Nothing is quite so inexplicably dreary as watching a relatively rich guy who has spent a lot of money on a trip to the Florida Keys or to a big western river like the Yellowstone and can't make the throw. You wonder why he bothered or if he assumed his enthusiasm would somehow allow him to overcome the twenty-knot wind, the moving skiff or McKenzie driftboat. Fly casting is most often a sport without second chances, and, like wing shooting, it requires the study of prescribed motion and the spirit of repetition. And if you can't afford a guide or, better yet, don't want one, your ultimate chore is understanding habitat. Both fish and birds hang out in their restaurants, but there are no signs out front.

So over a period of fifteen years you spent near a month per year on the flats of the Florida Keys fishing for permit and tarpon, your brain relentlessly mapping and remapping the area topographically to figure out where the fish will be, given specific conditions of date, weather, tide, water temperature. Even then you don't have it figured. Why is a school of two hundred tarpon coming in Hawk Channel under the absolutely wrong conditions?

And then one day you don't want to go fishing. You want to go to an art museum or a bookstore. How many times have you gotten up at 6:00 a.m. to meet the right tide after getting to bed only at 3:00 a.m. and not necessarily alone? There's nothing like a windless ninety-two-degree day on the flats to tell you exactly how you behaved the night before. The sweat dripping into your eyes and down your nose smells like whiskey and other not necessarily commendable substances.

And, of course, you forgot that you were simply fishing, and that when you had taken it to a magnum level it was still just fishing, despite the fact that you were fly casting to a 150-pound tarpon, which you can't really extrapolate by trying to imagine a 150-pound rainbow or steelhead. And this is not including stray shots at Pacific sails, striped marlin, and blue and black marlin off Ecuador and Costa Rica, where you had the suspicion that your body parts might detach. You had become not all that different from the humorless and somewhat doltish moguls who Leared into Key West for a few days of flats headhunting, as if their real quarry were just another form of arbitrage.

So you burned out, and the burnout on magnum fishing also slipped the soul out of the day-to-day fishing in the Upper Peninsula that was a pleasant balm when you weren't running your dogs to get ready for bird season. Burnout is endemic to our culture, whether in a job or in sport. I think it's actually traceable to brain physiology, if I understand Gerald Edelman's "neural Darwinism" properly, which I probably don't. Your responses become etiolated, atrophied, plain frazzled, and in this case you have quite simply fried your fishing neurons, except for the two weeks a year on the Yellowstone River near Livingston, Montana, floating in a McKenzie boat, which was more a retreat from your work life than anything else, and trotting with tadpoles in Kashmir would probably also do the same thing, except your grandsons were in Livingston.

In July I launch my new Poke Boat, a splendid and slender craft that weighs about thirty pounds and is perfectly suited for hauling into remote, uninhabited lakes in the UP. You can paddle it like a kayak or install a rowing contraption, which I did—or, rather, a friend did for me, as turning doorknobs stresses the limits of my mechanical abilities. I weigh either 130 or 230. I'm forgetful these days, but it's probably the latter, which makes getting in and out of the boat a trifle awkward. A beastly process, in fact.

But it's a crisp, virgin boat, and I feel younger than springtime as I fairly slice across a river estuary leading to Lake Superior, the body of water that not incidentally sank the seven-hundred-foot freighter *Edmund Fitzgerald* about seventy miles from here.

The first wave wrenches my bow sideways. The second, third, and fourth waves fill my virgin boat to the gunwales. How can this be? I'm nearly tits high in water and why didn't I leave my wallet in the car like I intended? Luckily my next stop, the Dunes Saloon, will accept wet money.

There's inflatable flotation in the bow and stern of the Poke Boat, so I manage to crawl it to a sandbar. At least I drown a swarm of noxious blackflies that were biting my legs. I wish mightily an old couple weren't watching me from shore. As a lifelong leftist I have always considered dignity to be faux-Republican indifference, but then everyone wants to look nifty. With a violent surge of energy and upper-body strength, I turn myself turtle on the sandbar, doubtless looking from shore like a giant beetle.

At the Dunes Saloon an especially intelligent Finn says, "You're wet," followed by a French-Canadian drunk who says the same thing. What's extraordinary about the experience is that I do the same thing the next day.

The only excuse, unacceptable anywhere in the world, is that I was working on a novella about a closed head injury and was living in a parallel universe where one doesn't learn from experience.

Luckily I moved inland in the following weeks and had a marvelous time drifting among herons and loons and on one lake at least

77,000 white water lilies. It was August, and the fishing was poor, though one day on my first cast with a streamer I caught a pike the size of a Havana corona, a truly beautiful little fish that nearly covered the length of my hand. Her (it had to be female) sharp, prickly teeth gave my finger a bite when I was about to slip her back into the water. With the gout of blood emerging from my finger, there was a momentary and primitive urge to squeeze her guts out, but then, I am a sportsman. If the pike had been a male, I might have done it.

During all my benighted years as a dry-fly purist, I occasionally did some slumming, partly because I was in my thirties and the molecular movement of hormones made any stupid thing possible. If you trek far out on the ice and spend an entire day in a fish shanty with a friend staring down through a large hole in hopes of spearing a pike, you are demonstrating that it's hard to find amusement in the Great North in January. You forgot the sandwiches, but you and the friend remembered two bottles of Boone's Farm Apple Wine and two bottles of Ripple made from indeterminable fruit, plus a half dozen joints of Colombian buds. Due to this not-very-exotic mixture, the day is still memorable.

When a pike finally made a pass on our dangling sucker decoy, I think we said in unison, "Wow, a pike," and forgot to hurl the spear. We wobbled toward the shore in a blinding snowstorm, our compass the church bells in our small village.

Of course, drugs and fishing don't mix. It's fun to mouth truisms that have become inanities. The tendency of boomers to tell older folks to "stay active," as Melvin Maddocks points out, implies the opposite: "stay inactive." It was certainly difficult to concentrate or cast well on LSD, but it made the rattling of gill plates on a jumping tarpon a fascinating sound indeed. And once, in an altered state, Jimmy Buffett revved his engine to the max when it was tilted up. I sat there in a questionable daze as the propeller fired out toward the Gulf Stream, glimmering in the blue distance. Mostly you couldn't fish well on acid because you became obsessive about the improbable profusion of life at the bottom of the shallow flats. A passing crustacean became as monstrous as it is to lesser creatures, which might have included yourself.

Recently, a few days before heading to Montana for my annual fishing vacation, I decided to go north, pretending I was an enervated businessman who had been strained through a corporate sheet and was desperate for a day of fishing. Parenthetically, I was only halfway to my cabin before I realized that except for my journal and poetry, I had never written for free, and a dense Martian might actually think I *was* a businessman. Many writers are as hopelessly venal as day traders. This is all the more reason to go fishing, which is a singular way to "get out of your mind" to where you might very well belong.

A friend of mine in the UP, Mike Ballard, had consented to act as a guide. We've been fishing together for twenty years and often have assumed different names to dispel the ironies involved in adults at sport. Mike is a consummate woodsman and occasionally refers to himself as "Uncas," the James Fenimore Cooper hero. In recognition of my own true character, I am just plain "Brown Dog." This is all plaintively idiotic, but to have fun the inner and the outer child must become the same, which is harder than it sounds. For extended periods of my life, I have condemned fishing to death by playing the mature adult, an illusion most of us live and die with.

It was one of those pratfall days. We boated five miles up the estuarine arm of a large lake, the fishing so slow we went ashore and walked a high ridge, which was delightfully wild. The sour note was that from the ridge we could see a huge, black rolling squall line approaching from the west, and by the time we made it back to the boat Uncas said, "Even our balls are wet." So were the sandwiches (capicola, provolone, mortadella), but the two bottles of Côtes du Rhône were secure. We stood under a tree and drank them both, making our way to the landing in a stiff wind and temperatures that had dropped from seventy degrees down to forty.

It's dreary to keep hearing that it doesn't matter if you're catching anything, it's the experience that counts. Well, of course the experience counts, and we spiritually thrive in this intimate contact with earth, but it's a whole lot better to catch fish than not to catch fish. You can't fry a reverie, and I like to fry fish in a cabin in the same manner as my grandfathers, my father, and my uncles did before me. I have supposed that at times you penetrate a set of feelings known intimately to your even more remote ancestors.

Probably 99 percent of the fish I've caught in my adult life have been released. I don't say "released unharmed," as a creature's struggle for life is indubitably harmful to it. We should avoid a mandarin feeling of virtue in this matter. It's a simple case that a variety of torture is better than murder for the survival of the species. The old wisdom is that the predator husbands its prey. "Catch and release" is sensible, which shouldn't be confused with virtuous. "I beat the shit out of you but I didn't kill you" is not clearly understood by the fish. This is a blood sport, and if you want a politically correct afterglow you should return to golf. Eating some wild trout now and then will serve to remind you that they are not toys put in the river for the exercise of your expensive equipment.

When you try to start over, you are forced to remember that enthusiasms that have become obsessions burn out rather easily. You think of the talented adolescent tennis and baseball players who withdraw when pushed too hard by their parents. I was pushing myself in my twenties when, as a dry-fly neurotic on a Guggenheim grant, I fished ninety days in a row. Such obsessive-compulsive behavior is supposedly a mental defect, but then I also wrote the title novella of my collection *Legends of the Fall* in nine days, which I view as worth the madness. It can be caused by back pressure—in the sense that I had been teaching for two years on Long Island and was longing for my beloved northern Michigan trout streams, thus the ninety-day binge. In the case of "Legends," I had brooded about the story for too long and had to write quickly or lose it.

Of course, certain fishing behavior is indefensibly stupid. Years of fishing permit and tarpon for thirty days back to back out of Key West naturally sours one, especially when augmented by bad habits. You need only to check into a hotel when a convention is in progress.

Having had my cabin in the UP for twenty years, I've been able to study hundreds of groups of men who have come north to hunt and fish. I've had the additional advantage of spending time studying anthropology. There is whooping, shouting, jumping, and slugging, along with countless manly trips to the toilet to relieve the mighty freight of beer. One could imagine Jane Goodall off in the corner making her primate notes.

This is all an extension of the mythologies of outdoor sport that begin in childhood, when the little brain fairly yelps, "Twelve-point buck! Ten-foot wingspan! Ten-pound brown!" Woods and water might very well be infested with "lunkers" of every variety. Within this spirit of conquest and food gathering, I have watched a fishing friend dance with a 350-pound woman so tall he barely nibbled at her chin while trying to kiss her. Early man and later man had become one under the feral pressure of a hunting and fishing trip.

As a language buff, I've been curious about how quickly speech can delaminate in the face of excitement. Years back, well off the northern coast of Costa Rica with my friend Guy de la Valdène and the renowned artist and fishing fop Russell Chatham, we managed one afternoon, using a rubber squid and a casting rod, to tease up a black marlin of about six hundred pounds and a blue marlin that certainly approached one thousand. First of all, it is alarming to look closely into a blue marlin's softball-sized eye maybe twenty or so feet away, and when Guy flopped out the fly, the fish sipped it into the corner of its mouth. The ratio would be similar to that of a very large man eating a very small brisling sardine.

Once hooked (it must have felt like a pinprick), the immense fish did the beginning of a barrel roll, its entire length emerging as it pitched backward, away from the boat. And to me the audio was as memorable as the visual, bleak screams, cries, yelps, keening, with each sound swallowed soon after it began.

An hour or so later we nearly had a repeat with the black marlin, but I was doing the teasing and lost the rubber squid to the fish before I managed to get him into casting range for Russell. It took a lot of yelling for me to console myself, but then finally I accepted the fact that we were fishing for the reasonably sized striped marlin, and the encounter with the two monsters, though lunar, was a doomed effort, a case of outdoor hubris similar to trying to take a Cape buffalo with a BB gun.

I have long since admitted that my vaunted maturity is in actuality the aging process. More than a decade ago, in a state of financial panic (fifty years old and no savings whatsoever), I began to work way too hard to allow for spending a lot of time on a sane activity like fishing. Saving money is even less fun than watching corn grow. My sporting life was reduced to a scant month, with two weeks of Montana fishing and a couple weeks of Michigan grouse and woodcock hunting. I don't count my afternoon quail hunting near our winter "casita" in Arizona, which mostly consisted of walking the dog. If your hunting is spliced between a double work shift, you're never quite "there" in the field.

Sad to say, this thoroughly nasty bourgeois work ethic, taken to my usual manic lengths, quite literally burned down the house of my fishing life. Years passed, and I began to envision my epitaph as "He got his work done"—something that fatuous. I think it was the novelist Tom Robbins who said that he doubted that success was an adequate response to life. Saving money, though pragmatically laudable, gets you in the garden-variety trap of trying to figure how much is enough. A straight answer is unavailable during a period in history when greed is not only defensible but generally considered a virtue. When overcome by greed, the fisherman tends to limit himself to headhunting, a kind of showy trophy search at the far corners of the earth. When living correctly and relatively free from greed, I did not differentiate between my humble beaver-pond brook-trout fishing and the stalking of large tarpon.

On one of my Poke Boat voyages I paddled into a ten-acre mat of white water lilies to protect my ass from gathering waves. As a lifelong claustrophobe, I experience an uninhabited lake as the ultimate relief from this neurosis that cannot clearly be understood.

I have, however, considered the idea that I might be somewhat less evolved than others are. After a severe childhood injury I quite literally ran to the woods, which has proved to be my only viable solution. When in Paris or New York, the Seine, the Hudson, and the East River present me with immediate relief from my phobia, as do the Bois de Boulogne, the Luxembourg Gardens, and Central Park. Even as a wacky young beatnik in New York City in the late fifties, I'd have to head up to the Botanical Garden in the Bronx.

Nearly all fishing takes place in a habitat that is likely to make you unable to think of anything but the sport at hand. In late August at my cabin I was brooding about my recent financial collapse and drove out to the gorge of a nearby river, basically a sand-choked mediocre river but nonetheless prepossessing. I sat down on a very high bank with a miniature fly rod and glassed a stretch with my monocular (the only real advantages of being blind in one eye are that I was 4F during Vietnam and I don't have to carry cumbersome binoculars). Under the shade of an overhanging cedar tree was a succession of decent brook-trout rises. I reflected on the gasping it would take to get out of the gorge, also the number of small grasshoppers in the area, which must have been what the trout were feeding on. I had only a small packet of flies with me and a single small Joe's Hopper from Montana. I made the long slide down the sandy bank on my butt, regathered myself, and took my first throw, only to hook a root halfway up the bank on my first backcast. I didn't yell "Gadzooks!" I climbed up to the root by pulling myself hand over hand on other roots. I detached the fly and managed to catch the smallest of the rising trout, scaring the others away. Now soaked with sweat, I took off my clothes and wallowed in an eddy. I paddled over an exchange, a blurred glance with several trout that seemed curious rather than frightened. Even the predictably gasping trip back up the bank was pleasurable indeed compared to important meetings in offices high above cities that I have experienced. As Thoreau said, "While I sit here listening to the waves which ripple and break on this shore, I am absolved from all obligation to the past."

Every few years I've taken to the idea of worms or minnows as bait or plugs for casting for pike and bass. The mood usually doesn't last and probably emerges from my modest egalitarianism, also an occasional sense of repulsion from being in the company of fresh- or saltwater fly fishermen when they are especially full of themselves, all fey and flouncing and arcane, somewhat like country clubbers peering with distaste over the fence at the ghetto bait types in the distance. However, I have sense enough to blush at my occasional proletarian masquerades at my income level. I still can't bear to "dress up" like the fishermen I see who, with an addition of one more gadget, appear likely to either drown or sink through the earth's crust from the weight of their equipment or, better yet, the outfits—the costumes, as it were—designed for a terrestrial moonwalk or perhaps for ridding an airliner of Ebola virus.

Of course, this is probably only an extension of my own childhood lust for first-rate equipment after I had judged those fifty-cent, fifteen-foot-long cane poles inappropriate to my future as a great angler. For a number of years, all of my earnings from hoeing and picking potato bugs went to rods, reels, plugs, and flies.

I suspect that I'm a fly fisherman for aesthetic reasons, adding the somewhat suspicious quotient of degree of difficulty. My father fished for trout using only a fly rod, whether with streamers or bait, and so I suppose it was all inevitable. He was a well-read agriculturist and fished incessantly, taking me along on every occasion after I was blinded in one eye at age seven. We were rather poor, but he was giving me the woods and the water to console me after a bad deal. Right after World War II, he and my battle-weary (South Pacific) uncles built a cabin on a lake, where we lived in the summer, with several trout streams in easy reach. I imagine millions of men are still fishing because they did so as children and it is unthinkable not to continue. And it is still a consolation in a not-quite-comprehensible world.

This quality of intensity in one's personal history can be unbearably poignant. After my father died in an accident along with my sister, I gave his fishing equipment—including a large, immaculately arranged tackle box—to a Mexican migrant kid named Roberto who lived with his family on the farm we rented. Roberto was about twelve and fished a lot in Texas when he wasn't working. In the tackle box there were at least one hundred plugs, antiques now, but I'm sure they were put to good use.

In George Anderson's fly shop in Livingston, you never hear fish referred to as "old fangface" or "waterwolves," nicknames for northern pike up in Michigan. This shop is as discreet as Armani's in New York. When I annually pick up my license, I ask an old acquaintance named Brant how the fishing has been, and he usually says, "So-so," having doubtless answered the question a hundred thousand times. He can't really say, "As good as your capabilities," which would be accurate.

A few years ago the Yellowstone River suffered serious flooding, but it has begun to recover. I simply love to float it in a McKenzie boat and have booked an expert guide, Dan Lahren, for the past decade. In that I have fished there nearly every year since 1968, I scarcely need a guide, but then it's a great deal more comfortable than stumbling over slippery rocks, and since I'm committed to the fee, I fish six hours every day. Ultimately the cost is nominal compared to evening meals in New York and Paris, where there's little fishing, though striped bass have been reappearing around New York and I've long promised myself the absolute inanity of fly casting the Seine right in the middle of Paris, particularly the stretch near the Musée d'Orsay. Lest you question my sanity, I should add that I don't value sanity very highly. Besides, we all know that every creature is confronted moment by moment with the question of what to do next, and casting a woolly worm out into the turgid waters of the Seine seems a splendid option.

I fish a total of about seventy miles of the Yellowstone, selecting a piece each day, keeping in mind the specific pleasures of scenery, habitat, the hydrologic shape of the water, the memories each stretch evokes. The novelist Tom McGuane moved to the area in 1968, and his friends followed, including Russell Chatham and Richard Brautigan, and in recent years I've fished a number of times with Peter Matthiessen. This year the fishing was mediocre, though I was distinctly more conscious, mostly because I've pulled back from the screenwriting business but partly because I fished a lot in the summer in my attempt to jump-start an old obsession. I had no forty-fish days, as I've had in the past, and no fish over three pounds, but each day was an unremitting delight. During slow periods I'm always reminded of McGuane's essay, the title work in *The Longest Silence*, on how angling is often filled with a pleasant torpor interrupted by truly wild excitement. My friend and guide Lahren likes to remind me of the time I pulled a dry fly away from a giant brown trout, thinking for truly inscrutable reasons that it was an otter trying to steal my fly. Its dense, massive arc seemed too large for a trout. This fall, the most noteworthy day brought a squall that turned the river into a long tidal riptide, and when we left the river, even the irrigation ditches had whitecaps.

It's now October 22, and there's a gale on Lake Superior, with the marine forecast predicting waves from eighteen to twenty-four feet. Perhaps I should get my beloved Poke Boat out of the shed, but first I'll knock off fifty pounds for ease of maneuvering. As a backup, a friend is building me a classic Chesapeake skiff. Also, I'm planning to go to Mexico to catch a roosterfish on a fly, a rare lacuna in my experience.

I won't say I've reached the location of that improbably banal word "closure." You don't start fishing a lot in the same place you left for the same reason you can't restart or renew a marriage back to a state of innocent, blissful passion. It's quite a different person baiting the hook or, better yet, tying on the fly. It is, however, fine indeed to know that if you've lost something very good in your life it's still possible to go looking for it.

(Men's Journal)

THE MAD MARLIN
OF PUNTA CARNERO
(1972)

It was first of all the strangeness of the water. If I didn't look at the receding shoreline it could have been Lake Michigan near my farm in high summer with a mild two-foot chop. But it was travel fatigue that made my mind wander: a late-afternoon Braniff flight that stretched deep into the night from Miami to Panama to Cali, Colombia, to Guayaquil, Ecuador. And from Guayaquil a two-hour taxi ride to the coast, eighty miles south of the equator, while I sweated in the back seat and tried to make out shapes in the dark—stilt houses, burros along the road's shoulder, cacti, pigs, dogs, goats. I felt mildly insane and bilious, for though I travel a great deal, I fear planes and this trip had taken a dozen or so drinks and I would be up and fishing within a few hours. Then we made a turn on the blacktop and I could hear the roar of surf and see the great, glittering Pacific.

Now, stretched out in the boat's fighting chair, I watched the rocks and caverns and crashing surf of Puntilla de Santa Elena disappear. I vaguely wanted to be home in bed in Michigan, where there was snow outside, on my own safe turf, rather than moving out at fifteen knots to do something I had never done before and considered in my exhausted state to be alarming. That is, catch striped marlin.

Marlin have always been the most distant of fish to me, the least accessible, and in some ways the most attractive. Growing up in the Midwest amid fresh water, I read about marlin in magazines and in the works of Van Campen Heilner, Kip Farrington Jr., Zane Grey, and Ernest Hemingway. Atlantic sailfish seemed manageable by comparison, though the larger Pacific sails appeared a bit over the borderline of good sense.

I tried mentally to multiply a five-pound rainbow by fifty, just as later, when I became fascinated by tarpon, I would multiply a largemouth bass of five pounds by twenty. The adjustment to taking tarpon with light tackle required a number of giddy months on the flats near Key West. Now I was going to up the ante considerably and try to take a striped marlin on a fly rod in addition to the more orthodox saltwater tackle. My introduction to marlin fishing was to prove even more violent than the tarpon expeditions.

The Carnero Inn at Punta Carnero was as far from roughing it as one can get in fishing. Part of their system is to have your lunches ready and a cab waiting when you finish breakfast. The short ride to Salinas was always pleasant, with hot Latin music on the cab radio, a fine view of the ocean, and, on the other side of the road, the sunblasted desert. Each time we came this way we passed the same osprey perched on a rock like a painting, looking out over the Pacific for his morning meal.

When you get to Salinas there are a number of beach boys, employed by Knud Holst's Pesca Tours, who relieve you of your gear and take you to your boat in a small dory. They expertly judge the incoming swells; I never got damp all week. The crews were always ready so that the minute you stepped aboard the boat at 7:00 a.m.

you were off for the marlin grounds, some fifteen miles out toward the Galápagos at the confluence of the Humboldt and the Niño currents. It is this mixture of currents over an oceanic canyon fifteen hundred feet deep that creates a great concentration of billfish.

That first day we had Captain Gomez, whose boat was an Owens called the *Haridor*. Gomez was relaxed but rather withdrawn. The brochure said the crews were fairly competent, but Gomez proved to be an incredible fish spotter and producer, as was Captain Capacho in the following days. In the first eight hours we spotted fifty-five striped marlin and by noon had caught three and lost three, one after an arduous half-hour fight when we had a "double," or two marlin hooked at once. With a double you have to fight the fish from a dead boat; my inexperience made me pressure the fish, and the fifty-pound-test line snapped. After the three we turned to fly rods, but had we kept on with ordinary tackle that first day out, we conservatively judged we would have boated seven.

Anyone who has read about or done any billfishing knows that this is nothing short of spectacular. In fact, it can be too much for one man. I quickly learned that a billfish takes more out of you than anything I had done except backpacking into the Rockies. After the first three I had not lost my nerve, but my arms were trembling involuntarily and the hot tropical sun was frying my brain. I began to dream of the hat I had left in my room. It was hard for me to believe that after an hour's fight you could slip the drag way up and the fish would still make two-hundred-yard runs as the mate continued dripping water on the line to cool it. I kept remembering what Hemingway had said—for every minute's rest you take, the fish gets the equivalent of five minutes.

Then a splendid surprise occurred; the first fish I hooked on conventional tackle proved to be a large Pacific sail. Eight hours later at the dock he still weighed 170 pounds despite the usual 10 percent dehydration. He was the simplest fish of the week to fight but for rather alarming reasons: he exhausted himself in a series of some twenty jumps, including a long, shattering stretch of tailwalking during which he kept himself aloft by smashing his great forked tail against the water. In my fatigued state this was all hard to comprehend. I wasn't really sure I wanted the fish in the boat after this demonstration of violence.

In addition to the sheer physical labor of the fight, striking a fish can be difficult. My main problem was my clumsiness in a rocking boat, increased greatly by an insane sort of excitement. Though a number of our striped marlin came from "under" on blind strikes, most were caught by trolling the skipping balao on an intercept pattern in front of visible fish. If the light is good, you can watch the strike on the two shorter lines and sometimes on the longer outrigger baits. Adding to the hysteria of the moment are the mates, standing on the bridge and shrieking, "Marleeen! Marleeen! Marleeen!"

The usual mistake is to strike too quickly, when the fish is merely mouthing and escaping with his prize. But it is hard to pause and count to five or more when you have seen a huge dorsal speeding toward the bait and then watched the line move out swiftly on a very light drag. It is even more awesome when you pick up the rod, flip up the drag to strike position, and reef the rod as hard as you can several times. At first it feels as if you have snagged a log, but then you are leaning back against a fish that is moving away so fast the reel screams and the spool becomes a blur. The first jump never fails to lift your head off, with the sunlight catching the water shedding from the striped blue back, the bill thrashing the air, and the depth-charge splash when the fish lands.

Experienced striped-marlin anglers prefer to fight the fish standing, held in with a belt harness. My inexperience and a bad back made this out of the question, though it would have been possible while fighting the fish on twenty-pound test. I spent a long time with a marlin on twenty-pound, and this line weight seemed much more sporting; but in order to stand up with heavier test the angler should be in great physical condition, preferably built like an NFL linebacker, and also have good sea legs. Even sitting in the fighting chair I could feel myself levitate when I slipped up the drag. And when a fish would sound for three hundred feet, the work could be brutal under the equatorial sun. I found out later, while reading about billfish, that a sounding marlin is best handled by letting him have line, then moving the boat well forward for a better fulcrum.

I would have been more interested in fighting the many large dolphin that struck the balao had not the billfish been so plentiful. In fact, the second day out with Capacho we saw sixty-seven striped marlin. The bait was skipping too fast for the many sharks, but a dolphin can catch anything, and the crew likes them for their delicious meat and the good price they fetch. Oddly, it is virtually unknown in these waters to lose a fish to the sharks, the opposite of the situation in the Bahamas. The hooked dolphin merely angered me and sapped the energy I was saving for the next marlin.

I was surprised how greatly the marlin varied in strength, with one of the smallest requiring the most time and effort and cursing. I kept thinking of Lee Wulff's thirteen-hour fight with a big tuna, and an account I had read of Farrington's eight-hour battle with a foul-hooked broadbill. The fact that Alfred Glassell had got his record black marlin a few hundred miles south of us, at Cabo Blanco, in less than two hours was astounding to me. But you pray the fish will jump a lot—in addition to being beautiful to watch, this quickly tires the marlin. We saw many free-jumping fish, evidently trying to get rid of sea lice or remora. On a free jump—without the nagging pressure of line—they are simply unbelievable, exceeding the height that a tarpon reaches and often against a backdrop of blue sky dotted with the graceful shapes of man-o'-war birds.

Photographer Guy de la Valdène is an expert on taking billfish on a fly rod. He has caught sail on large single- or double-hooked streamers, and we had hoped to add our names to the list of two or three others who have caught striped marlin with a fly rod. Briefly, here is the technique:

You use two teaser rods baited with either a large, hookless rubber squid or a flying fish. Plug-casting rods rather than boat rods are preferred because the fish often needs to be teased several times and the bait must be cast quickly.

You troll the teasers the same way you do an ordinary bait. When you intercept the path of a fish or group of fish, you take the rods from the gimbal holders and try to impart extra action to the skipping teaser. When a marlin becomes interested in one of the teasers, you quickly reel up the other one and grab the fly rod. (I suggest the use of a Scientific Anglers System 12 rod, called "the Great Equalizer." Anything less powerful would be disastrous.) The angler manning the teasing rod must be careful to keep the bait just out of reach of the fish, or just off the tip of his bill. A marlin is capable of a tremendous rush of speed and can easily rip the teaser off the line. (If he does get a good grip, you let him run with it and he usually drops it within a hundred yards or so.) Ideally, you tease the marlin up to within forty feet of the boat and tell the captain to kill the engine; then the teaser must be yanked clear of the water. At the instant this decoy is removed, the streamer must be cast into the immediate area, and if the marlin is sufficiently irritated, he will make a pass at the fly. It sounds involved, but the whole process usually takes place in a few stupefying minutes—though I teased one fish for Guy for thirteen minutes. It is hair-raising to bring a marlin this close to the boat; the crew, not used to such shenanigans, goes bananas.

It is as thrilling to man the teasing rod as it is to cast the fly. Several marlin made beeline rushes with their bills out of the water and mouths open, swerving away only a few feet from the boat. It should be added that the whole process must be rehearsed over and over because the moment itself is fatally swift and mistakes are final.

On the first day, when the fish were hungry and we boated the three, we set about preparing the teasing rods and fly equipment. (I don't suggest this stunt to anyone who hasn't boated a number of large tarpon; it is simply too overwhelming, almost nightmarish. And even tarpon seem a trifle lethargic compared to a marlin charging a bait.) Within ten minutes of stowing the boat rods, Guy had coaxed a large marlin within casting range. It made a number of aggressive passes at the squid, and I was literally numb from my skull down when the boat stopped; I false-cast once and let the fly drop. I watched as the marlin made one quick, open-mouthed lunge and grabbed the fly. I made sure he had the fly and then struck twice as he sped off. Unfortunately, I struck a third time, just as he emerged from the water shaking his great head. The leader snapped with an audible ping and I got fly line in the face. I had pumped enough adrenaline in one minute to supply a squadron of kamikaze pilots.

One afternoon soon after, we alarmed the crew when I brought a marlin in close and Guy went overboard to take underwater photos of the fighting fish. It would have taken a fortune to get me out of the boat. I had seen far too many cruising sharks that could have made an easy meal of me. And the occasional luminous, awful-looking sea snakes worked on my imagination. Too, we had been advised that morning by Peter Fischer, the inn manager, that one of the boats had had its planking punctured four times the year before by billfish. This is hard to believe until you see the speed of the fish, feel its strength on the line, and study the structure of its bill. But then, Guy is a trifle crazy, having fished far off Costa Rica in a twelve-foot whaler and having taken a small skiff from Palm Beach to the Bahamas. I was supposed to stop the marlin if it made a pass at him in the water, but this was clearly impossible. The mates and captain were screeching and laughing as they watched—this after I had fought the fish for an hour and was trying to increase the drag for Guy's safety. But every time Guy got close, the marlin would dart off fifty feet or so, and I soon felt my arms would pop from their sockets. As the fish finally tired, it was strange to look over the gunnel and see man and marlin eyeballing each other ten feet below in the clear water. The fish was much longer than Guy and clearly more suited to the water.

When I checked the inn's records to see if our luck was consistent with other parties', it was clear that our fishing was about average. From October through May the average catch ran about two and a half striped marlin per day, with a generous sprinkling of sails and a few black marlin. Swordfish or broadbill are also a possibility, but the trip to the grounds is longer. There are also plenty of big-eyed tuna.

A record black marlin had been caught the year before, but it couldn't be claimed because it had been fought by four Ecuadorians for thirteen hours. The fish had to be taken to Guayaquil to be weighed, and twenty-four hours transpired between the landing and the weigh-in. Despite the delays, the marlin weighed 1,760 pounds, well over Glassell's record but not by any means a fair fish, which is more important than any record.

For those enamored with sheer size, the trip to Punta Carnero is worth the shot at a black, though the odds are against it. Incidentally, the trip is no more expensive than some of those lake-trout-and-pike safaris into Canada and is easily arranged. But though Punta Carnero fishing is excellent, there are some discouraging aspects. Releasing a fish is virtually unheard of because pay is small and selling fish represents a good share of the crew's income—a marlin brings in from four to six dollars on the local market. The crews are very competitive in their search for fish, but they cooperate, as the money goes into a shared pool. I don't like to kill game fish any more than I would want to shoot twenty deer in a week. I think anyone who likes to kill a lot of them is an indisputable jerk and knows nothing of the soul of sport. Probably part of the problem in Ecuador, as in other places, is the "macho" sensibility attached to the sport. You combine this with economic necessity, and killing is inevitable. A solution exists, though: give the crew five dollars for each released fish. Everyone has a right to kill a fish for a mount, and often a marlin is injured badly and would not survive. But any notion that billfish are a resource of infinite supply is sadly wrong, as those who used to fish the Bahamas, Peru, and Chile know too well.

One of the blackest days in my sporting life occurred last year when I saw the carnage created by a "competition" between a Key West and a Miami fishing club. Among other species, there were a lot of three-pound barracuda, which would be pitched into the canal after pictures were taken. A fisherman who would do this ought to have his tackle destroyed and be confined to pitching marbles at a swine farm.

It is unfortunate that the political hubbub has kept a lot of American anglers away from Ecuador. In a number of years of extensive foreign travel, I have never been treated with such graciousness as I experienced among the Ecuadorians, and that without my knowing a single word of Spanish.

A nonfisherman could have a good trip just in terms of scenery and bird life, and some other more dubious possibilities, including the casino in Salinas. The coastline of Ecuador beneath Salinas is rocky and forbidding from a boat but broken by miles of paradisiacal beach. Rainfall is virtually unknown and there is no bug problem. The commercial fishing fleet that leaves the small harbor at Salinas every dawn is made up of sailing dories with two- or three-man crews; it all looks like the set for *The Old Man and the Sea*.

The first day out, the dories looked from a distance like a regatta, but I quickly realized this was not regatta country. There was the disturbing illusion of seeing men standing on the water between the gentle swells. These men are Peruvian fishermen, bottom fishing on small balsa rafts. Their modest mother schooner in the distance doesn't look much more seaworthy. They don't seem disturbed by the omnipresent sharks or the yellow-reddish sea snakes.

Punta Carnero is between Salinas and Anconcito, a desperately poor but beautiful fishing village situated on the edge of a cliff with a winding track down to the water. It was off Anconcito but within the reef line that Knud Holst Jr. saw many roosterfish ranging up to fifty pounds, but this inshore fishery is largely unexplored. Punta Carnero is a splendid spot for a hotel, and the Carnero Inn is built flush on the huge rock cliff, with a large swimming pool hovering over the Pacific.

On the way back to Guayaquil we passed through La Libertad, which was crowded with the Sunday-evening promenade. I was exhausted and melancholy, having stayed up half the night listening to the wild music in the hotel's Bar Roca. The band had been the equivalent of a Latin Rolling Stones, another fine surprise. It is hard, though, to celebrate a passing thing.

Ecuador offers fabulous striped marlin, an occasional black, broadbill, and sail, but the sport is in its twilight period and I suggest that anyone interested get at it fast. God might have made these "great fishes," but the Japanese are catching and eating them faster than God can replace them. The proof is conclusive—death by longline.

It doesn't seem possible in so huge and mythic an ocean, but it has happened. Cabo Blanco has been closed for a decade now. From Catalina to Chile the fish are running fewer and smaller. No one is "responsible" for the ocean; thus, it is pirated by all. The hogs of the sea are hyperactive, whether they be the Japanese with their five-mile nooses, the Russians off Cuttyhunk with their floating factories, the Norwegians chasing around the last whales, or the Danes off Greenland plundering the Atlantic salmon grounds. We will become old men with no great game fish to search for save tarpon, and them only because they have no food interest. But the black marlin, that great fish in whose maw has been found a 160-pound sail, and the broadbill swordfish, which has been known to chase a boat, are disappearing as viable game fish. In Japan these beasts, along with sailfish and striped marlin, are made into fish sausage.

Some of the Ecuadorian sights still haunt me. One afternoon we had spotted a large collection of man-o'-war birds and sped toward them because they are a good sign of bait concentration. A large marlin was herding bait toward the surface, then slashing through the fish to feed. The captain eased the boat close and we scrambled to the bow, where Guy cast several times. The marlin made several passes at the fly, then a bull dolphin grabbed it and Guy couldn't get him off. Under normal conditions it would have been splendid to have a large dolphin take a fly, but not when a picture-book marlin was thirty feet away, feeding as if it would never feed again.

Sadly enough, though we had several takes, we never landed a marlin on fly. We agreed to return, possibly next year, with a fast skiff to have another shot at it, even though it might take a month. I kept thinking of the marlin "balling" bait so visibly, as if we were on a platform above a clear aquarium pool with the great birds floating above us.

(*True*)

FISHING A WATERSHED
(CIRCA 1976)

Eight years ago I quit teaching forever. My swan song at the State University of New York at Stony Brook was the administering of a twenty-five-grand international poetry festival with over one hundred poets in attendance for a number of days. As might be expected, it was the sort of bombazine booze gala that tends to wound and petrify, mixed in with camaraderie, adulteries, fistfights, and general good spirits; the aftermath produced a kind of terrifying cultural exhaustion in me that I'm not sure I'm over yet.

Two weeks later—in the interim I moved to northern Michigan —I stood on the spine of a ridge some eleven thousand feet above sea level in the Absaroka mountains of Montana. Aside from the beauty, it was an acrophobic nightmare with visibility approaching the hundred-mile mark: to the north, the Crazy Mountains, and to the west, the Gallatin Range. Far to the south, peeking over the top of Yellowstone Park, there was a hint of the Tetons. At my feet a snowbank was melting into rivulets in two directions downward: one rivulet toward the Yellowstone and the other toward the Boulder River. It was an eerie moment, laden with vertigo and stoked with as much religiosity as I have ever mustered. It was merely the earth in pretty much the same state as we found it.

In my following eight annual visits to Livingston, Montana, I've never again quite matched that sense of seeing the world as do big birds and God. But this is mostly because I'm so involved with fishing the rivers of the valleys. To be honest, I also find mountain climbing and backpacking needlessly exhausting, a form of outdoor masochism engaged in and deserved by the young.

On that first trip a rancher friend of Tom McGuane took the three of us, including Dan Gerber, along on an expedition to check out his hunting camps. We rode horses for two hundred miles and saw only one other human, a lunatic forest ranger who scared me senseless with tales of recalcitrant grizzlies. My ass turned raw and plum colored. I favor only looking at horses, knowing that if God wanted something on their backs he would have grown it there.

The wilderness fishing that mountains offer requires no true finesse—the trout are willing virgins that any clown can catch—compared to the subtleties of dry-fly fishing for brown trout in the valleys. The real added onus to this current rage for backpacking is the freeze-dried food—tasteless bilge that only the most redoubtable nature freak or hippy could enjoy. One time in the mountains I caught seventy-five trout on fly in an afternoon, and this experience reduced fishing to something akin to a yo-yo tournament.

As a fisherman I have always been fascinated by the idea of a watershed. This might be partly because my father was a professional conservationist, and early in my life the word "watershed" had an air of strangeness to it. In the western part of the United States the terrain is topographically a great deal more obvious than in the east. In Michigan you have to be in a plane to sense how a river system is formed. In the West the watery courses that form the great Missouri watershed are as lucid and transparent on the map as those of the

Amazon basin. By mute fact of gravity every single raindrop tends one way or another.

Montana is a spectacular casebook for the births of rivers. The history of geological upheavals is such that within an hour's driving of Livingston you can find a half dozen fine trout rivers and an equal number of splendid spring creeks, those mysterious water courses that emerge from the earth nearly whole. The negative aspect of the watershed is, of course, the fact that any of our foulness—any impurities we produce—ends up in our watershed system. But Montana has little industry and an extremely slight population density, though trout rivers are readily destroyed by dams, both necessary and otherwise.

Just south of Livingston the canyon walls of the Yellowstone narrow to a few hundred yards; beyond this aperture you can see the whole broadening sweep of the canyon sixty miles south to where it narrows at Gardiner. This part of the watershed forms my favorite trout river on earth, though many favor the broader stretches from Livingston to Big Timber, after the waters of the Shields River have joined the Yellowstone.

Coming out of Livingston I often squint my eyes in a Cézanne effect to render out everything man-made. After the Civil War, the Story and Shorthill families pastured remudas of thousands of horses here. Before that, such illustrious names as Jim Bridger and Lewis and Clark passed through. At the far end, Chief Joseph paused in a doomed flight from the cavalry. In a dry creek bed near his ranch, McGuane found the silver snuffbox of an eighteenth-century Austrian explorer.

But the river itself, sometimes flowing placidly above great pools, sometimes hurtling over rocks in the narrows. It is superb for brown-trout fishing, particularly for the "headhunter"—one trying to catch a brown over four pounds on fly. Many fishermen, especially those from the East, prefer the confined waters of either Armstrong or Nelson's Spring Creeks, both emptying into the Yellowstone.

Oddly, and one learns it very slowly, purist fishermen are among the great bores of the world. They see with a pointillist's vision, similar to the professional dieter, the habitual dope smoker, the tennis fanatic, the granola muncher who forces their new crop of blanched alfalfa sprouts onto your plate. Or the hard-core Manhattan business drunk. You get the same shot of torpor from big-game fishermen who don't actually know anything about the ocean and from wing shooters who are ignorant of their prey. "Ecosystem" has become a profoundly homely word from misuse. It quickens again if you add the whole humanist notion, our own survival, preferably in a state of grace, along with other creatures who don't know we are trying to speak for them.

Thus, gradually over the years my vision of the Yellowstone valley changes. If I only wanted to catch fish, I would stay home—a few weeks ago on a food-gathering mission it took us only two hours to catch two chinook and six lake trout within five minutes of my front door. But a few times a year it is good to rid yourself of your average baggage, partly to see if it was worth carrying at all. You enter the new place with a little trepidation, fearing orthodontists might have bought the whole thing since your last visit. Within one hundred miles you get the grain and livestock reports on the local radio station. This reminds you of some of the faded, mildly crushed and weathered people you play pool with on many western nights, who insist on trying to make a living from a small ranch. You see the same people at the dozens of small county rodeos, and in numbers, seemingly unafraid of their own anachronism, of the way in which farming and ranching have become part of what the near-futurists call agribusiness. Just down the street from your favorite bar, the Wrangler, is Dan Bailey's tackle shop, with an immense collection of fishing flies and other sporting equipment, all of which you pore over as intensely as you viewed similar equipment in the Montgomery Ward catalogue in 1946, when your uncles returned unscathed from the South Pacific.

September in Montana is so definite with the deep greens of the aspen fading, and even the shadows become precise though liquid after the density of summer. There is frost on your sleeping bag and coffee owns some of the pungency of your first cup. There is a decidedly crazed though noncommunal sense in the gathering of fishing friends; "communal" most often means people who don't really like each other and are trying to figure out why. Real affection is in short supply between mammals. Once we gathered for dinner and pushed ourselves to a satisfying vulgarity: a dinner for eighteen that offered trout six ways, raw clams, oysters, Dungeness crabs flown in from the coast, roast pork, turkey stuffed with oysters, cases of a superb Burgundy—Côte de Beaune-Villages—and a case of Château d'Yquem, plus a mixed case of Calvados and twenty-year-old bourbon. Reeling eaters were lost in the woods and only found by bird dogs that had been fighting in the barnyard for scraps. Nobody wanted to dance for hours. Clothing was soiled. Nasty liaisons were begun but the meal was too splendid to allow for recriminations in the aftermath.

The next evening, with a mildly aching brain you notice the nightly powder snows are creeping down the slopes. The turbid waters of midsummer have become low and clear with the long chutes above the pools brilliantly defined. You don't mind getting cold, because you can soak it off afterward at the hot springs up at Chico. Meanwhile, you make long sweeping casts across the pool with your fly rod, mindful for the clear bulge and break in the skin of fast-flowing water that might mean a large trout.

THE BEAUTY OF THE JUMP
(2000)

A few days before I went down to Mexico in search of roosterfish, I was wandering through McCormick Place, the conventioneer's paradise in Chicago, which is the size of a hundred football fields, or something like that. This was a convention of book people, and it is hard to extrapolate the prospect of fishing when you are autographing books for a couple of hours. It's also hard to understand how you can become claustrophobic in such a huge place. The mind drifts, then recoils as the ceiling begins to sink. I had been troubled of late by the fact that a monarch butterfly's brain, about the size of a grain of salt, guides it all the way from my farm in northern Michigan to Mexico. Why have I found it so hard, especially in the winter, when I live virtually on the border?

Maybe it's because it's hard to divert an older dog with an ingrained bad habit like work. It's fine to work as hard as many others —and I do—if you're going to live two hundred years and there are free years in the offing. You can't prove that you get to smoke or go fishing after death, but it strikes me as unlikely. I had recently written an uncomfortable novella, "I Forgot to Go to Spain," about a successful man who makes a bunch of money but forgets his youthful ambition of going to Spain. Well, he finally gets to Spain, but he can't quite take off the blinders he's wearing, the kind that keep a draft horse on a straight furrow, a racetrack trotter from being spooked or diverted by the reality to its left or right. My hero, though a writer, tends to bark a lot, like the others who fly first class, stay in grand-deluxe hotels, and forget, like tertiary alcoholics, that the world is something other than an extension of their ambitions, a muddy mirror of their endless days of working or drinking.

But there I was on Sunday, boarding a Mexicana flight in Chicago, dreading the Mexico City airport, although, oddly, I had heard it had become marvelously efficient in my prolonged absence. Later, staring at the vases of fresh flowers in the Mexicana lounge before boarding for Zihuatanejo, I was already getting a tinge of the Otherness I needed. *Maybe I should simply stay in the lounge and stare at fresh flowers and drink free top-shelf*, I thought. In their current binge in favor of stockholders and executive compensation, our own airlines have made Greyhound buses a golden memory. It wouldn't be surprising if a copilot barged out and started pulling teeth as a pleasant diversion.

I could have flown to southern Baja, which is a better place to catch roosterfish on fly, but then I always think of Baja as owning a touch of banality, sort of the Budweiser Clydesdales of fishing destinations. I like to go to places where there aren't dozens of identically uniformed rich American anglers buying an outdoor adventure with an anal compulsive predictability. Admittedly, if I was as short on discretionary time as these folks, I'd do the same thing. There is a specific grace to being self-employed, though the rations were real short until I hit forty.

I got my first full hit of Otherness upon landing in Zihuatanejo, after flying through a thunderstorm that struck me as pleasant indeed compared with McCormick Place. Outside the airport I could hear distant surf, and the air was as moist, warm, dense, and dark as it had been in Key West in the early seventies, well before the tourism machine redlined. In those days they didn't pick up the garbage too regularly, Duval Street was vacant on weekday nights, and you didn't have to wait in line for a place to fish.

That night, several of my teeth began to hurt, but a secret mixture of ibuprofen and tequila did the job. I sat on my rooftop patio studying the distant thunderstorm over the Pacific, and also a gray-tailed grackle in a nearby palm that shrieked back at each clap of thunder and would continue to do so throughout the week. I liked the idea of replying to thunder. I began to recall that I had been in moderate to severe pain far from home in Brazil, East Africa, and Russia, not to speak of the month before in France on an extended book tour. In the case of teeth, I had grown up with a hammer-and-chisel-type dentist and wasn't eager to gamble on the Mexican variety.

The only plus aspect of pain is that, for unclear reasons, it makes one's surroundings far more vivid and memorable. A writer's consciousness should be relentlessly predatory, and any extra insight, no matter the source, is appreciated. I can see clearly three green flies on a baby elephant's right eyelid, the arch of a ballerina's foot as she dips a toe in the Neva River in Saint Petersburg, hear the throaty, catlike hiss of a Gaboon viper, all accompanied by the usual stomach cramps.

Here is what I saw the next day: a quarter-moon bay stretching perhaps three miles from north to south, with a broad beach of mostly sand but also splotches of grass closer to an improbably dense forest of palm trees that insisted on looking almost artificial, what with my single eye quite untrained for this character of sheer lushness in palm trees. Up beyond the trees was a succession of mountain ranges, a lattice of green mountains that were misty and rumpled in their unfolding and so striking that if photographed they would likely resemble a kitsch diorama of mountains. You simply had to be there to be convinced of their existence, especially at dawn, when they blotted out so much of the eastern sky and smallish isolated clouds dropped their own isolated storms. One morning a grand lightning stroke appeared, unrelated to anything else in the sky, as if it were the uniform signature of the Cihuateteo, the Nahua goddess women who are rumored to inhabit the area.

In the early morning, when our panga, a small fishing boat, arrived, there were three foals gamboling on the beach in front of a small white chapel at the south end of the quarter-moon bay. A mare came looking for them from the horse farm to the north, and it was still close enough to dawn that the foals cast skittering shadows on the beach in front of the chapel as they pretended to tease the Pacific combers sweeping in from the west.

It was often hard to remember that we were supposed to be fishing. Our culture is so sodden with irony that overwhelming beauty is often not quite palpable. We taste it and try to doubt, finding it a little difficult to accept an experience that banishes everything we are and have done in life. For instance, in the dawn after a night of explosive thunderstorms, a pent-up stream that had been blocked in the dry season by dunes had broken through, and now there were a thousand acres of pale-beige water with an irregular but defined border.

Adolfo, the captain, moved the panga along the edge of the troubled water, and I hooked a weighty fish on a fairly sturdy No. 11 Scott fly rod. I was startled to see it was a snook, somewhere between twenty and thirty pounds. The fish jumped three times, and after a twenty-minute fight the leader broke at the boat. It would have been my first large snook on fly rod, but I can't say that I cared, because getting the fish into the boat and clubbing it to death, or, more likely, releasing it, are technicalities compared with the beauty of the jumps.

The only nagging regret was that I knew how good snook tasted, and for the past four noons we had headed into an island where there was a small palm-frond-covered restaurant called El Indio, run by a local with the unlikely name of Marc Anthony, where the catch we offered would be cooked a number of different ways. Smaller roosterfish and dolphinfish (dorado) would be broiled over mesquite coals and served with a light red-chile sauce, and the two also were sautéed both plain and with a marvelously redolent garlic-and-lime sauce. (It should be noted that these limes are tree-ripened, thin-skinned, and have a tart sweetness unavailable in the US except in the bona fide Key lime.) The first course was invariably an instant ceviche, closer to sushi, made of black tuna, more commonly known as bonito. Included were thin slivers of jalapeño, so the iced buckets full of Mexican beer were especially good. The temperature was never lower than the midnineties at noon but was made tolerable by the ocean breeze, the icy beer, and the rare fact that you were doing something you had wanted to do for a very long time: catch a roosterfish. One lunch, Captain Adolfo idly said that we were eating better fish than the president of Mexico. "Maybe better than anyone," I added, thinking of the wretched sandwiches that were our noontime fare during twenty years of fishing tarpon, permit, and bonefish in the Florida Keys.

I first started thinking about roosterfish back in the early seventies, in the weeks before a trip to fish the waters off Ecuador, on which I hoped to become the third person (after Lee Wulff and Woody Sexton) to catch a striped marlin on fly. I called Kip Farrington, an expert and a virtual pioneer in the area, really at the top, along with the fabled Van Campen Heilner. Farrington had been with Al Glassell when Glassell caught a black marlin of more than sixteen hundred pounds off Cabo Blanco, Peru, near the Ecuadorean border. The film footage of this catch was later used in the movie version of Ernest Hemingway's The Old Man and the Sea. Farrington, though, was tired of marlin, and wanted to talk about roosterfish. He was quite old at the time, and his babbling about the roosterfish he and Glassell had caught was a bit disjointed, visionary, goofy, the talk of an ancient mariner who refused to diverge from a single subject.

Thirty years later, I was trembling from heat and exhaustion, blinking from the rivulets of sweat running into my eyes. The roosterfish on deck weighed a minimum of forty-five pounds. Adolfo disgorged the hook, then gently released the fish into the water, first feeding it a live minnow as a reward. It had taken just short of an hour to land the fish, because it had been lip-hooked, which gave it full freedom of movement. At one point I had gotten the fish close to the boat, the leader nearly in reach of our capable mate, nicknamed King Kong for good reason, but then the fish made another run of about three hundred yards and the work began again. Roosterfish are much stronger than tarpon of equal size, more on the order of a permit, where three quarters of the way into the battle you think, *This son of a bitch is trying to kill me*.

It turned out there was an extra reason for not taking any truly effective pain pills when my teeth were hurting the night before. Roosterfish are found in the wide, smooth trough where oceanic swells slowly become very large breakers. To fish there is to be on a lateral-sweeping elevator, a kind of sedate but unpleasant carnival ride. I noted that while we were concentrating on fishing, Adolfo never took his eye off the oncoming swells for more than a moment, even when he was sitting on the cowl of the outboard rigging tackle. In short, this was not a good situation in which to be dazed by painkillers. One could easily imagine a sleepy body trying to maintain control in the crashing surf.

Later that day, my friend Dan Gerber, who, not incidentally, is a writer who also races Formula One cars on the senior circuit, boated a roosterfish that weighed in the midsixties, which Adolfo said was the largest in recent years. I have known Dan well for thirty-five years, but at that point I was enjoying my distance from his struggles with the fish. We had caught several that morning in the ten-to-twenty-pound range, and given the heat of the day, that size seemed more appropriate. As a not altogether mentally stable poet, I thought, *Isn't a hundred-fifty-pound woman preferable to a four-hundred-pound specimen, generally speaking of course?* Besides, the small ones were delicious grilled over mesquite coals, better in fact than a three-hundred-dollar lunch at Le Bernardin in New York City, though beer is a poor substitute for Meursault, a wine that has caused certain expense-account questions:

"Why three bottles of Meursault?"

"I have a hollow leg from the Tet Offensive during Vietnam and a specific valve must have been inadvertently left open."

One day after catching roosterfish, jack crevalle, dorado, and bonito, and having a fine lunch of the same, I got into bed with a glass of tequila, making sure that the hard rim didn't click against my teeth. I pushed aside the two caressing swans that the maid had skillfully molded out of bath towels and covered with rose petals. This was a nice touch for a weary, sun-blasted geezer. I was still a little melancholy over a large sailfish (maybe ninety pounds) that had died on release the day before and a large roosterfish that had done the same. Adolfo took them home for a neighborhood barbecue, but it was upsetting to have them die that way.

Once you are freed from your own preoccupations, fish become astounding. An official or scientific description falls short with roosterfish: "A streamlined fish resembling jacks [not that much]; dorsal fin remarkable for spinous portion consisting of greatly lengthened spines nearly separate from each other, the fin connected by fin membrane only at the base except the last ray, which is free at its base. Caudal fin deeply forked; pectoral fin long, falcate; mouth rather large."

This is accurate, of course, though it sounds like a crime-show pathologist who slides the body back into the morgue bin with a resounding clack, then has a date at a fern bar in Santa Monica. I would add that the fins when you see them rising out of the cobalt-blue water cause a tremor in your rib cage. The fins wave and are heraldic; they shimmer, flop, become erect again. The eyes are very large and look at you with the comprehension that you are the enemy. When you hold the fish for a moment you are dumbfounded by its specific density, and the shadow you cast on its side trembles with its muscularity. You reflect that if they lived in rivers, it would be out of the question ever to land one over fifteen pounds. They are the ocean's equivalent of the avian goshawk. You are not part of their universe except by invasion.

The nap didn't work well, because I dreamed I was a fish, and it was pleasant to be without molars, so when I awoke I was a bit disappointed by my human form. I heard an acoustic guitar from next door that mixed nicely with the rattling of palm fronds in the evening breeze and more thunder arriving from behind the green mountains in the east.

Down at Elvira's, a pleasant restaurant on the beach, I ate small octopus stewed in garlic. I kept thinking of David Quammen's essay that depicted two male octopuses of different species screwing near a hydrothermal vent eight thousand feet deep. The perverse act was caught on videotape. What an incursion of privacy, but then I could scarcely tell if the delicious octopuses I was eating were male or female. I looked up for a moment and saw an attractive blonde at the next table reading Hermann Hesse. She was definitely a female. I was envious of Dan Gerber, and my son-in-law, Steve, and my friend and fishing guide from Montana, Dan Lahren. They were along for the trip and were chewing their food vigorously while staring at the blonde, which didn't seem to overly impress her.

After dinner I insisted we go to a strip club. If you write books, you don't want to go back to your room and read them after dinner. I am a connoisseur of strip clubs, what with my restless spirit while traveling. My favorites are the Night Before Lounge, in Lincoln, Nebraska, and the Crazy Horse, in Paris, where I was privileged to drink fine wine backstage with the lovely owner. Sipping wine, I am able to pretend I don't notice the loveliest butts in the Western world flouncing past.

At the strip club, I made a note of how healthy the citizens of Zihuatanejo looked compared with those up on the border. I deduced the availability of fresh fruit, rice, beans, and vegetables, the ready and cheap availability of certain species of fish, like mullet. I had noticed in the past the evident health of people in seashore villages of Ecuador and Costa Rica. I saw boys rowing in the harbor who made their American counterparts look like puffballs. Mexican kids are always well ahead of our own in the Kennedy fitness tests, probably because they can't afford our grease-sodden fast food.

The club lacked air-conditioning and was so hot that an attendant mopped the sweat off the floor after each number. The management was also sensitive enough to have a clear-glass-enclosed shower stall at the back of the stage so the girls could cool off after dancing. I managed to sit through eight numbers and fall in love eight times, an admirably perfect average. There were a lot of tough cowboys from ranches in the surrounding mountains, and I wanted to take an informal poll to see whether they thought looking at nude dancing women was sexist, but my son-in-law, who is a Montana lawyer, recommended against it. When I say these cowboys looked tough, I don't mean they were aerobicized or pumped gym iron. Maybe they worked.

Dawn came early. There was no breeze, and you worked up a dense sweat even walking *down* the stairs to the ground floor. Over morning coffee and Motrin, I reread Octavio Paz's magnificent *The Labyrinth of Solitude*, an essay on the Mexican national character. Anyone interested in Mexico should read this book, though it is vain indeed to ask those in Congress to do so. Like players of Pin the Tail on the Donkey, congressmen prefer to work blindfolded.

On the way out of the harbor, I noticed that the water near shore had been badly soiled by the storm sewers flushing from the night's rain. Of course, this happens also in our own port cities. Politicians are quite unable to see this as the moral equivalent of taking a dump on the floor of the Sistine Chapel. Both Miami and Key West have had many problems in this area, with the viable solution, for them anyway, of piping the sewage farther out to sea. One particularly grand aspect of visiting Mexico is that you quickly lose the sense of existing in an empire. Even our word "values" is an economic term.

We went out a dozen miles to check for sailfish, my lust for roosterfish having temporarily abated. Dan Gerber hooked a good sail on fly, but it was so hot that he didn't seem too disappointed when the fish broke off. After my sailfish died, I wanted to head back for shore fishing. My sadness was lifted amply by the sight of two green sea turtles making love. They didn't need black satin sheets with stirrups. The ocean provided them enough traction, and they looked over at us inscrutably.

The other thing that made me want to abandon sailfishing that morning was that I'd grown a little fatigued with approved species in the sport fishermen's agenda. In this mood, I once caught a large golden carp from the shore of Lake Michigan near my farm, and this pleased me as much as one of my tarpon fandangos. Limiting yourself to tarpon, permit, bonefish, marlin, and fly-fishing for trout can get as monochromatic as Minneapolis after a number of years. And after catching a goodly number of large fish on fly—even a three-hundred-pound shark—I prefer smaller fish because with them you know your nuts aren't going to pop out your eyeballs during the struggle.

The last afternoon, I had drinks with Stan Lushinsky, who had booked our two boats and our hotel, and who used to be in the trucking business in Pennsylvania. Lushinsky owns the manic glint of the fishing obsessive that I've seen in a number of friends and Keys and Montana guides. He told a local story as ghastly in its own way as The Perfect Storm.

A number of years ago, Lushinsky had been fishing some twenty miles south of Zihuatanejo along the surf line. He was watching a peasant fishing onshore, and his business partner, Susan Richards, was on the roof of the panga. The captain saw a tsunami coming in at high speed. He had to make a split-second decision. Beaching the panga was tempting, but probably would have been fatal to all of them. He headed at the wave, which Lushinsky estimated to be at least thirty feet high.

Unfortunately, Richards was still on the roof when the panga shot straight up the thirty-foot wave. The real problem came on the other side, when the boat became airborne. When it hit the water, it burst its ribs, and Richards hit the roof, then tumbled onto the deck. She required nearly a year of hospital treatment, including steel rods in her back. That night in the hospital, Lushinsky saw them bring in the peasant fisherman, his crotch wrapped around his neck. He'd survived his two-hundred-yard toss into the palm trees. After this story I drank rather deeply from my water glass of Herradura, my sore teeth shrinking in importance. As I looked off the patio at the Pacific, Mother Ocean, she seemed less than kind, just impersonal.

Lucky for us, there are different worlds within our singular, grand earth. I don't mean the World Wide Web, or anything perceived at a distance. Even an overguided jaunt is too distant: one of those isolated fishing camps with seven mini-moguls talking up the good bull-market leavings or Romanian fiber-optic opportunities. A nonspecific test is to see how far mentally and emotionally you can get from where you came from. That way you're less likely to plunge into the selfsame sucking bog on your return.

The other morning, back home at my cabin, I woke up cold though it was August; the temperature was a mere forty-five inside and in the midthirties outside. I actually shuddered with the desire to be in Mexico. All shudders are involuntary and can indicate physical craving.

By afternoon the desire for Mexico hadn't gone away, so I called my secretary, Joyce, and had her reserve Adolfo for next year. The excuse I gave myself was that I like to watch birds and I had forgotten my Mexican bird book on my trip. I knew the seabirds, the gavottes, and the grand and obvious frigate birds. But there were more I had to check out. A geezer fascinated with avian biodiversity, that's me, not

to speak of fish. A Spanish scholar had given me a new name last year
when I decided to become a Mexican poet who didn't really speak
the language (even English is difficult for me). Since the culture is
essentially matrilineal my Spanish name is Jaime Harrison-Walgren.
Just wait until my poems full of fish, birds, butterflies, strange fruit,
garlic, beige butts, thunderstorms, and night music hit the charts,
whatever they are.

(Men's Journal)

A RIVER NEVER SLEEPS
(1976)

Night fishing. In *The Snow Walker*, Farley Mowat observes what all linguists know, that the Inuit have over a hundred compound words to describe varieties and conditions of snow. The conditions of night are as various but there's never been any call for the thesaurus. Night is just night. Certainly not a time to be walking around in the woods looking for a river that you were sure abutted the end of a particular path. Your ears strain for the sound of rushing water. Nothing. You turn around and the path doesn't look like a path anymore. Above the whine of mosquitoes you hear your heart beating. If you pause long enough the owls will begin again. You make another careful tack into the woods. Your sweat mixed with mosquito repellent stings your eyes. Your fly rod catches in the tag alders and bends dangerously. But then you spot a landmark clump of yellow birch and stop long enough to hear the river just beyond.

There is a strange fragrance to a river at night that I've never been able to identify, some water-washed mixture of fern, rotting poplar, cedar, and the earthen odor of logjams. If you fish long enough alone at night and are a trifle unstable anyway, the moon that guides your casts across the river smells vaguely metallic, just as the sun that burns the first dew off after dawn smells copperish. This will sound far-fetched only to those who haven't been there. I knew a young Ojibwe Indian once who demonstrated to me how he could find deer by their scent. Then he got drunk one day and went to Vietnam and hasn't been heard from since.

Night fishing is best, though, with friends, barring those obvious times when you want to be alone and clean out your head. I fish mostly with a friend I used to work for, Pat Paton, who is a carpenter and block layer. He is very good at starting fires and it's a solace to sit looking at a fire when the fishing is slow. If we're camping and the night is particularly dark and impenetrable we drink a lot of whiskey. If either of us is in a violently hasty retreat from what is known as the "real world," we may even cook a steak. This is an unabashedly primitive coolant to a troubled mind—to eat steak and drink too much whiskey out in the woods in the middle of the night.

One night I caught a bat. The bat swallowed my fly and under the shaft of my penlight it was clearly suffering from the hook. The booze made the scene even more garish. I couldn't put a bat in the creel with my trout and I couldn't call Pat, who as a hardened country boy is afraid of bats and snakes. Luckily another friend was with us that night. This friend is somewhat of a gun nut and he was packing a .357 Magnum sidearm for no real reason other than he enjoyed doing so. Everyone knows that a .357 will blow a hole through an engine block and that police use the weapon in some cities because it shoots for keeps. It is good for close-range whale and grizzly attacks and for cutting down trees if you've forgotten your ax.

"Put this miserable bat away. He's swallowed a number-eight muddler minnow."

"Hold the light and stand back," my friend said.

There was a billowing blue flash and the kind of roar associated with a thunderstorm a foot away. We were covered with riverbank mud. The bat had vaporized; at least, we couldn't find it.

Night fishing for lake trout on the shores of Lake Michigan is even more likely to inspire hard-core buffoonery. It's best to have a driftwood fire because the water can be very cold. In this sort of fishing you get a definite release from the refinements of your sport and that's one of the best things about night fishing. You can forget the long delicate casts with a two-hundred-dollar bamboo rod, the minuscule fly drifting toward the water on a pound-test leader. The sophisticated trappings disappear and you're young again with a spinning rod and plug on some elemental mission. We caught ten lake trout one night, over a hundred pounds altogether, then discovered that my old station wagon had lost its brake fluid a half dozen miles from the nearest house. It was fine caroming off trees on the log road on the way out. The main thing was to try to make the blows glancing rather than direct. We returned to the yellow light of the tavern like blinking creatures wakened from a sleep.

My first memory of night fishing is as a boy in 1946 on a small lake we shared with a half dozen other cabins. One of the cabins owned a small military surplus diesel generator, while the rest were lit by kerosene lamps. I would row my father around at night while he cast plugs for bass. After the doctor turned off his generator our ears would slowly attune to the plop of the bass plug hitting the water, the creak of oars, perhaps a loon's cry and the frogs and crickets along the shore. When one sense is denied, another is enlivened, until you can actually hear the fish strike and know when to strike back. Without sight the world becomes almost unbearably tactile. The clownishness that creeps in is a reaction to a near embarrassment over how deeply the experience is felt, an escape from muddiness into clear water.

I stood one night in the Bechler Meadows in the southwest section of Yellowstone Park. There were no people for miles and in the moonlight I heard thousands of migrating herons calling. I had a bad toothache, the best toothache I ever had. My friends were asleep and despite a mixture of codeine and whiskey, sleep escaped me. I tried to fish in a branch of the Bechler River but my attention was overwhelmed by the sheen of thousands of acres of marsh grass in the moonlight, my throbbing jaw, the noise of the herons, and the presence of imaginary grizzlies. I was a night creature then as surely as I was a few years later in a boat with a broken-down motor out in Lake Okeechobee. There is a very particular "I don't care" abandonment to this kind of experience mixed with the raising of the hairs down the back of the neck that Matthew Arnold described as the test of good poetry.

When you fish at night, you are a pure sense mechanism. You are so far "out of your mind" that you are rather surprised, and not necessarily pleasantly, when you return. But that's what sport is supposed to do, and night fishing is a sport that colors all your other movements. From the boy catching bass at night to the man repeating the gesture three decades later is an inexhaustibly sensible step through time.

(*Esquire*)

FLOATING
(2003)

Back when I was a kid in the late 1940s there was a song that was relentlessly on the airwaves that said, "The best things in life are free." I was a gullible hick in northern Michigan but the thrust of the song wasn't apparent because I'd been hoping for a long time for a new Schwinn bicycle and with five children in the family there wasn't much in the way of "discretionary income" as they currently say. One hot afternoon while generally irked as only a ten-year-old can be I asked my dad just how the best things in life are free. He said that we listened to the Detroit Tigers baseball games for free, also the football games of the Detroit Lions and the Michigan State Spartans, I rowed our thirty-five-dollar rowboat for free, and the worms I dug for fishing cost nothing. I also rode Kilmer's horses free of charge, and all the bluegill, bass, and trout we ate didn't cost a dime. I got the Schwinn bike a few months later when my dad won big at poker at deer hunting camp, but the gradations of this homely lesson have never been lost on me because I know what to do when I have to run for my life.

Of course it depends on where you are when you are seeking relief from yourself and others. When I was spending a great deal of time in Hollywood as a screenwriter I felt like studio roadkill after a succession of daylong meetings where I sensed there might be a secret motorized shovel to scrape me up from the producer's floor. In stray, rare empty hours I did laps at the hotel pool or took long but not very pretty walks in Beverly Hills where I never saw the principals but only the service personnel like myself. Santa Monica was a good place to walk because I was reminded of things that are easy for a writer to forget like the ocean, and I liked watching a group of grubby old men who fished with very little success every day from the Santa Monica pier. Screenwriters are paid a fortune to be anonymous and I suspect it's a fair trade.

The best thing to do for a total purge, however, was to go see the Lakers game where the improbable grace of the game could draw you so far out of yourself that you were a little puzzled to have to rejoin yourself afterward. I remember one night when my brand new expensive linen sports coat had slipped to the floor without my noticing and I had jumped up and down on the coat tearing a hole and smashing my reading glasses. My friends Lou Adler and Jack Nicholson had four seats on the floor next to the visitors' bench so that you could easily have the illusion that you were part of what was happening. To me Laker basketball was the truest game in town, including the movie business.

Back to the question of where you are. The month of May always finds me at my cabin in Michigan's Upper Peninsula. You can take walks in a nearly limitless unpeopled landscape of forests, rivers, and lakes. Naturally work fills much of every day but in the evening at the local tavern you have the NFL playoffs and the Stanley Cup and also the NBA playoffs. In addition, if the weather isn't totally unreasonable, which it often is in May next to Lake Superior, you can also squeeze in a couple hours of trout fishing. It helps that the cabin is on the banks of a serviceable if undramatic river. Sure, there's a phone in your car but it rarely works in this isolation. It is finally the corny semantic notion that your recreation, your sport, should at least allow you in some minimal way to "re-create" yourself.

A friend of mine who is a pilot for a major airline said his work life is quite ordinary except for occasional periods of terror. These are rare but really get your attention, he added. I can collapse my own horror story into a few sentences: My wife of forty-odd years thought we should move from Michigan to Montana to be closer to family. It is important here to put most of the blame on someone else. I blithely agreed mostly because I had been thinking about moving there for over thirty years to get closer to prime brown trout habitat. I was also getting stale and nervous as a claustrophobe because of the iron noose of population growth around our one-hundred-acre farm in northern Michigan. In the past decade there had been an influx of the very wealthy replacing the farmers and commercial fishermen I had spent a big share of my life around, and I had this weary leftist notion that I no longer wanted to live on a farm I couldn't afford to buy. I didn't want to become the kind of stale geezer who orders a pamphlet from *Popular Mechanics* on how to carve a violin out of a single block of wood.

We put the farm up for sale and after a year and a half of lawyers, realtors, surveyors, banks, and courts the world has only recently stopped spinning in the wrong direction. It has become pleasant to spare friends and acquaintances the details because the whole story should be buried with nuclear waste in Nevada. However, I have lately begun to understand my nonuniqueness. I was being welcomed to the real world. It takes no more money and effort to make a good movie than a bad movie but sometimes a bad movie like life is in the cards.

I survived by floating. My wife survived because her nature is far more stable than my own. I didn't listen carefully to the real-tors, lawyers, and bankers. I mostly thought about fishing and left the nasty stuff to my aide of over twenty years who is the daughter

of a New York City meatpacker and can handle what the business
world has become.

Early each morning last summer in Livingston, Montana, where
things had reached their worst I'd leave our rental house and walk my
bird dog Rose. I hadn't lived in a town since leaving Stony Brook,
Long Island, in the sixties and I was essentially as far out of my ele-
ment as Rose. At least she wasn't having another close call with a
speeding Bentley like when we crossed the road to take a walk on
the farm the summer before.

After walking the dog it was time to ignore accumulated faxes,
phone calls, and emails and go fishing. I'd drive over to Danny
Lahren's house and we would decide on a stretch of river to fish,
tow his McKenzie boat to the launch site, and float and fish for a
half dozen hours.

You didn't wake up in the morning, eat breakfast, and check
out how your teams were doing because there aren't any professional
franchises in Montana. There's not enough population. I had to stop
checking on the Tigers in the *Detroit Free Press* as I had done for
half a century, and there would be no reading about the promising
summer training sessions of the Detroit Lions which would be like
flakking a Belgian or Clydesdale as a thoroughbred at Keeneland.
The Tigers and the Lions have been miserable for so long the fickle
heart of the remote sports fan finds it easy for his interest to wane,
while the Pistons and the Red Wings are still good enough to deserve
a peek at the Bozeman paper or the *New York Times*.

But the fishing. Water lightens us. Especially moving water.

More people fish than any other sporting activity but that can
give one illusions about the degree of difficulty. It's a skill that can't be
bought and despite the advertisements of tackle manufacturers, good
equipment isn't nearly as critical as knowledge of habitat. The degree
of difficulty in trout fishing or saltwater fly casting is daunting. There
are Michael Jordans in this sport, I've known a number of them, and
it's interesting to note that true excellence requires an obsessiveness
that takes over the entire life. I'm fairly good myself but more in the

manner of a semi-anonymous interior lineman. Anything more than that and I couldn't make a living though I've often been jealous of the glittery-eyed fishing "bums" I've met along the coasts of Ecuador, Costa Rica, and Mexico, or in the Bahamas and the Florida Keys, and on the trout rivers and streams of the American West.

So I fished at least forty full days last summer to get rid of my demons that weren't very demonic but spoke a language I had refused to learn. One afternoon in a Livingston tackle shop I overheard two high rollers from New York City muttering that the only way they could temporarily forget their market disasters was to trout fish. They had five days and I intended to spend eight times that many. My sympathies were mitigated when it occurred to me that they *were* the market and had blown their own poker game.

The rivers in Montana cleared early last summer because of the less-than-usual snowmelt. June was very good for brown trout, the best since the big flood of 1997 which had confused the fish by changing the shape of their favorite habitat. Rainbow trout are free spirits compared to brown trout which tend to be territorial.

In June we spent six days over on the Big Hole south of Butte, an old mining city which, if it can hold on, will be a major theme park in the future without changing or building a thing. The Big Hole is best fished early in the season while still vaguely navigable because in summer much of the water is drawn off to irrigate neighboring hay crops. In my six days on the Big Hole I never had the occasion to remember my own name let alone worry about the indefensible legalisms that were trying to strangle me. I became the seven-year-old boy who stared at his first brown trout with incomprehension thinking it the most beautiful thing on earth.

On the Big Hole one afternoon we saw at least a hundred nighthawks sweeping up and down the river catching mayflies. It's rare enough to see a single one of these birds on a summer evening. One soared past within inches of my face and I couldn't help but bid a goofy "hello." The natural world can draw you out of yourself if you're willing to let go. On a single day on the Yellowstone I've seen avocet and yellowlegs, snipe and teal, golden and bald eagles, herons, ospreys, and sandhill cranes. One day a fishing partner, the novelist Carl Hiaasen, told me that the recently arrived white pelicans we were seeing spent their winters near Naples, Florida. This seemed more interesting to me than the intricacies of laser surveying. Way back when I researched my novella "Legends of the Fall" I discovered that Native Americans were amused by the efforts of our surveyors to find out how tall all the mountains were to the final foot. They didn't play the game of inches with accountants.

Actually it's best not to be thinking of anything else when you're floating because the boat is usually going the speed of the river with only a modest amount of braking time offered by the oars. You only have one shot with your fly rod at the best places you are passing, the particular "lies" that larger trout live in because the confluence of currents and holes offer the best feeding possibilities. A good angler also has to learn to recognize dead water or he'll flog himself silly.

We often took Dan Lahren's dog Pete with us though he didn't make it through the summer. At age sixteen Pete was the oldest English pointer I had ever known. He would rest his grizzled chin on the gunnel and pay attention to our luck. Years before when Pete had more gumption we'd toss him a white fish and he'd bite off the head, shake out the guts, then curl up on the fish until it reached proper eating temperature, which made Pete a unique sushi hound.

We finally have a home to live in so I made it through my garden-variety crisis by the grace of trout fishing. The only time in my life it didn't work was early in our vacation the autumn before, September the 11th to be exact, when I had wakened in alarm at the timbre of my wife's voice. She pointed at the television and I watched for an hour but then decided I didn't need to see those planes hit the Twin Towers more than a hundred times. Once would last forever. I went fishing anyway though with a daylong lump in my throat. At the end of the afternoon I definitely didn't want to return to the real world.

EARLY FISHING
(2008)

There was a terrible mistake when I checked my driver's license today
and saw that I'd be seventy next week. At 3:30 a.m. I was only ten
and heard Dad with that coal shovel on a cool May morning in the
basement, his steps on the stairs, then he woke me for trout fishing
with scrambled eggs, a little coffee in my milk, and then we were
off in the car, a '47 Chevy two-tone, blue and beige, for the Pine
River about an hour's distance up through Luther, the two-track
off the county road muddy so he gunned it. He settled me near a
deep hole in the bend of the river and then headed upstream to his
favorite series of riffle corners. The water was a little muddy and
streamer flies didn't work so I tied on a bright Colorado spinner
and a gob of worms. In the next four hours between 5:00 a.m.
and 9:00 I caught three good-sized suckers and three small brown
trout. I kept the trout for our second breakfast and let the suckers go.
It was slow enough that I felt lucky that I'd brought along a couple

dozen Audubon cards to check out birds. Back then I wanted to see a yellow-bellied sapsucker and I still do. While I dozed I hooked my biggest brown trout, about two pounds, and wished I had been awake. When Dad came back downstream and started a small fire I fibbed about my heroism catching the trout, a lifelong habit. He fried the fish with bacon grease stored in a baby food jar. He cut up a quarter-loaf of Mother's Swedish rye bread and we ate the fish with the bread, salt, and pepper. Dad napped and I walked back into the dense swampy woods getting a little lost until he called out after waking. Midafternoon we packed up to leave with a creel full of trout for the family and I left my fly rod in the grass behind the car and Dad backed over it. I had paid ten bucks for it earned at fifteen cents an hour at lawn and garden work. Dad said, "Get your head out of your ass, Jimmy." They're still saying that.

(*In Search of Small Gods*)

PUBLISHER'S
ACKNOWLEDGMENTS

Putting together a book of this nature after an author has passed away is always a group effort, trying to judge alongside those who knew and loved him what Jim Harrison would have wanted in his lifetime. This is of course impossible, but I would like to thank the following people for help in selecting and balancing these pieces into a form that I hope gives the reader some of the pleasure it did me: Terry McDonell, Jim's editor for many of his magazine pieces; my colleagues Morgan Entrekin, Judy Hottensen, and Andrew Unger; Jim's French publisher Patrice Hoffmann; and most of all Joyce Bahle, who was Jim's right hand for thirty-five years; the Harrison archivists at Grand Valley State University, which holds his papers; and his daughters and longtime first readers Jamie and Anna, without whom this book would not exist.

The editors of *Esquire* and *Esquire Sportsman*, *Sports Illustrated*, *Men's Journal*, *Field & Stream*, *Automobile*, and *Outside* provided Jim with a home for his journalism for many years; he also enjoyed good relationships with the *New York Times*, *True* magazine, *Sports Afield*, and others. The original appearances of these pieces are credited at the end of each piece. Several of these pieces were written for publications and editors in France, including "The Man Who Ate

Books," which was published in the Salon du Livre special issue of *Télérama* in 2001. Others were written for the editors Joan Juliet Buck, of Paris *Vogue*, and Yves Jolivet, publisher of the French house Le mot et le reste.

Jim also contributed pieces to anthologies and other books; more detailed bibliographic information for these follows: *In Search of Small Gods* is a collection of Jim's poetry (some of them prose poems) published by Copper Canyon, to whom we are indebted for permission to reprint them; *Sports Afloat*, a Time-Life Books collection from the Library of Boating; the single volume edition of Pablo Neruda's *Residence on Earth* published by New Directions; Will Blythe's wonderful collection *Why I Write: Thoughts on the Craft of Fiction*; Susan Shillinglaw's *John Steinbeck: Centennial Reflections by American Writers*; Deborah Clow and Donald Snow's *Northern Lights: A Selection of Writing from the New American West*; John Leonard's *These United States: Original Essays by Leading American Writers on Their State within the Union*; and Joseph Barbato and Lisa Weinerman's *Heart of the Land: Essays on the Last Great Places*, conceptualized and published to benefit the Nature Conservancy.

For the beautiful images that appear in this edition, we thank Andy Anderson, Scott Baxter, Lea Chatham, Stephen Collector, Manny Crisostomo, Mary Dumsch, Jim Fergus, Danny Lyon, Paul Magnusson, Jürg Ramseier, Jill Sabella, Bud Schulz, Douglas David Seifert, Guy de la Valdène, Dan Gerber, John Zumpano, Kelly Wise, John Snell, Zulma, and Magnum Photos. For digging in the crates to find most of them, and so much else, Jamie and Anna Harrison. Every attempt has been made to contact the rights holders, but if we have failed to identify any photo here please contact us and let us know.

—Amy Hundley,
Grove Atlantic

PHOTO CREDITS

p. 87:   At his writing desk in Patagonia, Arizona. Photo by Scott Baxter.

p. 91:   With his infamous Airedale Hudley. Photo by Bud Schulz.

p. 100:   On the hunt with Rose and Tess. Photo by Jürg Ramseier.

p. 110:   With Philip Caputo. Photo by Jim Fergus.

p. 117:   Hunting with Guy de la Valdène. Photo by Douglas David Seifert.

p. 122:   With hunting friend Pat Paton, circa 1974. Photo by Guy de la Valdène.

p. 133:   With his dog Zilpha in the creek behind his Patagonia casita. Photo by Scott Baxter.

p. 157:   In the doorway of his Michigan granary/writing studio. Photo by Paul Magnusson/Zulma.

p. 178:   On board the *Osprey* off Key West with Scott Palmer and Tom McGuane, 1974. Photo by Guy de la Valdène.

p. 183:   In Michigan, 1980s. Photo by Paul Magnusson/Zulma.

p. 197:   With his daughter Anna at the cabin in Grand Marais, mid-1980s. Photo by Kelly Wise.

p. 205:   In the bottomland of Sonoita Creek outside his "border casita." Photo by Scott Baxter.

p. 223:   In his Lake Leelanau living room. Photo by Manny Crisostomo/Zulma.

p. 231:   Tarpon fishing, early 1970s. Photo by Guy de la Valdène.

p. 247:   Lake trout catch, Lake Leelanau, early 1970s. Photo courtesy of the Harrison family.

p. 249:   Swimming with his daughter Jamie, Clear Lake, Michigan, about 1964. Photo courtesy of the Harrison family.

p. 258:   Fly-fishing, drawn by fishing/hunting friend, the painter Russell Chatham. Image courtesy of the estate of Russell Chatham.

p. 271:   Cooking in Jimmy Buffett's kitchen with Russell Chatham and Guy de la Valdène. Photo by Stephen Collector.

p. 282:   The McGuane ranch at Deep Creek. Photo courtesy of the Harrison family.

p. 287:   Tarpon fishing in the flats, Key West. Photo by Guy de la Valdène.

p. 309:   Jim in foreground, with his sisters Judith (far right) and Mary (behind him) and a friend. Photo courtesy of the Harrison and Dumsch families.